Working with Children in Art Therapy

Two Tavistock videotapes, *Art Therapy* and *Art Therapy and Children* (Children with Special Needs) are available from Tavistock/Routledge. They are produced by Tessa Dalley, Diane Waller, and John Beacham. The tapes are for sale only. For details please contact Caroline Lane, Tavistock Videotapes, 11 New Fetter Lane, London, EC4P 4EE. Telephone: 01 583 9855.

Working with Children in Art Therapy

Edited by Caroline Case and Tessa Dalley

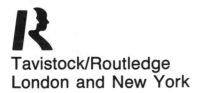

Tavistock/Routledge
London and New York

First published 1990
by Routledge
11 New Fetter Lane, London EC4P 4EE

Simultaneously published in the USA and Canada by Routledge
a division of Routledge, Chapman and Hall, Inc.
29 West 35th Street, New York, NY 10001

Filmset by Mayhew Typesetting, Bristol, England
Printed and bound in Great Britain by
Butler & Tanner Ltd, Frome and London

British Library Cataloguing in Publication Data

Working with children in art therapy
  1. Children. Art therapy
  I. Dalley, Tessa II. Case, Caroline,
  1948–
  615.8′5156′088042

Library of Congress Cataloging in Publication Data

Working with children in art therapy
  Bibliography: p.
  Includes index.
  1. Art therapy for children. I. Case, Caroline,
1948– . II. Dalley, Tessa.
RJ505.A715   1989   615.8′5156′088054   88-32538

ISBN 0–415–01737–8
ISBN 0–415–01738–6 (pbk.)

For double the vision my eyes do see,
And a double vision is always with me.
With my inward eye, 'tis an old man grey,
With my outward, a thistle across my way.

William Blake

Contents

Contents

The editors

Caroline Case has worked in clinical practice, particularly with children and adolescents with special needs, in the education and social services fields where she has carried out research into the expression of loss and bereavement in art therapy. Her current interests include small-group art therapy with children and the use of fairy tales and images from popular culture in therapy. Formerly she was senior lecturer and course leader of the postgraduate courses in art therapy at Hertfordshire College of Art and Design and a member of the British Association of Art Therapists' Registration Board. She has recently completed a visit to Hong Kong and the People's Republic of China where she lectured and ran workshops for a wide variety of professional groups, with assistance from the British Council. She also works in private practice and as a supervisor for art therapists. She was a contributor to *Images of Art Therapy* (Tavistock 1987).

Tessa Dalley has been working as an art therapist for the last twelve years and also has a training in psychotherapy. Recently, her interest in children has led her to work as an art therapist in a school, and she is also involved in child psychotherapy training at the Tavistock Clinic. Tessa is a part-time lecturer in art therapy at Goldsmiths' College, London, and at Hertfordshire College of Art and Design. She edited *Art as Therapy* (Tavistock 1984) and was a contributor to *Images of Art Therapy* (Tavistock 1987), and has made two videos about art therapy, the most recent being about children with special needs.

The contributors

Roger Arguile studied fine art at Loughborough and Exeter Colleges of Art before gaining a Master of Fine Art Degree at the University of Reading in 1978. He has worked extensively in residential social work with children in care and has some teaching experience in art college and a public school. He is a practising artist and has presented one-man lecture shows of his art film work and writings, besides exhibiting photographs and paintings. Since 1982 he has worked at St Mary's School at Bexhill-on-Sea, East Sussex, where he has established art therapy as a discipline (his work at St Mary's is featured in the video *Art Therapy and Children* (Tavistock 1988). He is a member of the Training and Education Committee of the British Association of Art Therapists.

Sarah Deco has a degree in psychology and trained as an art therapist at Hertfordshire College of Art and Design in 1980. Since then she has worked for the NHS as an art therapist in adult psychiatry. She has developed an interest in structural family therapy and has worked for Hammersmith and Fulham Social Services using this model. Sarah is also interested in dance and music, particularly Oriental and African dance, and has experience in the performing arts. She teaches dance for the Inner London Education Authority and also works part-time as an art therapist at St Peter's Hospital, Surrey.

Janek Dubowski is the Director of Studies of the Division of Arts and Psychology at Hertfordshire College of Art and Design. He is a qualified art therapist with several years' experience within the NHS, working with mentally handicapped people. He is a researcher and writer; his first degree was in Fine Art and he still regards himself as an artist.

Aleathea G. Lillitos graduated from Camberwell School of Art and worked as a part-time lecturer in art history at two London colleges while continuing with her own creative work. Since qualifying as an art therapist she has started an Art Therapy Department at St Thomas's Hospital, London, working with the Paediatric Department and the Child and Family Psychiatry Departments.

Ian McGregor originally trained as an artist. After qualifying as an art therapist in 1977 he worked extensively with autistic children. In 1986 he completed his master's degree in art therapy after writing his dissertation on anomalous drawing ability in autistic children. He is currently conducting doctoral research in the same subject.

Sigrid Rabiger is an art therapist at a school for children with severe learning difficulties. She trained as a painter and art teacher, then gravitated towards therapeutic teaching, with school phobic children, and later, autistic children at Family Tree. She gained the postgraduate diploma in art therapy in 1983.

Carol Sagar gained her diploma in art therapy from Goldsmiths' College, London, in 1984. Since then she has worked in child and adult psychiatry at the Bethel Child and Family Centre in Norwich. In conjunction with art therapy, she is concerned with the development of relaxation and rebirthing therapy as it is practised at the Kogyu Samye Ling Tibetan Centre under the direction of Chuje Aking Rinoche. She exhibits regularly with the Norwich Artists' Group.

Vera Vasarhelyi trained as a cellist and a painter in Hungary. She took part in Stockhausen's and Pousseur's masterclasses in Basle and, as a painter, has exhibited frequently. She gained her diploma in art therapy at Goldsmith's College, London, and has a part-time job in the Department of Adolescent and Child Psychiatry at Guy's Hospital, London. She has also established an independent Art Therapy Department in adult psychiatry at Crawley Hospital, Surrey. Her work consists of assessment and long-term, individual treatment and includes supervision of junior medical staff. She runs experiential workshops and seminars for senior registrars, social workers, nurses, psychologists, and GPs, besides lecturing extensively in England and abroad.

Editors' note

For consistency throughout the text, the word 'phantasy' is used when referring to the unconscious processes of the child's inner world as distinct from 'fantasy' which we understand as a conscious wish or daydream.

In the plate sections, illustrations have captions only in those cases where they have been given them by the children who made the pictures.

Introduction
Caroline Case and Tessa Dalley

The experience of childhood is universal yet extremely variable. This variability is due to the initial quality of parenting, early infant relationship with mother, and the environment into which the child is born. As the young infant grows, vulnerable and dependant, the child becomes initiated into the emotional, political, and social world of the adult. The child must develop and become integrated by trying to make sense of the conflicts experienced between inner needs, wishes, and phantasies and the outer constraints of this environment.

The idea of this book evolved out of our mutual interest, as art therapists, in working with children. The importance of using the art process in the communication of the inner world of the child is central to our work in art therapy. Also the environmental and social difficulties that the child encounters have come increasingly under scrutiny and therefore this book will interest all those people who come into contact with children either professionally or personally. It may also be of interest to those looking at the development of the child's consciousness in the formation of adult personality and hence therapeutic work with adults.

The child's position in society has become established by legal rights for education, health, protection, and also treatment, but this has been a gradual development. The concept of 'child' and 'childhood' has altered drastically over the last two centuries, from a Christian doctrine of original sin to a cult of original virtue expressed in the Romantic Revival. This assumption of original innocence was in its turn challenged and changed by the scientific investigations of the infant and child consciousness with the development of psychoanalytic theory. Freudian theory increased awareness of the child and attempted to give an objective appreciation of childhood consciousness. This was radically developed by child psychoanalysts such as Melanie Klein, Anna Freud, and Donald Winnicott, whose theories were more specifically concerned with the early infantile experience, most notably object relations and the concept of the inner world.

Art therapists working with psychoanalytic insight share similar views in

.erms of the consideration of the inner and outer world of the child. The various chapters in this book will describe different theoretical perspectives which are centred in the understanding and working with the images or art objects made. These hold many different meanings at many different levels and this multiplicity provides the essence of the depth of the communication within an art therapy relationship. Different theories essentially share the same foundation in that the role of art can offer the child an alternative means of communication which does not involve sophisticated speech. Indeed the art process can offer the child another language, non-verbal and symbolic, through which he or she can express, perhaps unconsciously, feelings, wishes, fears, and phantasies central to his or her inner experience. The art therapist is therefore ever present for the child in therapy, sensitive to the communication through the images or art objects working within the transference and counter-transference process.

Early British pioneers, largely working within a Jungian framework, placed emphasis on the inner function of painting and its process and less on the developing relationship with the therapist. 'Firstly imaginative material is given form; secondly, it "works back" on the maker and is experienced; and thirdly, one feels more alive' (Lydiatt 1971). The philosophy of working with children has largely emerged through the experience of these early practitioners and eminent teachers such as Michael Edwards and Diana Halliday but their work remains largely undocumented. The relatively recent literature on art therapy with children in the UK (Case 1987, Dalley 1987, Halliday 1987, Weir 1987, and Wood 1984) has also been clearly influenced by the child psychoanalytic theories such as those of Donald Winnicott and Melanie Klein. More specifically, the development of their ideas on play, symbol formation, object relations, the concept of the inner world, and children's phantasy have informed our work in art therapy considerably.

The children on whom we have chosen to concentrate are basically 'pre-latency' and 'latency' children. These are stages of development introduced by Melanie Klein, the first psychoanalyst to concentrate on working with very young children, and this work was essentially different from the Freudian approach of working with adults. For our purposes it is useful to use the Kleinian terminology and her description of pre-latency children, who are still under the immediate and powerful influence of instinctual experiences and phantasies, whereas the child in the latency period has already desexualized these experiences and phantasies much more completely and worked them over in a different form. As a result she describes how the analyses of children in the latency period present special difficulties.

Unlike the small child, whose lively imagination and acute anxiety enables us to gain access to and contact with its unconscious more easily, children in the latency period have a very limited imaginative life, in accordance with the strong tendency to repression which is characteristic of their while, in comparison with the grown-up person, their ego is still underdeveloped, and they neither have insight into their illness nor a desire to be cured, so they have no incentive to start analysis and no encouragement to go on with it. Added to this is the general attitude of reserve and distrust so typical of this period of life – an attitude which is in part an outcome of their intense preoccupation with the struggle against masturbation and thus makes them deeply averse to anything that savours of search and interrogation or touches on the impulses they just manage to keep under control.

(Klein 1932:58)

Interestingly, Klein used drawing extensively 'to gain access to the child's unconscious', such as in the case of Grete, and this is where the evolving work in art therapy with children of this age is proving to be so important. As can be seen by the various contributions in this book, the art work of the children in therapy is the central means of focus for the safe communication of conscious and unconscious processes. One of the unique aspects of art therapy is that there is a product, solid and tangible which can be kept and made sense of perhaps later in therapy. Children value these art objects greatly as they tend to hold the real significance for the child. They are a visual statement of their inner world experience.

It seems ironic, therefore, that this possibility of clearer communication for the child is itself being put at risk. Art therapists working with children are increasingly being turned to for 'evidence' in terms of what is revealed in the sessions through the child's drawings or art processes. Also other professions, in social work for example, are asking children to draw their experiences as concrete evidence, and this technique has long been used for purposes of psychological testing. This diagnostic approach where the child is aware of judgement and result does not involve the same process of communication as when the child is able to express aspects of their inner world in the safe containment of a relationship with a therapist.

For this reason, the use of drawings as 'evidence' in court, in cases of child sexual abuse for example, places the art therapist in a therapeutic and moral dilemma. The first priority must be the safety of the child and any indication that this is at risk must be shared with colleagues. But, in drawing and painting one is dealing with an overlap of inner and outer worlds, a mixture of reality and fantasy. Art therapists do not accept that drawings can be used automatically as literal statements and put the sanctity of the therapeutic relationship, trust, and space as paramount. There may be pressure from other members of a therapeutic team to contribute 'evidence' in this way because of the urgency and concern for the child, but what is fundamental is that the information is derived through the relationship and might be communicated through the images.

The experience of art therapists working with child abuse, for example, is that it is far more likely that the abuse will be expressed through 'making a mess' and an understanding can be reached through the transference and counter-transference process, rather than through a drawing depicting who did what to whom, on a particular occasion. The art therapist is trained to pick up communications of great sensitivity through the processes of image making, and more importantly waiting with, holding and containing the anxiety and uncertainty of the child struggling with the unfolding of their deepest difficulties. Therefore most art therapists hesitate to leap into early interpretation and judgement as to the meaning of the communication because of the very delicacy of the process. This would suggest that the art therapist may need to work to a point where the child can verbalize the experience with the support of the therapist through the ensuing months rather than use the actual art material obtained from one particular session.

The choice of papers was made for this book to include the three areas of health, social services, and education – the agencies which broadly cover the care of the child. Each contributor is an experienced art therapist working in a team with other professionals, although the membership of this group varies, reflecting the institution. But what of the child's natural group – the family? Any therapist working with a child must constantly be aware of this most influential factor in the child's experience. It is interesting how emphasis on the importance of the family in the art therapist's interaction with the child varies throughout the book.

For example, in the NHS setting, the sense of the families' involvement and of other members of the hospital team working with the family members comes through quite strongly, although the art therapist is mainly treating the child. In the social services setting one is more aware of the 'cycles of deprivation' where parental figures are caught enacting experiences of which they were themselves recipients. In this area of work one sees the emergence of the parents' trauma, which can also be treated, although many years after their own childhood; it is often first manifested as symptoms in the child. There is the possibility of family therapy, and a particular model of structural family therapy is put forward where patterns of behaviours, rather than insight into deeper levels of functioning, can be the focus of work. This section also describes work with the abandoned child towards healing and integration into new group structures, whether children's home or new adoptive family, underlining the need for preventative and supportive work before a situation has deteriorated. Finally, in the education setting there is a sense of the child 'alone' at school; even though a child's problems may have a strong emotional base they are often addressed as 'learning difficulties' and seen as the school's province. Here, although there is reference to and interaction with the parent, the emphasis on the family is much less central.

It is hoped that the expertise and professionalism of the contributors working in art therapy will inspire further interest in the important function an art therapist can hold within a team of professionals working with children. The first three chapters are based on theoretical considerations of the language of art in art therapy, and how this can be understood in terms of non-verbal communication (Dubowski, Rabiger, McGregor). The next two examine working with children in psychiatric clinics where posts are established for art therapists in the NHS (Vasarhelyi, Lillitos). Whereas the value of an art therapist has been acknowledged by the establishment of posts within psychiatry, therapists working in the social services (or education) are less common. Yet the next three chapters, based on social services, describe the depth of work needed in helping children who have suffered the deprivation and trauma of emotional, physical, and perhaps sexual abuse, which sometimes remains undetected at school, but needs specialist intervention to assist the child back towards 'normal' functioning and some degree of self-confidence and trust (Sagar, Deco, Case). Education, where art therapists are increasingly considered to be of value, is the area of concern for the last two chapters which examine the practice of art therapy in mainstream and special schools, with particular reference to working with children from ethnic minorities. The authors show how therapists working alongside teachers can both facilitate the learning experience of the child and make a strong contribution to the life of the school (Dalley, Arguile).

Art therapists in education and social services share a tentative status often subject to short-term or erratic funding. Therapists and their clients can experience an unstable situation where the termination or extension of the work is constantly under review. Until the status of art therapists is established with a salary structure commensurate with the depth of work being undertaken, many posts rely on pioneering therapists and sympathetic personalities within the system which can sometimes lead to the loss of hard-won ground when there are changes in personnel.

The whole book has been compiled in a process of unfolding and working together as editors. The subjects of the chapters were chosen to cover different ground but, interestingly, many cross-themes emerged, most notably, absence of fathers and the precarious balance of working between inner- and outer-world material. It seems that one mutual experience of all the authors was the degree to which their own feelings were aroused by writing in such depth and essentially re-examining the traumatic situation of the child. This was at times experienced as some mirroring of symptoms by the authors – Aleathea Lillitos for example mentions her blockedness in her anxiety to 'produce' the chapter. Other aspects such as resistance, anxiety, pain, secrecy, or even finding words for the images, caused problems for some contributors. There is also the difficulty of letting the reader into the experience of art therapy and indeed how to describe much of this process. Some of the images themselves are graphic descriptions of the process (Vasarhelyi), but where there is chaos and mess, central to some of the chapters (Case, Lillitos, Sagar), this is extremely difficult to describe – a point vividly made in the chapter by Sigrid Rabiger who works with children who may have reached puberty but remain at a developmental stage where they are not yet able to scribble.

Such is the depth and wide-ranging nature of the contributions but the central concern remains constant – the child.

© 1990 Caroline Case and Tessa Dalley

References

Case, C. (1987) 'A search for meaning: loss and transition in art therapy with children', in T. Dalley, C. Case, J. Schaverien, F. Weir, D. Halliday, P. Nowell Hall, and D. Waller, *Images of Art Therapy*, London: Tavistock Publications.

Dalley, T. (1987) 'Art as therapy: some new perspectives', in T. Dalley, C. Case, J. Schaverien, F. Weir, D. Halliday, P. Nowell Hall, and D. Waller, *Images of Art Therapy*, London: Tavistock Publications.

Halliday, D. (1987) 'Peak experiences: the individuation of children', in T. Dalley, C. Case, J. Schaverien, F. Weir, D. Halliday, P. Nowell Hall, and D. Waller, *Images of Art Therapy*, London: Tavistock Publications.

Klein, M. (1932) *The Psychoanalysis of Children*, London: Hogarth Press and the Institute of Psychoanalysis.

Lydiatt, E.M. (1971) *Spontaneous Painting and Modelling*, London: Constable.

Weir, F. (1987) 'The role of symbolic expression in its relation to art therapy', in T. Dalley, C. Case, J. Schaverien, F. Weir, D. Halliday, P. Nowell Hall, and D. Waller, *Images of Art Therapy*, London: Tavistock Publications.

Wood, M. (1984) 'The child and art therapy: a psychodynamic viewpoint', in T. Dalley (ed.) *Art as Therapy*, London: Tavistock Publications.

Chapter one

Art versus language (separate development during childhood)

Janek Dubowski

Language is a universal means of expression. With language we can communicate our experience, our thoughts, and even our aspirations to others. Language, however, is not only for communication. Words allow us to classify objects in the world. By the use of language we make sense of our experiences in a very structured and elaborate way. We can 'class' objects together and we can make subtle distinctions between them. We can predict certain qualities that may be found in an object by comparing our own experience with the internal list of objects that fits the same class as the object being observed. For example, a child's first confrontation with a puppy may result in a variety of experiences. If the puppy is friendly and quiet and allows the child to play or cuddle it, the child's first experience will, in the main, be a pleasurable one. If, on the other hand, the puppy barks or growls or even bites the child, the outcome will be quite different. Whatever the outcome the child will probably add to his or her growing vocabulary either the word 'dog' or 'puppy' (or perhaps 'Rover', 'Shep', 'Snapper' etc.). On the second occasion that this child comes into contact with a dog, the child will most probably remember the first experience. It is likely that the child will utter the appropriate label, 'dog' or 'Rover' although the experience may well be of a different dog altogether. What is important is that the child has started to classify his or her experience and by so doing can start to predict the potential outcome of the encounter and to act accordingly, either by attempting to play or by moving away in fright. The word 'dog' helps to classify differences; for example, 'cats' are often like puppies in appearance but do not fit the same class.

Language allows us to classify feelings and other experiences as well as objects in the world and perhaps it is this area that is first utilized by the young infant when he or she learns that very powerful word 'No'. Another powerful word learned and utilized about the same time is 'Mine'. The child often asserts ownership before stating an understanding of owner, that is, the word 'Mine' often precedes the word 'Me' although the child will have learned his or her name and use that instead.

As the child's linguistic abilities develop the more complex uses of language emerge. The use of metaphor allows for the exploration of complex ideas. We usually associate the metaphor with spoken language. However, pictures can also operate on a metaphorical level. When this occurs we have a clear relationship between two modes of expression, the iconic and the linguistic. Another example of this same relationship occurs when one asks a child, engaged in drawing or painting 'what is it?'. Here the request is that the child 'translates' the iconic mode of expression inherent in the picture to the linguistic by giving a title or other explanation.

In my experience this form of request is not always understood by the child. Sometimes an arbitrary word is used to placate the adult, sometimes the child appears puzzled by the request and simply says 'I don't know'. This puzzlement most often occurs when the child's art has not yet developed into fully fledged representation. These earlier stages are often referred to as the 'scribble' stages and are considered to be like 'babble' in linguistic development. This phenomenon is currently being researched by Trevor Jeavons (as yet unpublished). In his work with several under 5s he has found these children often have a 'favoured configuration' or complex scribble that is repeated over time. Further, certain children will continue to form this favoured configuration even after they have developed representation. Jeavons has hypothesized that these simple configurations may hold some specific meaning for children. However, when asked to give a verbal account of the work, the children have a variety of responses from looking puzzled by the request, saying 'I don't know', to even denying that they are responsible for the drawing. In my opinion the answer may be simply that they cannot say what it is because it has no linguistic counterpart.

I would argue, therefore, that during early stages of development, the iconic mode has a line of development that is distinct and separate from the linguistic. Later, when the child develops representational drawing skills, he or she can marry 'representational configurations' to linguistic classifications. Even a primitive stick figure 'corresponds' quite well to the word 'man'. We can see this relationship in the diagram (*Figure 1.1*).

The two separate lines of development converge when, at around 4–5 years of age the child starts to produce the earliest representational drawings, usually referred to as stick or tadpole men (*Figure 1.2*). These are clearly recognizable forms and therefore have a 'good fit' with what the child observed in the outside world. As the child's observational and classifying skills develop, more and increasingly complex features will be added to this initial scheme (*Figures 1.3 and 1.4*). For many children the marriage of iconic and linguistic modes is so convenient and exciting that the future development is entirely based on only developing forms (in drawing) that have a clear linguistic equivalent. Indeed, children will often talk through the drawing process (even if they are working alone). If an adult is present all the better, most parents become far more interested in their child's art if they

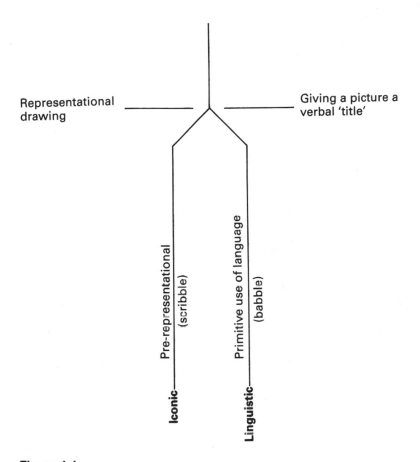

Figure 1.1

can discuss this with the child and of course the child is rewarded by the added parental attention that comes with this dialogue.

Jeavons has found that, when in the presence of adults, these older children will produce clearly representational drawings. However, in collecting and studying all the drawings produced he has also come across examples of the much earlier, pre-representational 'favoured configuration'. As when they were younger, however, the children are still not able to say anything about these drawings. Here I would argue that the line of iconic development is still exerting some form of independent influence (*Figure 1.5*). Of course we are aware that not all adult art is representational. Abstract art is made up of complex configurations that are not intended to 'resemble' forms in the observed outside world. In art therapy clients often use abstraction to express feelings and 'inner' expression as 'scribble' and I would argue that we should give the same amount of respect to children's non-representational art.

Figure 1.2

I have often heard it claimed of art therapy that painting, drawing, modelling, and other media, offer the patient a 'means of expression'. Sometimes this claim goes so far as to suggest that 'graphic expression' is nothing less than some form of 'alternative language'. The diagram in *Figure 1.5* does show how iconic expression can develop independently and therefore be an alternative to linguistic development. Further, in the absence of adequate linguistic development, as sometimes found in some mentally handicapped children, the iconic line of development may offer another way of making sense and order of an otherwise potentially chaotic world.

Indeed, such a notion is taken up by Howard Gardner in his theory of multiple intelligences (Gardner 1985). Here he argues that during development the child learns to make sense and order of the world, in several different ways, these include iconic, linguistic, musical, logical, and mathematical. All of these, (and this is not by any means a definitive list), allow the individual, in a separate way, to make sense of 'self'. Gardner calls these different ways of ordering the world 'separate intelligences'. Of course, these separate modes of mental activity do interrelate with one another. However, in the absence of one (or more) because of mental disability, brain damage, etc., the others can still function on an optimal level.

Figure 1.3

In order to explore further how these separate modes can correlate to one another I will be focusing on a particular linguistic phenomenon, the metaphor. We understand a metaphor as 'a figure of speech by which a thing is spoken of as being that which it resembles, not fundamentally, but only in a certain marked characteristic' (*Chambers Everyday Dictionary* 1975).

In 1952, Professor Gombrich, the aesthetician and art historian, suggested a far more elaborate definition:

The possibility of metaphor springs from the infinite elasticity of the human mind; it testifies to its capacity to perceive and assimilate new experiences as modifications to earlier ones, of finding equivalence in the most

Figure 1.4

disparate phenomena and of substituting one for another. Without this constant process of substitution neither language nor art, nor indeed civilized life would be possible.

(Gombrich 1952)

So, according to Gombrich, the possibility of metaphor precedes the development of language, of art, and without these two, of civilization.

So it appears that we need to look at pre-linguistic development in our search for the origins of metaphorical processes. Piaget places his focus clearly on play.

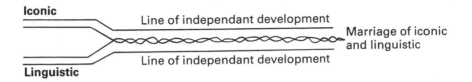

Figure 1.5

It is indispensable to his (the child) affective and intellectual equilibrium, therefore, that he has available to him an area of activity whose motivation is not adaptation to reality but, on the contrary, assimilation of reality to the self, without coercions and sanctions. Such an area is play, which transforms reality by assimilation to the needs of the self.

(Piaget 1951)

As art and language offer the opportunity for expression, so does play. Play is observed in infants very early on in their development. Even the complex type of play known as a 'game' which requires adherence to rule structure, can be observed in infants as young as 7 months of age who actively participate in the game of Peekaboo (Bruner and Sherwook 1979). Play clearly precedes the development of language as a mode of expression. However, the infant has even earlier modes of expression in the smiling response and in crying. Both of these are clearly recognizable as expressions of emotions.

Expression can now be divided into three categories. Emotioning, languaging and, in art therapy, picturing. (This idea has been put forward by Humberto Maturana, a biologist whose work in systems theory is influencing many group and family therapists. I was introduced to this idea during one of his lectures and to my knowledge, he has not published this work (Maturana 1980).)

Emotioning may precede languaging but these two modes of expression differ quite significantly. The expression of emotions, as in the case of the smiling response and crying already cited, are innate or instinctive responses, that is, they will develop in the infant even in the absence of conventional learning or practice. Language, on the other hand, as Chomsky has shown us, is governed by a structure of grammatical rules and although we all inherit the capacity for language, this capacity is not realized without exposure to other language users and this interaction includes conventional learning and practice (Peattelli-Palmarini 1980; see also *Figure 1.6*).

At this level, we might consider that all expression is a form of representation. The cry 'represents' the unpleasure experienced because of hunger or

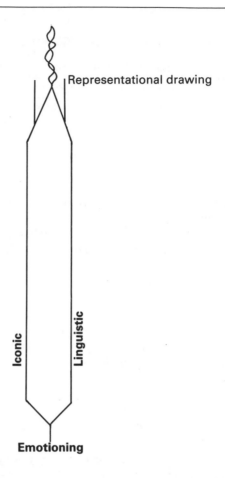

Figure 1.6

the painful discomfort that accompanies a filled wet nappy. The smiling response represents the anticipation of the pleasure afforded by the body of the mother. In all types of representation there are two elements, the signifier and the signified. The signifier 'stands for' the signified. In spoken language the signifier is usually a word and as such it in no way resembles that which it signifies. (This is of course because words have no substance in the way that material objects do.)

Patricia Marks Greenfield of the University of California, Los Angeles, has pointed out that the most *basic* aspect of all representation is 'correspondence' between these two elements – signifier and signified. She points out that:

Such correspondence is a feature of the earliest type of object manipulation. Its origins appear to lie in the bilateral symmetry of human beings.

Typically in the fourth month of life the infant begins to play with her hands; she discovers that one hand corresponds to the other . . . the child discovers her two hands which are the same, yet distinct. Such similarity can be considered a basic type of correspondence.

(Greenfield 1978)

Here we can note that the capacity for representation originates in the discovery of correspondence. Language is a particular and highly complex representational system. As a system, this has to be learned by the child. The child also makes use of earlier systems such as emotioning but also at the period when language acquisition is taking place (between the ages of 6 and 11 months the child starts making spontaneous vocalizations, these are soon replaced by single words; by approximately 18 months to 2 years these develop into two-word sentences, then short complete sentences; and between 2 and 4 years the child gradually acquires grammatical structure), the child starts to develop the capacity for representation using images with the beginnings of drawing. And this development, like language, is also based on conventions that need to be learned.

Sometime between approximately 12 and 18 months of age the child will have developed enough hand–eye co-ordination to allow for the manipulation of objects. The child discovers that when certain objects are moved over certain surfaces they leave a trace. The earliest traces are often referred to as 'locomotor scribble', a term suggested by Victor Lowenfeld (Lowenfeld and Brittain 1974). During this initial stage of 'locomotor scribble', the child is experimenting with movements of the limbs, interest being shown more to the movements than the traces that these leave behind. However, the child does start to notice that specific types of movements leave specific forms of marks and gradually attention becomes focused on the mark-making activity itself. Here we have a recurrence of Patricia Marks Greenfield's notion of 'correspondence'.

While drawing, the child starts to experiment, repeating the same locomotor movement over and over again, sometimes producing several very similar drawings all from a uniform repeated single movement. Here, Kellogg (Kellogg 1970) could argue that the child is starting to learn what might be considered a vocabulary of marks. She herself identified twenty so-called 'basic scribbles', these include the dot, vertical lines, horizontal lines, roving open lines, single and multiple loop lines, and finally imperfect circles. At first the child will make only one 'type' of mark or 'basic scribble' on any one drawing but gradually two or more forms of marks will be combined together. At this stage, although the child has not produced what might be considered a recognizable configuration, he might name the drawing and this stage is sometimes referred to as one of 'named scribble'.

Most models describing this development, including those postulated by both Kellogg and Lowenfeld, as I have already shown, suggest that the developmental sequence culminates in the child being able to arrive at a particular configuration of marks commonly referred to as a 'tadpole-man' or 'stick-figure'. Prior to this 'picture', the drawings produced are often referred to as pre-representational or scribble. The idea has been recently challenged by John Matthews:

> The prevailing notion of children's drawing development is one in which the child more or less thoughtfully assembles a vocabulary of marks which are eventually used for figurative purposes . . . . During this 'scribbling period', the child has been considered a 'failed realist' displaying 'synthetic incapacity' . . . yet while there is indeed a level at which the child investigates mark-making for itself, independent of any symbolic meaning, it would be nonetheless anomalous in the light of the child's other burgeoning symbolic capacities and activities . . . if the infants did not glimpse symbolic potential in the earliest marks they make.
>
> (Matthews 1984)

Matthews goes on to describe a notion of 'action representation'. An example of this is when the child uses the actual movement of the implement across the picture surface to 'correspond' with other movements remembered or imagined. For example, a roving line represents the passage of a motor car on a journey and this might be followed by a vigorous circular scribble corresponding to an imagined crash. Matthews writes further: 'In fact, right from the onset of marking behaviour – from drawing in vomit or spilt milk – experiments in symbolization are occurring.' (We can apply this assertion to our work with the mentally handicapped, as even what appear to be primitive 'scribbles' are nevertheless potentially operating on a symbolic level.)

The correspondencies utilized for symbolization in these cases of 'action representation' are not at the visual or 'pictorial' level but, as Matthews points out, are to be seen as 'depictions of a topological nature'. He concludes: 'the child builds iconography on a substratum of symbolizations which are as much to do with movement and time as they are with configuration'. Here we can see that the child's use of mark-making and his or her understanding of the subsequent drawings is based on a complex series of developments. Some of these developments are directing the child to view drawing in terms of making marks that correspond with objects that he or she views in the world. (This may be a parallel to our use of the term 'literal' when applied to speech.) This line of development is towards the production of 'pictures'. Another line of development explores movement and events and this line may best be described as 'mapping'. The use of colour can often express certain feelings, line movements and tones can also be used this way and this development follows a separate line. It is difficult to label this and perhaps the word 'mood' is as good as any. These are just three of a potentially much greater number of ways that a child may use mark-making, all of these lines offer the opportunity for symbolic use to the child. However, when, as adults, we view the subsequent piece of work we almost invariably ask the same question: 'What is it?' and expect an answer that corresponds with an object and by so doing start literally to rob the child of all the other potentials inherent in the drawing.

Even at the so-called 'scribble stage' the child is actively participating in a process of representation. As early as between 12 and 18 months of age the child begins this exploration. According to Piaget, this exploration coincides with the end of the sensory-motor period and the beginnings of the period of concrete operations. Here he describes the beginning of what he terms the 'Semiotic-function' (Piaget and Inhelder 1969). Unlike Gardner, Piaget lists Drawing together with Imitation, Symbolic Play, Mental Images, Memory, and Language under this single term.

When turning specifically to the development of drawing skills within the semiotic-function, Piaget brings in the observations made by Luquet while he was studying the drawing development of the child in the 1920s. Luquet calls one of the early stages of drawing 'fortuitous realism' and he describes this in terms of scribble 'whose meaning is discovered in the act of making it' (Luquet 1927). He suggests that at this stage (approximately 18 months of age) the child has not yet grasped the concepts necessary for graphic representation and therefore embarks on a drawing with no conscious intention to produce a depiction. Experimenting with line (locomotor scribble) the child places her or his marks in a more or less random fashion. However some of these combinations of marks might suggest a visual resemblance (correspondence) simply by chance. As the child pays attention to the drawing she or he is producing the 'meaning' (resemblance/correspondence) is discovered. Because of the child's yet undeveloped skills she or he cannot reproduce this configuration and this leads to Luquet's next stage, that of 'failed-realism'. What I find exciting about this concept is not that it leads to some sense of failure but that it is a genuine course for discovery. For me, what Luquet has pointed out is a mechanism for symbolic resemblance. This mechanism, which is indeed fortuitous, continues to occur even following a stage in drawing development that allows the child to produce representational images.

I have already pointed out that one of the most common early pictorial representations produced by children is the tadpole-man. I have also suggested a sequence of stages that may precede this. Clearly, prior to the child being able to produce this configuration she or he must first have mastered the circle. This usually corresponds to a combination of head and body. Following this, radials emanating from the outside of the circle correspond to limbs. Children often 'learn' to produce this configuration in a sequential or 'schematic' way. I have worked with several children who are at this stage of drawing development.

As an art therapist, one of the questions I have in mind when I first start working with a child concerns my understanding of drawing development. I often ask children to 'draw a man' as part of my initial assessment. One occasion was while I was working at a family centre that catered for single parents and their children. I was introduced to a small boy of 2½ years of age, Peter, who had just started attending that day. He had been accompanied by his mother who was a single parent. Most of the staff of the family centre are women and on this day I was the only male in the building. We had drawing materials available and I noted that Peter's drawing contained circular configurations. I asked, 'Can you draw a man?' he said 'Yes' and proceeded to produce a tadpole-man. He seemed keen to continue and so I prompted him by asking 'who will you draw next?' he replied 'Daddy' and started the next drawing, in the same way as with the previous figure, by producing a circle. The next mark in his sequence (or schema) was a radial line that corresponded to one of the legs and he drew this next. At this stage he stopped and took a long look at his drawing then said 'balloon'. I suggested that he might continue with the drawing but instead he said 'Daddy is a balloon'. He did not make any further marks on the drawing and seemed clearly satisfied with his productions, both pictorial and verbal.

As a therapist I could suggest interpretations of this session on several levels but what struck me was the poetical nature of this young child's state-ment. 'Daddy is a balloon' works on a metaphorical level. This sentence came about fortuitously. The child noted a resemblance in his incompleted schema and named this 'balloon', his intention still complying with my request that he draw a named figure, 'Daddy' is still active in his mind. And he makes his statement 'Daddy is a balloon'. On a symbolic level this suggests associations that potentially link with his experiences of a man, his father, whose visits are infrequent, have little substance, and are prone to burst or fly away. I did not make these or any other interpretations to the child as I regarded his statement to be insightful in its own right. His discovery at this metaphorical level was therapeutic as it allowed him to make further sense of experience.

For me, one of the important aspects of this attempt is that the metaphor was discovered at the iconic (pictorial) level. If we accept Gardner's arguments concerning separate development for separate 'intelligences' we can start to argue that this metaphor might have been made in the absence of linguistic development. Further, if we then take the evidence presented by Matthews suggesting pre-pictorial 'representation' we can see that the child who has not been able to develop pictorial skills can still possibly function at a level of sophistication that even allows for metaphorical thinking.

In my experience, many art therapists who work with people who have a mental handicap (and consequently have not developed linguistic skills or a level of pictorial sophistication in art work), still feel that the drawings and paintings produced by these people suggest some form of order or meaning.

Plate 1

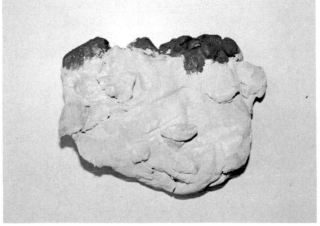

Plate 2

Plate 3

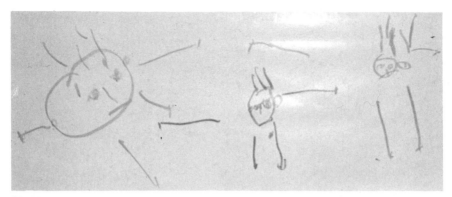

Plate 4

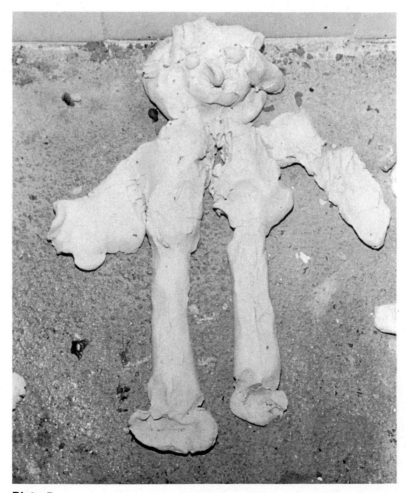

Plate 5

Plate 6

Plate 7

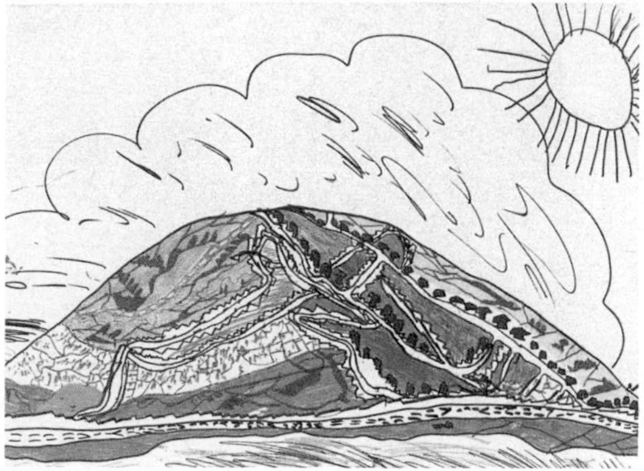

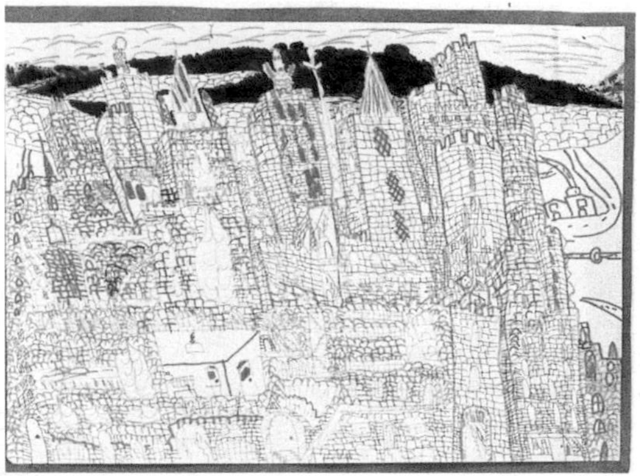

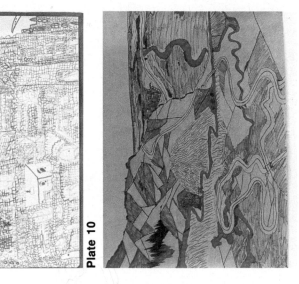

Plate 10

Plate 11

Plate 8

Plate 9

It has been widely held that if an individual cannot develop language then that person's competence of thought is also affected. What I hope to have shown is that this may not be the case. Further, I feel very strongly that as therapists, teachers, parents, etc., we should be encouraging disabled people to develop as many skills or 'intelligences' as possible. For some people art may offer a channel for further development leading to a true sense of self and of a place within the world.

Within the theory of multiple intelligences we can see some form of hierarchical organization taking place. At the earliest stages of development, during infancy and early childhood, we can observe a large degree of flexibility in the way in which an individual learns. However, sooner or later the sophistication, complexity, and economy of language exert their influence. As a means of communication language is unrivalled. One consequence of this is that if our experiences cannot easily be translated into words we find it difficult to share it with others. How can the art therapist start to understand and work with products produced by children who have limited linguistic skills and who cannot make representational pictures? I have suggested one possible clue. If a non-representational configuration is often repeated this may suggest that it has a special meaning to the child. At this stage it is as important to observe how the 'favoured configuration' is arrived at as simply viewing the finished object. It may be a form of 'action representation' or may be produced by rhythmic movements of hands. It may correspond with the posture of the child while he or she is drawing. If this is the case then we may have something like a 'literal' self-portrait in that the configuration is directly related to the child's body. If configurations include enclosures, circles, etc., then the child may be exploring concepts of 'inside and outside'. I have also suggested that colour rhythm and tone can be used as an expression of feelings or 'mood'.

All of these can be combined or kept separate and this may hold potential meaning for the child. We should remember that learning plays a large part in any development process and that much learning takes place in the form of play. Further we must understand that it is during the earliest stages of development, during infancy, and early childhood, that the child is most flexible and can therefore make the most use of developing real skill in all areas of his or her potential 'intelligence'. This flexibility is partly due to neurological factors (during infancy and early childhood the brain is still growing and changing), and therefore in some respects the infant does not get a second chance if certain things are not learned during these early stages of development. (An example of this is language acquisition; we all know how difficult it is for an adult to learn a second language, while during childhood it is possible for an individual to learn several languages simultaneously without getting them mixed up.) It is therefore very important that handicapped children be given the opportunity to start exploring with mark-making as soon as they are able.

This is at the time that the individual has developed enough hand–eye co-ordination to be able to bring a marker into contact with a sheet of paper (or other picture surface). Most children will have managed this before 18 months, and it is not uncommon for infants as young as 8 months to start playing with crayons. Even the most primitive mark made with the imple-ment is an act of creation. Adults should meet these acts of creation with uncritical and unconditional regard. It is important for the child to recognize this act of creation. This discovery amounts to the child realizing that he or she is responsible for the mark that has been created and by so doing the child is enabled to see him or herself as an agent of change. This can be very exciting for the child and the heightened excitement will improve the child's attention and concentration.

These earliest marks will probably be executed with simple movements, perhaps a movement of just the fingers holding the crayon, or the wrist. The child can make a movement from the elbow or from the shoulder or even use the whole body to make an arc or other gesture across a picture surface. In this way we can see that the child uses his or her body as a vehicle for expression. The posture of the child determines the type of mark that will be made. The child will gradually build up a repertoire of marks (or iconic vocabulary) and in the process learn that different movements of the body produce different marks. The child learns to master his or her movements at the same time as paying attention to the new and exciting things that are happening on the picture surface. Realization of the causal relationship between body and mark in itself has potential meaning for the child and it is possible for certain profound marks to take on a special symbolic meaning for the individual.

I think it is therefore important that the child is given a picture surface large enough to enable full expression of movement. As a rough guide the sheet of paper should be at least as wide as the distance between the child's fingers and shoulder. We should also have in mind that the plane of the picture surface will influence the types of movements that are possible. A sheet of paper pinned to the wall allows for expressing the body while stand-ing up, the sheet of paper on the floor allows the child to get down on all fours. As adults, we tend to look at the blank sheet of paper as if it is a kind of window. Although this can be a very useful convention, it can also be very limiting. The young child is not bound by any such convention and we should not imagine that the mark made by the child must necessarily stand for a movement or a feeling rather than an object. Several marks on a sheet of paper may form some kind of map in the child's imagination, the child may be exploring the space afforded by the sheet of paper in the same way that he or she explores the physical space of the environment.

The child should be given help and encouragement in playing with all the possibilities I have mentioned and this can often be done non-verbally; I have already shown that asking 'what is it?' can be less than helpful. I have always found it useful, during these early stages of development, to materials that offer maximum visual feedback to the child. I also feel that at this stage, line is perhaps more important than tone (particularly as the child is building up a repertoire of different types of marks). Some marks, such as lines, demand a continuous movement across a picture surface and paint does not always allow this as the brush needs frequent rechanging. I have found that simple black (or other dark coloured) wax crayons on good quality white paper give excellent results. The use of colour can be very important, especially because of the emotional effect that it has on the individual. Children can release much feeling when they use colour and this can enrich the developing iconic vocabulary a great deal.

Jeavons has made an excellent study regarding using art with children who suffer from cerebral palsy (Jeavons 1977). I have worked with children who suffer from a wide range of neurological damage and have found that the majority, even the most profoundly handicapped, can grasp an implement and direct it toward a picture surface. This is the start of making a statement, a statement about one's individuality. A statement that does not need words or language but can eventually express the most profound, sensitive, and complex feelings of the human spirit.

© 1990 Janek Dubowski

Note

This chapter is based on a paper entitled 'Daddy Is a Balloon', presented during Image and Enactment in Childhood, Art Therapy and Dramatherapy with Children, a conference held at Hertfordshire College of Art and Design in 1987.

References

Bruner, Jerome S. and Sherwook, V. (1979) 'Peekaboo and the learning of rule struc-
tures', in J.S. Bruner, A. Jolly, and K. Sylva (eds), *Play: Its Role in Development and Evolution*, London: Penguin Books.
Chambers Everyday Dictionary (1975) Edinburgh: W. & R. Chambers Ltd.
Gardner, H. (1985) *Frames of Mind: The Theory of Multiple Intelligences*, London: Paladin.
Greenfield, P. (1978) 'Structural parallels between language and action in develop-
ment', in Andrew Lock (ed.) *Action, Gesture and Symbol: The Emergence of Language*, London: Academic Press.
Gombrich, E.H. (1952) *Meditations on a Hobby Horse*, London: Phaidon. First writ-
ten for a symposium entitled 'Symbols and Values', New York.
Jeavons, T. (1977) *Art and Cerebral Palsy*, London: The Spastics Society.
Kellog, R. (1970) *Analysing Children's Art*, Calif.: National Press Books.
Lowenfeld, V. and Lambert Brittain, W. (1974) *Creative and Mental Growth*, London: Macmillan.

Luquet, G.H. (1927) *Le Dessin Enfantin*, Paris: Alcan.

Matthews, J. (1984) 'Children drawing: Are young children really scribbling?', *Early Child Development and Care* 18.

Maturana, H. (1980) *Antopoiesis and Cognition: The Realization of the Living*, London: D. Reidel Publishing Co.

Peattelli-Palmarini, M. (ed.) (1980) *Language and Learning: The Debate Between Jean Piaget and Noam Chomsky*, Cambridge, Mass.: Harvard University Press.

Piaget, J. (1951) *Play, Drama and Imitations of Childhood*, London: Routledge & Kegan Paul.

Piaget, J. and Inhelder, B. (1969) *The Psychology of the Child*, London: Routledge & Kegan Paul.

Chapter two

Art therapy as a container
Sigrid Rabiger

I aim to describe ways of working in art therapy with children who have little or no sense of an 'as if' and to try to differentiate between this lack being one of developmental delay of a severe kind, or that of psychotic or borderline defence structures. The kinds of approaches I use with both groups, as with those who show marked autistic tendencies, are equally appropriate and helpful, in that they offer a firm base from which to begin.

I wish at the outset to make a clear differentiation between the concept of mental handicap and the so-called 'severe learning difficulties' (SLD) which describe the various children in the SLD school where I work. It seems to me that the term 'mental handicap' is far too broad, encompassing as it can, a 'slow learner' in a moderate learning difficulties school (MLD); a well-functioning, imaginative, and verbal Down's Syndrome child, or a multiply-handicapped adolescent of weeks'-only developmental level. In actual fact, one of the major handicaps with many of our children seems to be a severely impaired sense of self, a degree of traumatization or of developmental delay, both of which seem to contribute to an inability to play, thus handicapping the ability to learn, or indeed, to use art. Thus, our children are not so much 'slow learners' as 'non-learners', either because of psychological problems blocking any meaningful input, or because their developmental delay has not enabled them to progress in ways of even a pre-school child. This is not so much a question of 'intelligence' as of a far deeper psychological, emotional, or even neurological imbalance.

Until recently there has been a sharp demarcation between 'mental handicap' and 'mental illness' but it seems lately to be more widely accepted that the one can greatly contribute to the other. Now that these concepts are fusing more constructively, I hope we will be able to help these children to a more meaningful extent. Perhaps we also need to question the wisdom of the view that *all* children have a 'right' to 'education'. For the deeply psychiatrically-disturbed, or the severely multiply-handicapped, school often seems to do little for the child and can create a negative effect on other children and the staff. For these children, 'school' seems at best inappropriate, at worst a form of near-torture. In my experience in this kind of setting, I have discovered that the only way to help these children is to establish their developmental level and begin there, whatever their actual age might be. To do otherwise seems to create a gap filled only with robot-like responses, little comprehension, or aggressive outbursts.

Melanie Klein writes:

> In my experience, excessive persecutory fears and schizoid mechanisms in early infancy may have a detrimental effect on intellectual development in its initial stages. Certain forms of mental deficiency would therefore have to be regarded as belonging to the group of schizophrenias. Accordingly, in considering mental deficiency in children at any age one should keep in mind the possibility of schizophrenic illness in early infancy.
>
> (Klein 1946:104)

Helen Deutsch describes the inability of comprehending an 'as if' concept, and writes of primary identification in people who have been 'exposed to chronic emotional deprivation and inconsistency in primary relationships at the time preceding the ascendancy of the Oedipus complex' (Deutsch 1942:301). This has left them without the necessary cathetic energy to internalize and integrate the various fragments which go to form the superego. 'In their pregenital development they devalued the objects that could have served them as models for personality development, and thus failed to obtain a sense of personal identity' (Deutsch 1942:301). She also observes that these kinds of impairments implied developmental failure rather than regression.

These two descriptions illustrate well the intractable problem of the so-called 'senior' class existing in the school when I arrived. Many of these youngsters, mostly male, had been hospitalized from their earliest years, thus they did not even have the possibility of anchoring to a stable mother figure. Given the 'chance' of education in their early teens, their defences and regressions were already too entrenched to allow realistic benefit. There was a further problem of which I became aware only relatively recently – which is that many of these children are barely through their infancy stage, in terms of comprehension and response, before actual, hormonal puberty overtakes them. Thus, they are deprived of experiencing the relative quiescence of latency. Most of these lads responded to this physical bombardment of sensation with rage and bewilderment – the reactions of a 2-year-old in an adult-sized body. The usual school strictures, such as 'time out', did little to contain these eruptions, and it certainly seemed too late to introduce a once-weekly art therapy session, although I was expected to attempt to do so. It is interesting for me to see how much better they are faring in the day centres they now attend, and in their residential settings, where expectations are more realistic, and are perhaps geared to a more appropriate level for them, with less unbearable pressure in the form of well-meant frenetic activities; in effect an altogether calmer, quieter atmosphere pervades.

I have written elsewhere (Rabiger 1984) about the inadvisability of over-stimulation, of assuming this is a 'teenaged' group, and the bewildering impact on youngsters who are already confused and vulnerable. I have found identical equivalents in art therapy techniques: that many art activities can trigger negative responses of a damaging kind. Victor Lowenfeld (1965), describes this very well when he advises against the use of finger paint with too-young a child, as this can cause regression to more primitive levels. It is regrettable that many teachers and their training colleges assume that as children with severe learning difficulties may be unsuitable for cognition, they can do lots of lovely art instead, not realizing that both are dependent upon emotional readiness. Exciting art techniques can be both confusing and destructive if not properly understood by the child, and if the adults involved assume too much imaginative symbolism where none might exist. This can create a gap in the child's understanding and experience because the input has been projected by the adult, not the child.

Viktor Lowenfeld also describes the various scribble stages, and says longitudinal scribbling is indicative of the relationship between motor and vision, and that learning controlled scribbling can affect the whole child's motor ability. I would say further that it can indeed affect the whole child; that it is a primary means of expression, and an advance for many of our SLD children, whatever their actual age. For this reason, it seemed important to establish regular displays of children's work, including scribbles by some more able seniors, for whom this was a major achievement, equivalent to drawings in perspective by a similar age group in mainstream education. Further, I felt that by doing this, the staff of each class were shown not only the level of ability and the point at which these children were functioning, but also that there arose thereby a symbolic acceptance of the child himself for what he could achieve rather than for what he could not. Conversely, it can be surprising for many people to see how 'able' in art some children in fact are, when they do not appear so developed cognitively, and *vice versa*.

It is extremely hard for adults to fully conceive of there being a total inability to play, so there is a universal tendency to project 'play' interpretations upon a child's behaviour and activity. We pretend the child is pretending, whereas for him the activity may be all-too real, or quite incomprehensible. Working with autistic children, with their extreme concretization, has helped me to see this manifested in other forms of developmental impairments or psychosis. I have been greatly helped in this by the writings of Frances Tustin (1972, 1981, 1986) and also by my experience at Family Tree, where I saw that the apparent restrictions and direction aided meaningful development. This can be translated into similarly structured approaches in the art room, and concrete use of art materials.

Frances Tustin pinpoints the need for atypical interventions in her psychotherapy with autistic children, and I have found similar needs in the art room, equally applicable to children who are either developmentally delayed, or have psychotic features, or both. Somehow structure, and intervention, seem to make possible a degree of relaxation and creativity in former stereotypic uses of art media.

From this awareness of the very beginnings, it was necessary to eradicate any suggestion or expectation of figuration or things-representational. This is more difficult to put into practice than it may appear, but once achieved, releases all sorts of potential. For instance, clay can be used as a substance to be manipulated, to help acknowledge just *something* outside the self. It is also an area, like finger-paint, where the child may be helped towards autonomy, by imprinting and wiping away his own marks at will. Some need help, as with finger-paint, in recognizing its difference from 'dirt', or faeces, to feel confident enough to handle it. Clay can also be cut, by children who may still have difficulty cutting their food. I do try to encourage aggression to be more overtly expressed, for instance by offering a heavy mallet to a child, but it is an interesting paradox that many of the more aggressive children often seem hesitant to use such tools, like the more resistant autistic children, who will also not exert enough energy to use even woodwork tools meaningfully. Most children are surprisingly able to recognize that it is the clay which is to be banged, rather than the table. I provide various shapes, circular, oval, square, rectangular, for imprinting and to help the more cognitively-aware children familiarize their differences and their names – many non-verbal children will signify their awareness by pointing to the shape they have just made, or by looking intently at the article itself.

On the basis of Tustin's recognition that autistic children can be helped into awareness of 'insides' and 'outsides', the children are asked to put the clay away in its bag. This too can be helpful, as an assessment of intelligence or problem-solving capacity – one young child knew that it was necessary to prop the bag against a firm surface! It is also a revelation of just how many of our children 'go through the motions' of an activity without understanding its aim or end result, so that there is much shaking and rustling of the bag but no clay actually enters it; many shoot the clay right past, through lack of any eye–hand co-ordination. One little girl needed to be encouraged to *put* the clay inside the bag, rather than throw it, as one of her more psychotic manifestations was to suddenly lose her original concept of an activity and jerk her arms around, throwing objects and letting them fall, obsessively and manically.

This is the very basis, but even such a fundamental approach can only be used with children who are ready to acknowledge art materials as substances to be handled, rather than eaten. For the more able, and those beginning to use figuration, clay can be a useful way to develop body image. Those who still place legs and arms away from the head, when drawing, are able, with verbal question-reminders from me, to put in a body, sometimes even a neck, in their almost diagrammatically built-up clay figures. Concepts such as 'more' and 'less' can be experienced in a concrete way, aiding total awareness and development – using art therapy educationally to help the whole child advance to his or her maximum capacity. All these methods can also be helpful indications of which stage a child may be at – though this may be 'lost' a week or two later, to be resumed again. There is a considerable amount of fluctuation in the child's abilities. One little girl at the infant level who had hitherto played 'tea-parties' with clay, elected to make her first conscious form, calling it 'house', but portraying a recognizable 'figure'. One autistic boy, with a late onset of puberty, made clay shapes which were equivalent to his new bodily interests – first phallic, later mammary.

Clay can also encourage a form of 'sharing' play, so that little bits of it are broken up and distributed among various pots, pretended to be eaten, rearranged, and then handed to me. Children will often rather ritualistically say 'cooking' and 'cakes' while rolling and patting. Having no awareness of size, they frequently attempt to cram pieces which are too large into impossibly small containers. (One stocky autistic boy at Family Tree used to regularly try to squeeze himself into a cardboard box, quite unaware of his own body image in relation to its size.) Clay can help the beginnings of symbolic awareness, as when an adolescent girl still at the pre-figurative stage, called out: 'Don't touch! Hot!' after handing a visitor a small piece. Another, greatly disturbed and aggressive 'senior' would, towards the end of his last year, continually cut pieces of clay with a knife, saying 'cheese' – one of his few words.

Clay is also a good way to encourage manual dexterity in our children who need help in every facet of their lives, so that art therapy cannot detach itself from this universal need to develop motor co-ordination. It surprised and interested me to discover how few children can actually roll a ball of clay, an activity which is perhaps similar in ability to drawing a circle? Once a ball can be formed, the concept of a face, or even a thumb-pot is easier. Yet even this is not a consistent indicator of ability, as an otherwise fairly low-functioning and wheelchair-bound girl knew how to pat the clay from hand to hand to form a ball shape, even though she could not master the rolling of it. Another, an able 8-year-old who can draw (*Plate 1*) and make up a clay face (*Plate 2*) with features, seems to have more difficulty in rolling a 'sausage' shape than a ball, which he can manage with ease.

This is another continual reminder that there are no 'answers', that there is no magical 'key' or even a consistent pattern. Once I had freed myself from this expectation, the work became more meaningful and exciting. To imagine there *is* a solution which has eluded one, tends to make one feel a failure – as these children can already cause one to feel, by their dismissive and apathetic attitude to the contents of the art room. But to be flexible to the needs of the moment, to be able to adjust to what seems most urgent in any particular session, keeps one more in touch with the individual child and less likely to be swamped by the sometimes apparent impossibility of the task. Similarly, to help children to concentrate and focus, even within half-an-hour, is to help them relax and reduce tension. For the more psychotic, naturally, this period may be a matter of minutes only. It is interesting that my expectation of thought and effort seems to encourage greater confidence, where one would have expected hesitation and withdrawal. Yet almost universally, these children tend to panic at direct questioning or overt expectation. This governs most forms of learning within the school, for instance a child unable to form a conventional number concept, when asked to lay the table, and reminded there would be seven people, was well able to lay seven places!

But for many, even these concrete, primary uses of clay are far in advance of their capacity, being still at the stage of needing to mouth every object, though not in the enquiring manner of a young baby, but in a sort of automated fixation. For this group, mostly adolescent, mobile, but very severely mentally handicapped and functioning at a very early stage indeed, I devised 'water play' – although the word 'play' is a misnomer. For the children to recognize that a container could be used as a cup was a high-level of response indeed. There was either total inability to make eye-contact with the water bowl, eyes fixed on mine, or gaze-avoidance of everything, negative insistence on dropping things to the floor, or no response at all. Most did not react or even notice if I blew bubbles. For these children it seemed too late to make any impingement on their awareness, while at the same time they had all the mood-swings and lability of hormonal adolescence, thereby showing how very much physical states can influence emotions.

For the multiply-handicapped even this level was too advanced, and it really seemed to me that they were at the stage of development where feeding was the priority, so that I began to encourage an anchoring of a one-to-one feeder, same feeder, same child, to try to promote the beginnings of a sense of a continuing relationship, and also to motivate any degree of mobility to assist in self-help. Over the years, this has been seen to have helped them to develop a greater consciousness of the environment, but they have not yet reached a state where art would have any relevance at all.

Daphne

However, one 9-year-old girl responded extraordinarily well to this technique of using water, taking it far past its initial stages and proceeding to art forms of a scribble kind. This has reinforced my conviction of the need to establish developmental levels in considering what may be a suitable art activity. Because she presented such behavioural problems, I was required to work with her almost daily at first. She was able to come through this very needy stage and progress to more external interactions with the art materials.

Daphne is microcephalic, and lived with her family until the age of 5. She was put into care, with tenuous links still maintained with home. At this point, a brother and, later, a younger sister were born (she already had a much older sister, now in her 20s) so that she has had to bear the pain of actual separation from her mother, and intense sibling rivalry. Thus this little girl is suffering from both severe mental handicap and severe emotional deprivation, which she seemed only to be able to verbalize in temper tantrums and aggression towards her peers.

I had an early glimpse of her ability to relate when I saw her on the lap of one of her care workers, fingering her face like a baby; and her need for containment when I had to hold her firmly between my knees in a classroom situation, during which time she resisted violently at first, and then capitulated, relaxed, and laid her head on my lap.

Everything I had offered in the art room she had thrown, smeared over her face and hands, and eaten. She seemed to find being reprimanded hilariously funny. Given my present freedom to select children on a clinical basis for art therapy, I might well have declined to work with her, and yet this child has taught me so very much, not least about the need to begin at the very beginning.

I decided all I could meaningfully offer would be water, and kept the objects to a minimum. At first her response was manic. She drank at a rapid rate using all her fingers, dunked her head, throwing and spilling, and finally urinated all over the floor. I tried to encourage greater consciousness and control, offering a separate cup for drinking from the tap. As I felt her become more ready to understand and accept, I removed objects she had thrown, and much later, objects she had drunk from, trying to encourage a differentiation between the 'play' element and the practical need for a drink – also recognizing that many hyperactive children do seem to suffer from excessive thirst. I felt there was a possibility of therapeutic change when one day, eyeing me fixedly as she slowly poured water on to the floor, she then accepted my invitation to pour it into a cup held by me. After this, I offered increasingly smaller containers for her to pour water into, playing with her, and trying to promote greater manual dexterity and focus. She became far more able to look at her own activity, sometimes really concentrating and becoming involved, and I may well have stayed at this stage, refining the pouring techniques and emphasizing the difference between drinking and 'playing', if she had not rushed to an easel on her way out and swiped it with a brush. After only one term, it seemed she was telling me she could use 'art' now.

The first paper I gave her was small, not too threatening, and her first marks were tentative and hesitant. Soon I gave her paper the size of the table, to avoid predictable issues over boundaries, and still began each session with a period of water-play. She quickly became able to scribble vehemently and expressively, and with variety (*Plate 3*). Her confusion entangled with her apparent negativism showed in the way she would forget whether she had just removed a felt-tip pen top to use, or was replacing it. We went through a long period of this 'off–on–off'. She delighted in the skills required and became increasingly able to use her eyes more to look at what she was doing, and less to gaze at me. I began to realize how much greater her verbal comprehension was than her ability to convey it, and began to commiserate with her feelings at having to leave her sister behind with her mother. Her response was to scribble violently! (Her visits home had increased by now, to twice a week.) Daphne is very musical and tends to control adults by insisting they complete a song she has started. I began to sing my own tunes to her, using made-up words to describe her situation and possible feelings.

Over three-and-a-half years, Daphne has become quite able to resist putting any materials to her mouth, and can wait while I fetch paper, with a tray of paints on the table in front of her. She can replace the pens in their right places, point to what she wishes to use, return the brushes to their correct pots, stay on the paper, listen, and walk about the room without going out of the door. She understands far more, screams far less, and is more able to hold some sort of dialogue instead of snatching. She has found clay the most difficult to resist putting in her mouth and continues to do so as a tease, and is still least interested in using this as a medium. But her original intense oral need has gone, as has her compulsion to drink. After graduating to fetching her own drink and staying at the sink by herself to do so, she has not signed for one for an entire term. This reinforces my view that apparent 'greed' and thirst are of emotional origin, which makes the question of attempting to diet this overweight, pre-pubescent girl very problematical, as she will only be able to perceive such controls on her food intake as 'punishment'.

During one of our calmest sessions, in our second year, Daphne was able for the first time to desist from putting the clay in her mouth, even as a testing-tease. When she left the session, there was a large turd under her chair! I felt this was an act on several levels: an earliest infancy form of 'gift' possibly; an unconscious association with the symbolic similarity of clay and faeces, observed in several children; and also a 'sock-it-to-you' as the price I had to pay for her agreement not to eat it. The links between me and internal substances have become clearer recently, when she seems to need me to take her to the lavatory at the beginning of every session. This not-surprisingly severely-constipated girl is able to perform, often saying 'Mummy' the while. It seems that through our long association in frequent art therapy sessions, I have come to represent many roles for her.

Since we first worked together, our sessions have reduced to three a week. She now goes home every day on the coach with most of the other children.

After one-and-a-half years of daily visits, subject to school breaks and her parents' holidays, Daphne is still unable to hold this as a certainty, and is quite frenzied during the day. Yet it is acknowledged by all who work with her that since these daily visits, she is dramatically improved in behaviour, and is relaxed enough to allow greater cognitive development, verbal comprehension, and more single words. In the children's home she signs 'conversations' such as 'going for a walk?'. She can now use finger paint appropriately and loves it, as genuine 'play' and knows to lift her hands up for a print to be taken. Her shapes have become far more restrained and her capacity to wait is remarkable. I, too, have ceased to feel I need to rush about making sure she has some activity before her – so greatly can one be affected by these children.

To help with her problems of sibling rivalry, I set up a threesome to try to recreate the family situation. When she shared sessions with a 'sister' substitute, she seemed to find this easily bearable, but now she tries to drown us all in noise, and hits out at the very innocuous 'brother-figure'. Yet on two occasions, she detached herself from this group and went to an easel to make a really expressive painting (*Plate 6*). She certainly seems to draw and paint now for her own pleasure, the beginning of 'play', and less for compliance. Her moods are still unpredictable and disruptive and her behaviour needs much more work, e.g. one continual and worsening trait is that of hurting more vulnerable children. Yet paradoxically it has been through art therapy that she has learnt control and restraint, structure and boundaries, as well as being able to experience a continuing constant and consistent relationship with me, against the perpetual and unavoidable staff changes both in the children's home and at school. The strength of her ego carries her forward and enables her to convey the intensity of her needs. It was noted at the children's home that when only she and one other child were taken for a week's holiday, she presented no behaviour problems whatsoever. Her communication is clear, but circumstantially impossible to meet.

The very ego-strength of this child is unusual in our school, but not the mix of sensitivity and handicap, awareness and incomprehension. Opportunity to offer a child intensive, regular, frequent art therapy sessions builds up over a year or more into providing that child with a sense of belonging and continuity often not found in the rest of his or her life. The accumulated sense of trust enables the work to progress, and enables me to push harder for greater relinquishment of manipulative techniques that have become entrenched with time. This sensitivity pervades the school, and also the children I teach only once-weekly. The most bombastic children have responded delicately to the good quality paper donated by a printing firm, and taken greater pains when using it. Two children make motions of drawing in the air, saying 'Nice!' to indicate their choice. Several children choose 'sugar paper' for its word association with sweetness and pleasure, but when shown the difference, often realize that was not their choice after all. An autistic adolescent, when asked who his clay figure was of, replied with great dignity: 'J— G—' giving his full name! Some years ago a very difficult boy with Down's Syndrome who resisted even coming to the art room, was offered farm and jungle animals to play with. He relinquished his macho stance to exclaim 'Elephant baby!' with great tenderness. When I had been ill for many weeks just before the long summer break, every child I had worked with in the last few days made enormous efforts to refrain from their more usual testing and malpractices – though this could also indicate the phantasy that it was their 'misbehaviour' which had caused my 'disappearance'. But in either case, it showed a sensitivity of response.

Daphne, who like several others, farts as an expression of defiance (though also laughing), observed that I sprayed the room with a deodorizer, and began to fetch it beforehand – also identifying it from other, similar cans of fixative. She also, on hearing the particular tune I always sing to her played during Assembly, searched the hall for me, with a real 'They're Playing Our Song' expression on her face! On a slightly different level, but equally sensitively and with intense feeling, she went nearly berserk recently, when I played a tape which she, too, obviously had at the children's home. She seemed to feel it was 'her' music, and how could I possibly have it too? Without adequate language, it was difficult to explain, but I am sure understanding her dilemma helped. The most handicapped child who can use paint, will search painstakingly for the right pot to which to return the brush – though no child can yet deduce that it will be the empty one! Most children will now pause in a doorway, at least aware there is another person (me) behind them, liable to be squashed, and not merely an object to be discarded.

Observations of these small awarenesses and sensitivities can be most encouraging and enable one to hold a greater sense of a functioning person in the child, rather than an assemblage of intractable behaviours or inertness that these children can so easily become, as part of their overriding management problem. Developing this sense of normalcy from within, rather than superimposing it from outside, and especially in the younger children, has enabled me to realize how little I have allowed for the more usual Oedipal stages, while attending to more immediate and apparent problems. Once again, it has been the children who have alerted me. A well-functioning 8-year-old boy with Down's Syndrome first made a breakthrough from a rather sulky-seeming incomprehension and apathy when one day he painted 'Sigrid Dead From Snakes'. Frequent attempts at figuration have since emerged. Lately, he has been drawing 'car crashes' and 'babies', with many phallic shapes. Because of these children's inadequate language, verbal interpretations are sometimes not appropriate, but it seemed helpful to offer a Sasha doll dressed in boy's clothes, although without specific male genitals. This child made no comment or reaction, but there was a rather prolonged removal of the doll's underpants, so I asked what he could see that was different from himself? He euphemistically replied, 'knees'! One comprehending but non-verbal boy dashed an anxious glance at his own crotch, so that I was able to offer an explanative reassurance. Another, highly chaotic boy, made lavatory noises once the doll was undressed, so I offered a pretend potty. To my surprise, however, he stood the doll up to 'wee', as he is now learning to do himself. Years ago, a very inhibited and verbal boy using water-play as an extended activity, rather than as a preliminary stage, suddenly called out: 'Like wee-wee!' This very well-behaved boy is surprisingly unable to contain his water-play, or acknowledge when a bottle is full, and continues pouring, alarmed at the mess, but seemingly unable to stop without intervention. Yet his classmate, usually very disruptive, is extremely organized with water, spilling not a drop. This work is full of surprises!

Some children only seem to attain a 5-year-old level of sexual curiosity as they enter puberty, and will now begin to choose to undress the dolls, and also hold on to themselves anxiously, like a far younger child would. The stages are so intermingled, that it is difficult to understand the child's level. A 16-year-old who reacted excessively to the onset of puberty, seeming to come through very well after all, has now begun to 'expose' himself, with what appears to me far more the pride of a 4-year-old than an act of 'perversion'. Once again we are caught up in trying to disentangle the mixed stages in any one child, and also maintain acceptable social norms.

I have begun to link the apparently accidental spillings and droppings, both in the art room and in the classroom, with probable sexual anxiety and unexpressed sexual curiosity. Where children can draw and play, it is more possible to attempt to provide outlets for expression and to try to verbalize when it seems helpful. But with greater handicaps it is at least as important to try to understand the possible turmoil within a child, which may well explain apparently inexplicable outbursts of aggression or hysteria. There is a strong need for physically demonstrative affection in many children, both to give and receive, yet in older children this can be sexually provoking, although they may be simultaneously needing the comfort one would offer a toddler. It is the importance of identifying and differentiating the need that is so crucial in being able to offer real help, not only in art therapy but also throughout the school.

In a similarly unconventional and irregular way, one cannot apply the 'draw-a-man' test, developmental-level assessment to children with severe learning difficulties. Many will be able to put in details such as eyebrows and pupils before thinking of adding a body. There is another interesting phenomenon, in that some children, after initially attaching legs and arms to the head, as in normal development, start to leave a gap. At first I was worried and puzzled by this rather schizoid manifestation, but watching carefully, it seemed that there was a dawning awareness of a body which they were not quite ready to put in, so a space was left for what they were aware *does* come in between (*Plate 4*). This was verbalized for me some years ago by an able Down's Syndrome child who explained that the hole in the middle of his clay figure was 'tummy' (*Plate 5*). There is also a progression from controlled circular scribble, with random dots in, leading eventually to a definite face. Some will put legs inside the face, or join them, so that they could also represent a neck. Several children have begun to draw hair all round the face. When I questioned this, thinking it was typical dreamy absent-mindedness, one child assured me he did have hair all round! Several have started to do two kinds of hair, a rather stereotyped, sticking-up variety, and then something more specific, such as a fringe, is added. One boy with an organic perceptual imbalance has moved from a clear representative face to a vast circle with a 'face' within it. Some children seem on the verge of attaining the ability to draw figuratively and then lose it regressing into mindless or decorative scribble through adolescence, and then at 19, often in their last week before leaving school, may resume greater signs of figuration.

As well as the hyperactive, noisy, demanding, verbal, and non-verbal children, there are also the more withdrawn, autistic or psychotic, who either negate any meaning of art materials, or become lethargic and catatonic as a reaction to a sense of internal pressure. One such boy, diagnosed as deaf, though often smiling at things said to him, but certainly not acknowledging language, had come a long way towards integrated art work (*Plate 7*), which I hoped would also affect his responses to the total environment. However, as Greenacre (1953) describes so well, outside life does get in the way. In this case, the decline seemed to come after one intensely frenetic preparation for the Christmas Show, where lack of 'holding' due to staff preoccupations has a negative effect on more needy children. This boy never recovered, and came almost to a standstill in his catatonic resistance, possibly exacerbated by the onset of puberty. In the art room, he would lethargically cut up pieces of clay, or scratch his grid-like designs on it, either working best with my close support and presence, or, according to his state, by my distancing myself. I put out a series of options for him, being unable to remove his hands from his eyes for even a signed selection of choice. The first week I reintroduced water colours in blocks, which require the brush to be rinsed between each colour change. I stayed with him, to remind him of the method, and he worked slowly, but was affected by the natural flow of the paint. He came to an abrupt halt, and the following week I left him to work on his own, though making constant signed reassurances of the many times he sought 'permission' to proceed. He made his most completed and committed design for over a year.

It has become quite possible for me to assess confidently which are the autistic children by their similarity of approach, or denial, of the art media. Tools are used as a continuation of autistic objects or stereotypies, flicked in the air, or stared at with a semblance of examination, but with no real curiosity. There is no hand–eye contact and marks are made with total indifference and apathy. Those who are able to use the art materials appropriately, will be capable of concentrated eye–hand co-ordination, but have total gaze-avoidance with people. They will make rigid stripes, often progressing to an arc of stripes, or will paint a whole sheet one colour, and if not removed, continue the same process with another colour *ad infinitum*. There is a universal tendency to obliterate any meaningful marks made, usually in black, and not to complete a circle or any specific shape. There is a hesitancy over allowing colours to touch, or an insistence on painting-over where paint has just been applied. There is a need to test everything by smell, putting every object first to the the nose, or bending to sniff at the paper or clay. These phenomena *can* be seen in the more handicapped or psychotic children also, but not the whole, insistent combination. In fact, it surprised me when I first arrived from a purely autistic unit to see how many autistic features were displayed in severely delayed children; this ties in with my observation that many autistic tendencies are, in fact, early infantile stages not yet relinquished, including the pronoun-reversal so frequent in early normal speech patterns.

There are also superficial similarities in deaf children, which are quickly sorted out – so that one severely deaf little boy soon revealed his high intelligence as he became more confident, and unusually, *painted* his name and figures up to ten, as well as his first number. (I say unusually, because most advances are habitually attained in graphic media rather than paint.) It was in the art room that his intelligence was first noted, and he has now transferred to a school for the hearing impaired. Another child, designated deaf, shows increasingly autistic patterns the longer we work together. It is sad that autism is seen as an incurable condition, for if work is commenced on it early enough and in very specific ways, important interventions *can* be made on the defences which hold potentially able children back from normal development.

It is very difficult to engage most autistic children in art activity, by reason of their very concrete perception of the environment and lack of ability to symbolize. Yet I have noticed, that after puberty, a kind of appropriateness of response does seem to occur in autistic children, and with it, a greater social awareness. A very echolalic, now pre-pubertal boy on the verge of adolescence, is suddenly becoming able to volunteer his own words and sentences, after years of being quite unable to do other than parrot an adult's remark.

Each class in the school usually contains children with a wide variety of difficulties, for example, one highly autistic-type child; one child with Down's Syndrome usually with a good prognosis due to creative potential and ability to play; one child too severely handicapped for any meaningful impingement to be made, especially in art therapy; one child who is generally delayed developmentally and also sometimes physically impaired, usually functioning at the scribble stage, with a few single words and some verbal comprehension, whose art work is very repetitive; and one child with acute behaviour problems which are difficult to contain in a classroom setting with even as few as six children. The children in this last group need and are offered almost daily art therapy sessions, however brief. With varying degrees all these children seem to acquire, and respond to, firm structure, containment and boundaries, and to an 'outside–in' approach. The stabilizing of external behaviours seems to set the pattern for internalization of an increased sense of reality, clarifications of confusions, and interruption of the need for omnipotence stemming from acute anxiety. With the more apathetic children, quite sharp demands for focus and acknowledgement, and often non-art tasks, such as those which depend on eye–hand co-ordination, can help free their entrenched resistance.

Those working with psychotic or borderline patients describe very well 'psychic bleeding' and 'organic insecurity' (Stern 1938). It is often difficult to hold an awareness of the underlying terrors when they are expressed in anti-social ways, such as spitting and head-butting. Yet since analysts working with borderline cases emphasize the need for non-confrontational approaches, and lessening of pressure, it seems those in a special school such as ours have the same requirements; that it is not good enough to say 'school is school' when many children are in no state to endure 'school'. Stern describes very well the deep-seated and recalcitrant lack of self-confidence and self-assurance; he points out that projective mechanisms can easily arise from these accumulated feelings. This, together with a 2-year-old's sense of omnipotence and justification, can be very difficult with a physically powerful adolescent. Anything less than daily or frequent art therapy sessions cannot make much impact. If we continue to apply a uniform standard to each child irrespective of his difficulties, we are likely to produce only an automaton, who may well become physically violent as his only available means of communication.

Summary

The need to establish developmental stages is paramount. Confusion arises when children have attained normal physical growth for their age, so that it becomes difficult to realize their emotional and cognitive levels.

In the most promising infant group, it is hard to remember that these are not 4-year-olds; most are 7, and one is 9. They are at a unified stage of their physical, emotional, and cognitive development, and have the capacity to play and symbolize. Yet the meaning of developmental delay is illustrated by an epileptic, Down's Syndrome child, who is now 11 and has only recently made enough progress to join this advantaged group. When I first arrived, she was 7 and still crawling around on the floor, eating the contents of waste-paper baskets. Later, when she became an increasing disruption in her classroom, I was able to anchor her daily, for brief, regular art therapy sessions. Once again, it was in the art room that restraint and structure were attained, through using the art materials symbolically, in a concrete way.

Thus, I offered her scratchy chalks on rough sugar paper, to encourage effort and help externalize more direct aggression. When she became able to use finger paint without smearing and mis-using, I poured sand into one end and washing up liquid into the other, for textural experience. Frances Tustin (1981) advises that autistic children need to be helped to differentiate between 'hard' and 'soft', 'rough' and 'smooth' – as most children are able to do through play experiences. But this does not only apply to autistic children, as I have tried to demonstrate, and is one of the many ways that external intervention can become internalized – but only when geared to the observed needs of the individual child, and not offered, as Edith Kramer (1971), in a quite different context, so aptly put it – as mere 'busy work'.

Another way, the 'outside–in' approach seems to work is with the universal ambivalence expressed by many children, possibly due to their early emotional experiences. This takes the form of changing hands, places, ideas. I try to promote agreement to take the brush or felt-tip with the hand they use, so that no swapping is required, and to persuade those with established hand-predominance that they can reach across with the same hand, rather than use the left for the left side, and the right for the right, in a rather opportunist way. I remove the need for giving up a first choice of media by assurance that there will be time for both, or indeed all. I try to reinforce confidence in an initial action or intention, which can often be immediately retracted. All these rather trivial-seeming mechanisms do indeed appear to help build up greater stability and a sense of continuing rhythm, so that not allowing dithering, as it were, eventually depletes the need for it. I also try, in this familiar and secure setting, to practice experience of the unexpected, interrupting rituals and routines that threaten to become entities in themselves.

There is another factor with children who have more than one session a week, and who are still mechanically scribbling, rather than expressing or developing even anger – similar perhaps to mere outpourings in psycho-therapy. I have found, first in an effort to attain hand–eye contact, that simple buttoning and popping techniques can anchor a child emotionally by the process of the need to focus, on a practical level. This seems to greatly help those autistic children who make no use of art materials, and those with severe restlessness and behaviour problems. Their very agreement to the task, and their frequent volunteering to do it, confirms my conviction.

So, although art therapy with such children is of necessity extremely concrete, the importance of attempting a psychodynamic understanding cannot be over-emphasized if true therapeutic change is to occur. It does not seem helpful to sit by while these children circle in their own confusion, reinforc-ing their muddled perception of the outside world.

© 1990 Sigrid Rabiger

References

Axline, V. (1947) *Play Therapy*, New York: Ballantine Books.
Axline, V. (1964) *Dibs – In Search of Self*, London: Pelican.
Boston, M. and Szlur, R. (eds) (1983) *Psychotherapy with Severely Deprived Children*, London: Routledge & Kegan Paul.
Bowlby, J. (1969) *Attachment and Loss*, vol. 1, London: Hogarth Press.
Bowlby, J. (1973) *Separation: Anxiety and Anger*, vol. 2, London: Hogarth Press.
Bowlby, J. (1979) *The Making and Breaking of Affectional Bonds*, London: Tavistock.
Bowlby, J. (1980) *Loss: Sadness and Depression*, vol. 3, London: Hogarth Press.
Deutsch, H. (1942) 'Some forms of emotional disturbances and their relation to schizophrenia', *Psychoanalytic Quarterly* 11: 301–21.
Greenacre, P. (1953) *Trauma, Growth and Personality*, London: Hogarth Press.
Klein, M. (1946) 'Notes on some schizoid mechanisms', in *Envy and Gratitude*, London: Hogarth Press.
Klein, M. (1961) *Narrative of a Child Analysis*, London: Hogarth Press.
Kramer, E. (1971) *Art as Therapy with Children*, New York: Schoken Books.
LeBoit, J. and Capponi, A. (eds) (1979) *Advances in Psychotherapy of the Borderline Patient*, New York: Aaronson.
Lowenfeld, V. (1965) *Creative and Mental Growth*, New York: Macmillan.
Mahler, M.S. (1971) 'A study of the separation–individuation process and its possible application to borderline phenomena in the psychoanalytic situation', *The Psychoanalytic Study of the Child* 26: 403–24.
Mahler, M.S., Pine, F., and Bergman, A. (1975) *The Psychological Birth of the Human Infant*, New York: Basic Books.
Mitchell, J. (ed.) (1986) *The Selected Melanie Klein*, London: Penguin Books.
Piaget, J. (1973) *The Child's Conception of the World*, London: Paladin.
Rabiger, S. (1984) 'Some experiences of art therapy in a special school', proceedings of a two-day conference 'Art Therapy as Psychotherapy in Relation to the Mentally-Handicapped?' St Albans College of Art, 29 and 30 November 1984.
Rabiger, S. (1987) 'Value of Educational Factors in Art Therapy', proceedings of a one-day conference 'Image and Enactment in Childhood', St Albans College of Art, May 1987.
Rubin, J. (1978) *Child Art Therapy*, USA: Van Nostrand Reinhold Co.
Sinason, V. (1986) 'Secondary mental handicap and its relation to trauma', *Psychoanalytic Psychotherapy* 12(2): 131–54.
Stern, A. (1938) 'Psychoanalytic investigation of and therapy in the borderline group of neuroses', *Psychoanalytic Quarterly* 7: 467–89.
Tustin, F. (1972) *Autism and Childhood Psychosis*, London: Hogarth Press.
Tustin, F. (1981) *Autistic States in Children*, London: Routledge & Kegan Paul.
Tustin, F. (1986) *Autistic Barriers in Neurotic Patients*, London: Harnac.
Ulman, E. (ed.) (1975) *Art Therapy in Theory and Practice*, New York: Schoken Books.
Winnicott, D. (1964) *The Child, the Family and the Outside World*, London: Pelican.
Winnicott, D. (1965) *The Maturational Process and the Facilitating Environment*, London: Hogarth Press.
Winnicott, D. (1971) *Playing and Reality*, London: Pelican.
Winnicott, D. (1984) *Deprivation and Delinquency*, London: Tavistock.

Chapter three

Unusual drawing development in children: what does it reveal about children's art?

Ian McGregor

All children draw spontaneously. In its most basic form making marks is as natural as making sounds, gestures, and movements. Given a surface and a means of making a mark, any child will leave a trace of its drawing activity, a visual record of its contact with that surface. This is true of children regardless of their cognitive, social, visual, or even physical abilities. Children will also draw on virtually any surface regardless of whether that surface allows for permanent record of their activity. They will for example draw in food or sand using their finger of a stick, they will also use any substance that will leave a trace, often to the chagrin of their parents. In short it is rarely if ever something that they have to be taught. Why do children draw and what are the characteristics of this universally innate activity?

These questions have formed only part of any systematic study in the last 100 years. It was with the Victorian interest in education that the study of child art began. The ability to draw was seen as a necessity for the educated person, especially young women. This led to an attempt to understand the principles by which art could be successfully taught to children as part of a balanced curriculum. There was also a growing interest in fostering artistic sensibilities amongst the manufacturing classes. In 1835 the government appointed a Select Committee to investigate ways of promoting knowledge of the arts and the principles of design amongst the population. This Select Committee concluded that it would be beneficial to make art a component in elementary education as it already was in Germany and Switzerland.

It was not until 1850 that this was actually achieved in Britain. The first systematic study of child art was conducted in France in the early years of this century. Luquet (1913) made the first serious attempt to develop a theoretical understanding of what children are doing when they draw. However, as with many of his contemporaries he tended to see child art as a primitive attempt to achieve the realism of adult drawing. He saw the stages he observed in children's drawings as logical steps on the path to visual realism. This view prevailed until the development of modern art and the interest aroused by primitive and ethnic art at the beginning of this century. At the same time psychoanalysis promoted a growing interest in childhood experiences which, in turn, led to psychologists becoming interested in children's drawings and a recognition of infant art as a study in its own right independent of the study of aesthetics as a whole. It was to a large extent as a result of this decoupling of child art from art history that a growing interest in its study as a method of yielding answers to questions regarding the perceptual development of the child arose.

This has tended to lead to a concentration on the activity as a manifestation of the child's conception of the world. Particular attention has been paid to the process of construction of drawings as symptomatic of how the child constructs his view of the world. Much of the recent investigation of child art has attempted to define the 'laws' by which child art is made. As drawing amongst children is common to western cultures it was assumed that some definition of these laws would produce a failsafe set of criteria providing insight into the world of children. Educators obviously hoped this would provide a universal yardstick for understanding how the child's knowledge of the world develops. Tests were formulated based on these 'universal laws', the Goodenough (1926) 'draw a man' test being the best known example although many intelligence tests contain variations. Indeed by the late 1960s it seemed that the problem was solved and could be summarized by the axiom 'the child draws what he knows rather than what he sees'.

During the 1970s increasing interest focused on cases of children whose artistic development seemed very advanced at a young age (Selfe 1977). Their drawing ability did not seem to fit into the watertight laws that had been formulated to describe child art. As the children were mostly diagnosed as disturbed or handicapped in some way, these cases further undermined the assumptions which had been carefully assembled over the previous 50 years, that artistic activity reveals intellectual maturity. Such cases, while not necessarily forcing a total disregard of previous tenets have nevertheless created an atmosphere of disquiet as to whether the right questions are being asked in relation to what children are doing when they draw. They certainly undermine any notion of immutable laws regarding the development of child art.

I can make no promises of solutions to this problem, however, at this time solving the problem depends on confidence that the right questions are being asked. A re-examination of the evidence relating to child art is necessary for this process to begin. Any study of children's art and particularly any study of anomalous drawing in children poses questions about the child's perceptual world and how it differs from that of an adult.

The exact nature of the child's perceptual world and how it is affected by growth can really be no more than educated guesses as opinions differ greatly on what the young child is actually capable of perceiving. However, a brief review of current thinking might be useful before we move on to examining theories about child art. The central questions are to what extent the perceptual system consists of innate factors and to what extent perception is changed or formed by growth and experience.

Certain factors do not seem to have to be learned. Perception of distance is a seemingly innate phenomenon. From very early on in development, babies can differentiate between stimuli that are close and can be interacted with, as opposed to those that are far away and have to be approached. The perception of where an object is in relation to the viewer or perceiver does not need to be learned and the perception of the movement of objects seems to be innate. Tangibility or to what extent an object can be touched or interacted with again is a very primitive ability as is the ability to discriminate between new stimuli and stimuli to which the perceptual system has become habituated. This latter ability is very important in viewing children's drawing ability; it is often explained in terms of the formulation of mental schema. In the most simple terms one could describe these as maps of experience created by the perceptual system in order to assess to what extent stimuli need to be attended to.

That babies can recognize and mimic the gestures and facial expressions of their mothers is a well attested phenomenon, Carpenter (1975). The fact that babies can match their own expressions with that of their mothers' may seem fairly self-evident but it is still a significant achievement for the immature perceptual system. It strongly suggests that the new baby is able to identify itself as similar to its caretakers. The infant also recognizes continuing identity in its mother. This social aspect of perception or perception of social relationships is also fairly central to many theories of child art. It accounts of course for the fact that the human image is one of the most common in children's art in western culture.

On the other hand there are many aspects of perception that are clearly not innate and are seemingly to a large extent dependent upon experience. The length of human childhood is often cited as a necessity because of the amount the developing child has to learn before independent living is possible. The first 6 months of life seem to be particularly important, and any restrictions in perceptual development during this period are exceedingly difficult to compensate for later.

The central question psychologists have attempted to answer is how does experience affect perception and how is meaning achieved? This is of course assuming that meaning is not a 'given' as some might argue (Gibson 1970). To see a table as a table seems to be an achievement of perception. In the beginning we may assume that what the neonate perceives is a layout of surfaces of up and down, vertical and horizontal, near and far, edges and planes. This world is highly structured, there is no reason to assume it is chaotic, but it does not consist of discrete objects which in themselves are meaningful and recognizable. How this meaningfulness is achieved is still open to speculation. It would seem to develop through either increasing perceptual experience and growth, that is by recognizing what changes and what stays the same in perceptual experience, or it may be closely related to the development of language. These questions are still unresolved.

The study of child art can be divided into four main schools of thought. We have already discussed some aspects of the notion that children's art should be viewed as the primitive steps towards an aesthetic goal namely that of the mature adult artist. In this view particular emphasis is placed on the art object and the child is thought primarily to learn about 'making pictures' from looking at other pictures. In other words, the development of artistic activity depends primarily on learning more about the rules and conventions of picture-making than it does on the external world. H. Read (1943) has perhaps been the most renowned exponent of this view in recent years and this idea has tended to be proposed by art historians attempting to make sense of child art in the context of art history.

This view is of interest in that to a large extent it can avoid the problems of relating child art to perceptual or cognitive development save in so far as they are related to the apprehension of pictorial material. It is after all only a recent assumption that art has anything to do with perception and there are attractions in trying to understand art as a consistent set of rules for graphic activity within a certain context which do not need to be related to anything beyond that context. Art for art's sake as it were; this view also allows art to be seen as a kind of language which has grammar and syntax. The early scribbles of children can be thus related to their babbling and the development of fully-formed images can be likened to the development of words. The naming of objects and the creation of contexts and relations for images is similar to the creation of meaningful sentences. This similarity may be more apparent than real and the cases of anomalous or unusual drawing ability in young children would in many ways seem to undermine this assumption.

An equally influential account of child art and its function is the *Gestalt* or holistic school of thought, Arnheim (1954) and Harris (1963) having contributed a great deal to the field. Arnheim's view of perception was that it 'proceeds from generalities from which the particular is differentiated'. The point of view put forward by Arnheim and many other influential writers such as Piaget and Inhelder (1971), Harris (1963), Goodenough (1926) and Kellogg (1969) is that perception is preceded by knowledge. This leads to the tenet of child art that children draw what they know in preference to what they see.

By looking at children's drawings we do tend to see a preference for unambiguous description. Objects, their relationships and functional qualities tend to be set out in the simplest and most readily comprehensible format. There is also a close relation between mark-making and intention. One observes this in that most children tend to resist any interpretation of their drawings other than the one they intended, and are rarely reticent at correcting an adult observer's misinterpretation of their drawing. Some writers such as Matthews (1984) suggest this is equally true of a child's earliest scribbles.

The drawings of children are from this view invariably expressive of concepts, Harris (1963). The process is to a large extent more important than the object. One of the difficulties with this view is that children are probably never able to draw all they know. They clearly know more than they can express graphically. It can therefore be quite misleading to infer too much about their mental representative ability from their graphic representative ability.

Another significant contribution to the study of child art has been made by writers looking at the problem from the standpoint of affect. What part do experiences of the self play in artistic development? Victor Lowenfeld and Lambert (1975) have written extensively on child art and from a wealth of case studies of children's drawings have attempted to show the links between drawing and personality. They try to illustrate a relation between states of mind and consequent graphic activity in children. For example, they make a broad distinction between the visually orientated who tend to be detached spectators with little emotional or kinaesthetic response to events in the world as opposed to the haptically-orientated individual who will tend to interact with things and be more able to experience affectively and kinaesthetically. That graphic activity consists of visual and motor aspects cannot be doubted, whether these can be differentiated on the basis of personality is open to question. However, defining the relationship and interaction of these aspects or perceptual modes is of fundamental importance in understanding children's art.

In reality all of the various theories of child art have something important to say on the subject of what children are doing when they are drawing. One is not safe in assuming that one definition of children's drawing holds true in all cases. It is in a sense the nature of art that it exists on many levels simultaneously. It is a satisfying activity for the child because it blends many aspects of experience together and gains its power from the fact that it operates on many levels. This is as true for child art as it is for the highest pinnacles of artistic achievement. Children's drawings are not always the result of the same processes. This is clearly illustrated by the examples of unusually talented child artists several examples of whose works have gained publicity and generated much interest as well as perplexity in recent years. These drawings are described as unusual or anomalous because they display certain features which normal children find difficult or tend to avoid. They also display a maturity of artistic vision which does not seem commensurate with the artists' ages, and in most cases they are produced by handicapped or autistic children with low IQs.

There are four distinct features to these drawings with which most normal children have difficulty. First, the depiction of proportion is a problem for normal children, it is however, a distinct characteristic in these children's drawings. Young children will generally exaggerate certain features in drawings which are usually related to the importance they attach to that particular feature, such as the head in figure drawings. The sense of proportioning tends to improve with age but even at 10 years old, proportion within figures and single objects are not depicted very accurately. There is also a difficulty with proportions between objects, especially in depth. That an object that is further away looks smaller and one that is near looks larger is a distinct problem and most children resolve this by using the top and bottom of the paper to represent far and near respectively. By contrast the anomalous draughtsmen can, from a very early age (5 to 6 years) represent objects in depth in proportional relation to each other.

The second feature to note is dimension. Normal children tend to make two-dimensional representations of objects in a 'canonical' format and then add any salient features. In other words they have a basic representational format for a person or a house or a ship or whatever and then add on particular details that specify that particular view of the person, house, or ship. It is only much later that a child is prepared to deform its canonical representation. Most people indeed continue to make canonical representations throughout adult life. The anomalous draughtsman on the other hand is quite prepared to draw from a single viewpoint and does not seem concerned at all about the ambiguity that might result from something that is assumed to be of concern to the normal child artist.

Linear perspective is one of the most striking features of these young anomalous draughtsmen. In contrast, the normal child has difficulty in estimating the true size of objects in pictorial relations. The phenomenon of occlusion is another one that seems to pose problems for normal children. They tend to represent an object partly hidden by another as two separate objects or as transparencies. This phenomenon is well documented by writers such as Arnheim (1954) and is a central feature of the schematization of children's drawings and the resulting maxim that children draw what they know. Lorna Selfe describes the situation regarding normal children's drawings succinctly, 'Drawings of normal children are a record of the conventional visual experiential features that are often important to all children in a shared culture' (Selfe 1985:150).

For normal children drawing seems to be closely related to language development and an uncluttered and meaningful symbolic representation appears to be more important than attention to idiosyncratic detail. In contrast the anomalous draughtsman records objects in his optic array as patterns, edges, contours, shapes, and surfaces, rather than as representatives of classes or symbols.

For some time I had been working as an art therapist at a unit for autistic children as part of a research project I am conducting into autistic children's drawings. I was particularly interested in unusual drawing ability in children and I therefore became very excited when one of the teachers in the reception unit at the school showed me some very unusual drawings produced by a 6-year-old within the unit and invited me to work with him. Peter had been a pupil in the special unit within the school for several years. He had suffered a fairly severe trauma in his relationship with his parents who had neglected him. He would be left on his own while his mother and father went to the pub. Peter was roughly handled as a child and was eventually taken into care by the local authority and ultimately placed in the care of his grandmother whom he refers to as 'nanny'. Peter's grandmother and mother did not seem to get on well and Peter's mother had to a large extent lost interest in him since remarrying, and having two more children.

Peter is very small for his age, when I first met him he had, in fact, just turned 7 although he looked about 5 years old. He was obviously not autistic as I had expected him to be, in fact he showed no social avoidance at all and his language was suitably advanced for his age. He was clearly a very bright child and was interested in virtually everything around him. There were, however, signs of disturbance in his behaviour and in conversation he would introduce neologisms and meaningless phrases which at times became almost a 'word salad'. He seemed continually anxious, needing constant reassurance. Peter had been well-known within the school for a couple of years for his drawings (from age 5) which were clearly much more sophisticated than those of his peers. He seemed quite conscious of the fact that his drawings were somehow special. When I first met him to conduct fortnightly art therapy sessions with him, he was convinced I had come to take his pictures to a museum.

The drawings of his that I had seen previously and which had impressed me were landscapes and town scenes which had included all the elements such as perspective, and occlusion which are mentioned above. They were also impressive in that many of them displayed a very sensitive and well-observed use of colour. Further, many of his drawings were exceedingly large, and this added greatly to their visual power.

However, on the first occasion I worked with him he started off by drawing a face. When he had finished a rather primitive figure he said, while pointing at the drawing that, 'Peter's nanny is exactly like this'. It is interesting to note that it is often in drawing the layout of the environment that these anomalous draughtsman display their talent; their drawings of figures are often more age appropriate. Peter is quite conscious of producing a 'nice drawing' for my benefit. He is, however, extremely distractable often stopping drawing and looking blankly around him as if preoccupied with something else. When his concentration returns, however, he picks up precisely at the point he left off. This was something I noticed on most of the occasions I worked with him. In returning to the figures he was working on he said 'need to put some arms on' and drew on the arms with a single line without taking the pen off the paper. This was another feature I often noticed when he was drawing. He seemed to have a virtually complete notion of the final drawing, from the start he always knew what the next mark, line, or image was going to be, almost as if he were copying an idea in his mind; however, he was also able to exploit unforeseen opportunities with which the drawing process provided him.

He next began to add a background or context for his figures. Starting on his right-hand side looking at the paper, he drew a horizon of trees and hills in silhouette. He clearly understood the notion of vanishing point which is displayed in his drawing of lines diminishing from the foreground into the distance which is plainly a road or path. Peter also understands the relational sizes between objects in pictorial terms, in that some objects appear bigger because they are nearer to the viewer. He is also very sensitive to changes in texture and how these can create space in that things that are nearer seem more textured and therefore more solid. I was also struck by the strong sense of composition he displayed, knowing for example, when to add a cloud to balance the picture. In many ways this drawing he had made seemed like that of a trained landscape painter with a knowledge of many of the tricks needed to create a large sense of space felt when viewing a landscape. At first I wondered whether he had been deliberately taught any of these. There were several particular features in these drawings which are worth noting.

First the general impression his landscapes create are that they are viewed from quite high up (*Plate 8*). Somewhat similar to the viewpoints gained in the hilly countryside in which he lives and indeed through which he often journeys on bus rides with his 'nanny'. There are also differential aspects in the way he represents features in these landscapes. The horizons are drawn in true perspective as are any buildings included in the picture. These are combined with roads and rivers being drawn as plans, he blends these approaches very effectively and there is no jarring visual discontinuity in the drawings (*Plate 9*).

In a subsequent session I asked him to make a drawing of Oxford which I knew was a favourite subject (*Plate 10*). In this particular drawing he started with two lines which narrowed towards a vanishing point. He then drew two lines bisecting the previous two to form a crossroads. This seemed to give him the basic structure for the 'scene'. Buildings were added in perspective along these roads. Peter named the most significant buildings which were well-known aspects of the Oxford skyline. He still used an elevated viewpoint but he was able to capture the quality of streets receding into the distance with the use of the vanishing point. This made me feel he had a clear understanding of the way perspective works over different kinds of terrain; how it is less and almost imperceptible in rolling countryside and how striking it is in the harsh geometric pattern of a townscape.

In another drawing he represented Oxford as a silhouette on the horizon as if seen on a hill some 30 or 40 miles away. He drew the M40 and was very precise about the number of bridges over the motorway and although I cannot say whether he was accurate, there was no doubt that he was very certain. Next he drew a patchwork of fields, which was one of the most common features of his drawings and he described these as 'hills'. He then said 'do it like this because its going down through the hedges', while adding more and more fields until the impression of an agricultural landscape was complete. I noticed when Peter was drawing that he varied the kind of marks he made, sometimes using large shoulder-generated movements to make lines across the full length of the paper, but more often he would make a series of shorter lines as if he were feeling his way along the edge of the object. At other times he would draw a line around the object to be represented without taking his pencil off the paper (*Plate 11*).

Two weeks later when I visited the unit again Peter seemed much more disturbed and confused than on the previous occasions I had seen him. When I gave him a piece of paper he made a half-hearted attempt at drawing a landscape but soon started to try to make a hole in the paper saying he was making a hole in the hill. He banged the pencil up and down all but breaking it, making a hole in the paper. I then asked him if he could draw a hole, to which he responded by drawing two lines disappearing into the actual hole and coming out the other side which he then drew a bridge over. I had decided prior to this session to see how Peter would make something in three dimensions. Consequently I had brought some chicken wire, paper, and glue with me to see whether he would make a papier mâché model. I showed him how he could manipulate the wire into different shapes. He said he wanted to make an 'island', so I helped him to bend the wire into a lump. My only other assistance was to show him how to tear the paper into strips and dip them in the paste, and to point out parts where the chicken wire was not covered with papier mâché about which Peter did not seem too concerned.

Peter calmed down a lot in making the hill as his interest in the model seemed to overcome his previous disturbance. He told me the island was Scotland where apparently he was going for his summer holidays. Peter said he wanted to paint the island and so I got out a palette and put a selection of colours in it. He proceeded to carefully paint in the different geographic details of the island; the shore, the grass, rocky outcrops, etc. It was painting these details that seemed to interest him most, almost as if it was a painting rather than a piece of sculpture. I asked him at one point if he was going to put some people on the island, he replied 'no because they would be too small, so you could not see them'. This statement seemed to reveal how viewer-centred his perceptions were and his refusal or inability to include material inconsistent with this viewer-centredness. Whenever I asked him questions regarding the relations of objects in space he always seemed to be able to describe them verbally as well as graphically. It seems reasonable to assume that he actually had a fairly complete understanding of diminishing size with distance and it therefore seems reasonable to say that his drawing ability was not purely eidetic.

The theoretical questions that cases of special drawing ability have raised are both perplexing and apparently paradoxical. This has been especially true in those cases of autistic and handicapped children where exceptional ability in drawing seems at odds with their overall level of cognitive functioning. Peter's case is of particular interest in this context because he is neither autistic nor handicapped and is in fact an extremely bright child who in many ways is very accessible although he is emotionally disturbed and at times shows symptoms of childhood psychosis.

Special abilities in autistic and handicapped children (idiot savants) have been observed for some considerable time particularly musical and arithmetical abilities which seem to be more common than drawing ability. Anastasi and Raymond (1960), Lester (1978). Although it must be said that many of these special abilities are apochryphal and may be purely the result of a willingness to engage in certain activities as opposed to others, and this is then interpreted as a special skill. Scheerer *et al.* (1945) distinguished between persons who are retarded but who develop a special skill and those normal children who suffer impairment in all skills save one. The most important point about these children with truly anomalous abilities is that they are qualitively as well as quantitively different from those of other children. It is not just whether, for example, they draw all the time but that these children's drawings have completely different characteristics from those of other children. Possibly the most straightforward explanation of these special abilities would be a genetic theory. Unfortunately, although this has often been asserted there is no evidence for it. A specific cerebral lesion has also been offered as an explanation although again there is no specific evidence. It is true, however, that many autistics and idiot savants are brain-damaged. Currently, difficulty with this approach to the problem is that brain science is still somewhat imprecise, so it cannot be discounted although it naturally seems easier to accept brain damage as responsible for deficits rather than special skills.

Some commentators, Horowitz (1965) and Lindley (1965) have suggested that the handicapped condition itself promotes the special skill. Lindley suggests that development of special skills may be enhanced because there will be less competition from other behaviours or distracting stimuli. Consequently, stimuli in the special skills' area will have increased reinforcing power; there will also be less competing behaviour to extinguish while developing the skill. The problem with this learning-theory approach in my experience is that the skill when first displayed, especially in autistic children, seems to be fully formed and it is not clear how much if any learning was required in its acquisition. A study by Viscott (1970) noted sensory hyperacuity in idiot savants and in some cases where sensory hyperacuity was present, psychosis later developed.

Perhaps the most significant theory as to why these special talents develop is related to these children's limited capacity for abstraction. Scheerer *et al.* (1945) observed that autistics and idiot savants appear to suffer from an inability to abstract. Lorna Selfe (1977) in her work on *Nadia* first suggested that special drawing ability was probably related to autistic children's retardation in terms of symbolic abilities. This is most obviously manifested in terms of the children's language deficit. Nadia's drawings seem to become more age-appropriate as she began to develop language. According to Tustin (1974), many autistic children, when they begin to draw, are preoccupied with problems of perspective and the drawing of three dimensional objects to a degree that amounts to an obsession. She viewed this phenomenon as a developmental problem. Tustin indeed proposed that these autistic children are unable to conceptualize the notion of 'inside' and until this awareness has been achieved, inner life is not possible. She sees this lack of development as serving the pathological function of blotting out awareness of separateness and thus of space inside and outside.

These children it would seem are not drawing objects as such but lines, edges, contours, and angles of a frozen fixed viewpoint. The ordinary child artist is primarily concerned with a canonical and unambiguous representation to which any defining characteristic can be added, as in adding adjectives to the verb in a sentence. Anomalous draughtsmen, however, are more concerned with surfaces seen from one fixed viewpoint. This naturally leads to objects being partially occluded, truncated, and represented in perspective as the scene is not really made-up of objects in the conceptual sense, but of surfaces and edges. How can one see these differences in developmental terms? David Marr (1982) has produced a computational model of the processes of image analysis involved in visual perception. He starts with what he describes as the 'primal sketch' which makes explicit the intensity changes and local two-dimensional geometry of an image. From this is derived what Marr calls the '2½-D' sketch. This is a viewer-centred representation of the depth, orientation, and discontinuities of the visible surfaces. However, being viewer-centred it changes every time the viewer moves. It would suffice in order to manipulate objects and avoid bumping into them, but it could not produce object recognition, for this we need an object-centred description which would also have to be volumetric as opposed to surface-based.

The object-centred description must be canonical in the sense that the same object, seen from any point of view will always yield the same unique description. To obtain a volumetric description, that is independent of view-point, according to Marr some axis intrinsic to the object has to be selected to which the rest of the description can be referred. Marr called this the model axis. For an elongated object it will be its longest dimension; symmetry can also be used to yield a canonical model axis. For many objects found in the same orientation the model axis may be provided by the gravitational vertical. The object is then broken into subsidiary axes, and the shape of each part is described as a generalized core centred on its axis. The relationship between axes is hierarchical. Recognition of an object involves computing a 3-D representation of the object in viewer-centred co-ordinates, and adjusting the estimates of the orientation of the model axis by moving backwards and forwards between this representation and the representation stored in memory in object-centred co-ordinates. This is of course purely a computational model and its limitations must be borne in mind when thinking of children. It does, however, offer a possible mechanism to explain how when looking at an object, we are simultaneously aware both of its visible structure in relation to our viewpoint and also of the volume of space it occupies regardless of viewpoint.

It seems to be precisely this constant and unchanging volumetric structure of which autistic children are unaware. They seem to be functionally blind to objects while showing very acute sensitivity to and memory for small details and aspects. It could well be that the developmental problem Frances Tustin refers to in autism is an inability to progress beyond this '2½-D' stage of visual processing. They have difficulties with object-centred perception which consequently leads to the often-observed ritualized and stereotypic use of objects and possibly their apparent difficulty with symbolic thought. On the other hand, this viewer-centred perception would seem to predispose them to being accomplished draughtsmen as they are always seeing something as if for the first time. Any art student will know the advantages in making drawings if the object can be seen as edges, lines, and forms within forms rather than as a person or a chair. Much of the content of teaching someone to draw is helping them to develop strategies to overcome the conservatism caused by seeing an object in relation to the class of objects to which it belongs.

Some interesting experiments conducted by Van Sommers (1984) illustrate the effects of conservatism on children's drawings. He took two groups of children. Group one was shown an intact object and then given a structural description of the object and asked to make a drawing. The second group was shown the intact object and asked to make a drawing, then given a structural description and asked to make a second drawing. Group one produced a significantly greater number of structurally sophisticated drawings than group two. It would appear from these results that making a previous drawing of an object would seem to inhibit the possibility of using new strategies for representing it. The only additions that were found in groups two's second drawings were surface details; there was no attempt to employ new strategies to represent structure on the basis of the new information given. Van Sommers concludes that this phenomenon is due in part to the development of a 'motor routine'. These motor routines obviously have an adaptive purpose in other contexts but they tend to have a restricting influence on the development of new graphic strategies. He also found that attempts by the children to pre-plan their drawings, provoked by asking them to think about how they would represent an object, also has a retarding influence on subsequent drawing strategies.

So what does this tell us about Peter's ability and why it has developed? In some senses it tells us very little primarily because he is not and has never been diagnosed as autistic. Almost all of the previous case studies have been of autistic children and for this reason his case is useful to compare with the previous cases. It may be that his case illustrates that special drawing ability is not solely related to autism and it may be misleading to look too much

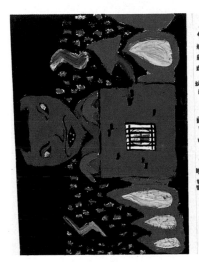

Plate 13
Top: Living in an internal prison: Claire's nightmare world
Bottom: The little girl who held up the globe in the loneliness of outer space

Plate 12
Top: The cat, the fish, the man, and the bird
Bottom: The bee circus

Plate 15
Top: The 8-month-old Claire
Bottom: Claire's tip up

Plate 14
Top: The visit of the terrifying lady of darkness and flames
Bottom: Lost and alone in the maze

Plate 17
Top: The black dwarf departs
Bottom: The journey back to childhood

Plate 16
Top: The picture of the family
Bottom: The teacher and the blackboard of riddles

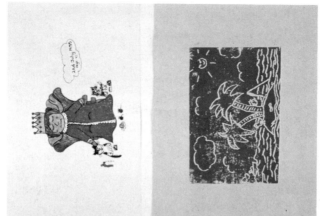

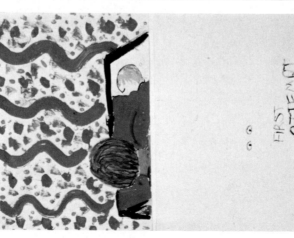

Plate 18
Top: Claire and baby sister
Bottom: Self-portrait: first attempt

Plate 19
Top: Self-portrait: second attempt
Bottom: Self-portrait: third attempt

Plate 20
Top: The queen says farewell and returns to school
Bottom: The ship's final departure from the magical island

to autistic symptomology to provide an answer to this perplexing problem. It is also of course true that this phenomenon is rare enough amongst autistic children. One possible explanation could be that in this phenomenon there are certain features that autistic children are prone to (the majority of the cases are autistic) but which are not exclusively related to autism as such.

Peter is social and does not have any significant language difficulties. He does however, have certain features in common with autistic children. He does not play imaginatively and seems to have little or no interest in toys. In all the fortnightly art therapy sessions I had with Peter any attempts to lead him into symbolic play failed. He is often obsessive and ritualistic in his behaviour and is also resolutely omnipotent. At times this displayed itself in his inability to learn new things as he always seemed to start from the premise that everything worth knowing was known to him already. Pronominal reversal, a common feature in autistic children whereby the pronouns you and I are reversed the self being referred to as 'you' is another symptom displayed by Peter. Bosch (1962) thought this showed the autistic child's inability to differentiate between itself and other individuals as separate entities. I feel that it is within these features that some clues to Peter's remarkable abilities might lie. These aspects of his case as with those of other children with special abilities, must be seen as predisposing factors but obviously cannot be used to predict the development of a special talent as there are undoubtedly opportunistic features that would be almost impossible to calculate.

The trauma Peter suffered through his early neglect and the lack of a significant first relationship with his mother has led to a lack of individuation on his part. One sees the same phenomena in autistic children although possibly for different reasons as it seems clear that their lack of response to their mothers is not caused by environmental trauma. This lack of individuation has severe developmental implications for children, in that it inhibits the development of symbolic and imaginative play and, consequently, retards the development of abstract thought. Paradoxically, these special abilities are to a large extent probably the result of a lack of imaginative and symbolic development. Some evidence for this assertion comes from recent research into the content of pre-representational drawings by children and the developmental function (Matthews 1984).

Children's earliest scribbles are now seen not as meaningless experimentations with mark making but rather as a symbolic substratum upon which representation develops. Matthews describes these scribbles as 'action representation' by which he means that the child at this stage is not trying to represent objects but is representing his understanding of the way objects operate in the world, the way they behave in space and time. A scribble, for example, would represent for the child the movements of an aeroplane or a car rather than the object itself. It is closely related to what the child is doing in its play at that time. 'Graphic properties' are, according to Matthews, 'only a by product of what is mainly a symbolic enactment using paper . . . as a terrain for a pretend adventure' (Matthews 1984: 28). It is only as the child recognizes that these graphic properties correspond to the features of the objects, and exploits them as such, that he begins to attempt representations of objects in themselves. In contrast the anomalous draughtsman invariably starts to produce fully formed representations without a preliminary scribbling stage. Just as he does not engage in symbolic play. Most children use this scribbling to enhance their understanding of the way objects are and behave in the environment in a viewer-independent way. It is out of this that attempts at representations of objects develop. As Matthews points out, however, both types of representation overlap so that the normal child is still trying to incorporate aspects of his 'action representation' in his attempts at representing objects. The anomalous draughtsman, however, does not have his vision cluttered by this need to incorporate experience in what he represents and it can thus remain truly viewer-centred as we can witness in Peter's drawings.

At the end of the day, it is clear that much further research needs to be carried out to confirm these various hypotheses both in relation to normal children's drawings and to the drawings of those children who display anomalous abilities. It is essential to observe development in the anomalous draughtsman before they display their abilities to confirm the hypotheses set out above, although this is obviously difficult as they only gain attention when their talent has fully developed. For a child like Peter his empty landscapes are symbolic, for me as an observer at least. They symbolize a lonely world where his search for his lost mother is conducted. Sadly the attention he receives for them is scant recompense for his loss.

© 1990 Ian McGregor

References

Anastasi, A. and Raymond, F. (1960) 'Intellectual deficit and musical talent', *American Journal of Mental Deficiency* 64: 695–703.

Arnheim, R. (1954) *Art and Visual Perception*, Berkley: University of California Press.

Bosch, G. (1962) *Der Freuhkindliche Autismus*, Berlin: Spring.

Carpenter, G. (1975) 'Mother's face and the newborn', in R. Lewin (ed.) *Child Alive*, London: Temple Smith.

Gibson, J.J. (1970) *Ecological Approach to Visual Perception*, London: Houghton Stodder.

Goodenough, F. (1926) *The Measurement of Intelligence by Drawings*, New York: Harcourt, Brace and World.

Harris, D.B. (1963) *Children's Drawings as Measures of Intellectual Maturity*, New York: Harcourt, Brace and World.

Horowitz, W. (1965) 'Identical twin idiot savants', *American Journal of Psychiatry* 121: 1075–9.

Kellogg, R. (1969) *Analysing Children's Art*, Palo Alto, Calif.: National Press Books.

Lester, D. (1978) 'Idiot savants: a review', *Psychology* 14(1): 20–3.

Lindley, O. (1965) 'Can deficiency produce specific superiority?', *Exceptional Child* 31: 225–32.

Lowenfeld, V. and Lambert, W. (1975) *Creative and Mental Growth*, New York: Macmillan.

Matthews, J. (1984) 'Children drawing: are young children really scribbling?', *Early Child Development and Care* 18: 1–39.

Luquet, G.H. (1913) *Les Dessins d'un Enfant*, Paris: Alcan.

Marr, D. (1982) *Vision*, San Francisco: W.H. Freeman.

Piaget, J. and Inhelder, B. (1971) *Mental Imagery in the Child*, London: Routledge & Kegan Paul.

Read, H. (1943) *Education Through Art*, London: Faber & Faber.

Scheerer, M., Rothman, E., and Goldstein, K. (1945) 'A case of idiot savant', *Psychological Monogram* no. 4: 58.

Selfe, L. (1977) *Nadia*, New York: Academic Press.

Selfe, L. (1985) 'Anomalous drawing development: some clinical studies', in Freeman and Cox (eds) *Visual Order*, Cambridge: Cambridge University Press.

Tustin, F. (1974) *Autism and Childhood Psychosis*, London: Hogarth Press.

Van Sommers, P. (1984) *Drawing and Cognition*, Cambridge: Cambridge University Press.

Viscott, D. (1970) 'A musical idiot savant', *Psychiatry* 33: 494–515.

Chapter four

The cat, the fish, the man, and the bird: or how to be a nothing. Illness behaviour in children; the case study of a 10-year-old girl

Vera Vasarhelyi

Introduction

It has always been difficult to justify art therapy as a viable and legitimate option in the treatment of distressed children within the multi-disciplinary team, since children are supposed to be able to draw without much inhibition anyway, and can do so with anyone, given a reasonably relaxed situation. This of course assumes that for children drawing is a natural activity, without any specific investment of the child's inner world in these pictures. My own experience would suggest however, that the symbolic content of images produced in a well-defined and contained therapeutic space is far from being just playful or arbitrary. Rather – as I have come increasingly to realize – it can facilitate a unique insight into the dynamics of the unconscious and allow us the privilege of seeing hidden processes which would otherwise remain largely inaccessible to exploration.

The case study of the 10-year-old girl – whom from now on I will call Claire – should illustrate a further, vital point, namely that the images she created were not only instrumental in understanding and expressing the depth of her desperation, but also played a crucial role in her recovery. Whilst she herself remained mute, her pictures spoke vividly about the terrifying threat of an imagined, hostile, external world. Entering and exploring the realm of images, she could safely re-enact and resolve her hidden wishes of destruction. Her yearning to become 'nothing' would be encapsulated in symbols and images and thus changed through a process of slow metamorphosis into the design of her true identity.

However, on her admission I knew only a few facts about Claire's history. At that stage it seemed that her difficulties started with a viral illness at the age of 8, from which she found it increasingly difficult to recover. She spent a long time in convalescence, needing a lot of attention and care. Her parents noticed a slow change in her personality, as she became more and more withdrawn. She refused to go to school despite the class teacher's attempts to assist her return. On the few occasions she attended, she screamed in terror, so that finally she was asked to leave.

It was at this time that she was admitted to the child psychiatry ward. The diagnosis was 'illness behaviour', an elusive diagnostic criteria, which has a history in its own right. According to Dubowitz and Hersov, 'The paediatric literature contains very little on the management of such cases.' There is, however, one common theme in all forms of 'illness behaviour', namely that 'symptoms are often made more intractable by repeated, fruitless, physical investigations' (Dubowitz and Hersov 1976:366).

In his paper 'Hysteria in childhood', Goodyer draws our attention to the fact that although, 'Since the early work of Charcot the intimate relationship between physical and psychological symptoms has been widely studied . . . hysterical disorder in adults has been the subject of much research, less attention has been paid to childhood hysteria' (Goodyer 1985:103).

Despite much research and preoccupation, hysteria seems to defy our striving to find an acceptable definition. 'As with many psychiatric syndromes. no satisfactory definition exists. As well as its medical meaning, in itself poorly delineated, the concept of hysteria is further obscured by the lay use of the word' (Reed 1971:237). In the same paper on 'Hysteria', Reed spells out that:

Hysteria is a condition that has been recorded in medical reports from the earliest times and must be virtually the only psychological illness whose history goes back nearly 4000 years. Despite such a lengthy history, it remains an enigma with many disparate theories as to its nature.

(Reed 1971:237)

The preoccupation with the nature of hysteria was the focus of Freud's early studies, influenced by Charcot's research and demonstrations of hypnosis during the 1880s in Paris.

In the course of these early studies with hysterical patients in particular, Freud came to conceptualize the neurotic symptom as representing the break-through of pent-up unconscious forces which could not be expressed in more direct ways. . . . Thus Freud invokes the concept of psychic energies which may vary in quantity, which are generated or stirred up by certain kinds of experiences, can be 'damned up', 'escape' in roundabout ways, and might require the physician's assistance if they are to be properly discharged, allowing the organism to return to a state of psychic calm.

(Feldman 1975:558)

Feldman then concludes: 'The analytic task was seen as striving to understand the hidden or unconscious meaning not only of the symptoms but also the patient's behaviour, his free associations and his dreams in particular' (Feldman 1975:558).

The idea of understanding the nature of hysteria – or (rather more precisely) the origin of physical symptoms without any detectable medical condition – proved to some clinicians unsatisfactory. The focus shifted from definition towards classification. Dubowitz and Hersov in their paper on 'Management of children with non-organic (hysterical) disorders of motor function' use Creak's classification of hysteria in childhood:

(1) True conversion hysteria, where neurological symptoms were due to conversion of anxiety into somatic manifestations; (2) hysterical prolongation of a symptom originally part of an organically determined disease; and (3) undoubted organic disease in which nervous (psychological) accompaniment plays an important part.

(Dubowitz and Hersov 1976:358–9)

Finally Kendell removes even further from the wish to define the underlying cause, in order to fully concentrate on the behaviour manifested. He offers a 'tentative classification of illness behaviour', in which he recognizes three main groups: 'Unrecognised organic disease; illness behaviour motivated primarily by fear of disease or death; illness behaviour rewarded by the advantages of the invalid role' (Kendell 1983:1616).

The incessant drive to find the 'ideal', all-encompassing model is probably not so much motivated by the wish to become aware of the true nature of the relationship between the human mind and body, but rather fuelled by our anxiety as helpers and therapists. The question is whether we will be able to make sense and facilitate changes in a realm where our comfortable assumptions seem to have completely lost their validity. The pictures Claire created during our therapeutic relationship neither confirm nor deny any of the above theories. Much more important, they communicate the intensity, formulate the pain, and remind and warn us of the risks of an experience, the outcome of which is far from predictable, and where the dividing line between achieving the equilibrium of a true self, or becoming 'nothing' is very thin indeed.

I intend to follow the sequence of Claire's pictures in strict chronological order. An invisible pattern, coherent in structure and image – both the expression and the resolution of her conflicts in one – should emerge, without my attempt to over-rationalize it, since pictures have their own language, which will resist our wish simply to translate them into words or verbal concepts.

The beginning of therapy: the first appearance of the cat, the fish, the man, and the bird *(Plate 12, top)*

It is some years ago that I first met Claire in the waiting room of our clinic. Saying good bye to my previous little client gave me just enough time to accustom myself to her desperate, monotonous crying, which seemed to have no beginning or end and had the effect of keeping everyone in the waiting-room in anxious and uneasy silence. After greeting her I exchanged a few words with the nurse who had accompanied her from the ward, then asked Claire to come with me to my office. She got up hesitantly to join me and I could see that her thin body was wrapped in protective layers of clothing: including an oversized pullover, long scarf, woollen cap, and baggy overcoat. Whilst she was preoccupied with desperately hugging her teddy bear, I could watch her strange, insecure 'pigeon walk' as we climbed the stairs and walked down the long corridor leading to my room. Claire did not seem to notice either my room or the surrounding space and as I helped her to remove her coat I first became aware that her eyes were almost totally closed. They were to remain so during the whole hour. I explained to her the nature of our session, gave her some paint, a box of felt-tip pens, some pastel crayons, and a few pencils with a collection of coloured and white paper to choose from. 'You are welcome to paint whatever you would like to', I said. I could feel how painfully aware she was of my presence, so I reassured her: 'I have got a few things to do, so I won't watch you while you paint. I will come back in about fifteen minutes to see how far you have got. I am looking forward to seeing your picture!'

I turned away and listening to her incessant crying I gave up any hope of her producing any painting. I knew all too well that she was totally lethargic in her existence, hardly ate or spoke, and that any wish to communicate had been absent for a long time. I was amazed when, after a short time, feverish activity seemed to have started. I heard the rustling of paper, and the scraping noise of crayons rubbing against the rough surface, her activity clearly undisturbed by the simultaneous accompaniment of her relentless crying. I had difficulty in keeping my own word to wait for 15 minutes, and when I finally looked, I was astonished by what I found. At the centre of the page a cat had appeared, whose open lips dripped with saliva in the excited anticipation of a meal, and who stared with menacing intensity at a fish, which was carelessly swimming in his bowl, obviously unaware of his impending fate.

I expressed my surprise and encouraged her to continue. Without any acknowledgement of my comment the feverish activity behind my back continued. By the next time I turned to her, new figures had joined the cat and the fish in her picture. Right behind a window an oversized bird peered through the glass with an intense and inquisitive glare, whilst slightly more in the background, a man was just about to turn away towards a crooked tree, which was one of the most prominent objects visible from the room in the picture. This space strangely lacked any depth. Although it was supposed to be the external world, it had the unmistakable flavour of dreams and nightmares; it was both two-dimensional and unreal.

Inside the room of Claire's imagination, a picture hung on the wall. This was a picture within a picture, twice unreal, yet within its frame a world of three-dimensional fields opened up, a healthy tree grew out of the grass, and ordinary birds were flying in the sky. The complex yet precise juxtaposition of spatial ideas, the violent undercurrent of emotions contained in a cool, mature, and strictly formulated pictorial style seemed to be in total contradiction to her overwhelming anxiety and continuous crying, in which virtually any sign of her will to exist seemed to be dissolved. Yet her picture was perfectly finished by the end of the hour. As I helped her into her overcoat she reached out for her teddy bear and left my room without having said a single word to me during the entire duration of the session. She was still crying as she returned to the waiting-room to meet her nurse. She left me in the silent company of her puzzling friends, wondering about their significance and the role they played in her secret world. Were they to be allies or enemies on the road to her recovery?

The astonishing performance of the 'bee circus' (Plate 12, bottom)

Our next session took place a week later, on Monday afternoon, which was to remain 'our time' for the rest of her stay in the ward. It is a crucial day for all children, as it marks the beginning of another week on the ward after a weekend at home with their families. Claire was desperately unhappy to return. Her arrival was a distressing event for everybody. She had to be carried by her father – screaming, kicking, and biting – through crowds of bewildered onlookers. Later in the afternoon I found her in the waiting room, she was in the same mood as the week before: fragile, withdrawn, crying as if her grief could never be left behind.

On arrival in my room Claire needed no re-introduction to the art material and assumed that as in the previous week, I would provide her with a space of her own, safely delineated by an agreed time which had to elapse before I would be allowed to intrude into her world again. I sat down, avoided looking at her and quietly read my notes, whilst the sound of her crying competed for supremacy with the noise of her creative activity. When I first looked I just caught a glimpse of a huge poster held up in the sky by two oversized insect-like creatures. 'Bee circus', it declared proudly, ready to disappear again, since both announcers were visibly swinging backwards and forwards on their trapeze.

It didn't take long, however, before the whole extravaganza unfolded. There were two distinct groupings of bees. Two mature looking ones performed on the ground, whilst three younger bees were busily buzzing in the air above them. The first one from the left was just about to begin his (or her) tightrope-walk, blue flag in his right hand and a huge, multicoloured umbrella in the other. It was difficult to imagine him successfully completing his task, since it seemed he was just about to start off his walk sideways.

The middle bee was obviously in a good mood. Suspended in the air, barely touching a petal of a giant daisy with his right toe, he was performing his act of juggling with utmost virtuosity. I was not sure whether his props were intended to be light, blue balls, or some transparent bubbles. The third bee on the right was not amused. Standing on a high platform with a bunch of balloons in his hand, a mixture of a clown and a somewhat morose magician, he was clearly not destined to be the star of the show. On the ground a flamboyant figure, elegant and composed – this time unmistakably a lady bee – was approaching from the right, smoothly gliding on the back of a huge snail, who was carrying her without any effort on the top of her neatly decorated house. The snail – contented and smiling – had a red ribbon tied onto her tail, which she held up gracefully in the air. It was obvious that they both took great pride in their appearance. The last person in the 'ménage' was the ringmaster. With top hat and moustache he cut a manly figure. Firmly standing on top of a large drum, whip in his left hand, there was no doubt that he was in charge.

As in the previous week, she cried through the whole session, but finished her picture exactly on time. When I asked her whether the picture might have had anything to do with her family, she shook her head and said nothing at all. I could not accept her denial, since the three small bees (herself, her brother, and younger sister) and the male and female grown-up bees were an exact parallel to Claire's family.

The picture of the family *(Plate 16, top)*

As in the following week my assumption still appeared to be a relevant one, I decided to ask her to paint her family. When I turned to her after our firmly-established ritual of 15 minutes, the unexpected change in her style astonished me. She used felt-tip pens exclusively this time and her visual vocabulary seemed to have undergone a complete change. The five members of her family were lined up in sequence from the smallest to the tallest one. Each held the string of a balloon in their hand and each balloon had the same schematic sketch of a smiling face, hovering above each member of the family, like a somewhat grotesque, collective alter-ego. Everybody – old and young – had the same protruding, intense, glazed eyes, transfixed in time in an aimless stare, oblivious both to each other and their pets. The cats and the gerbils were to gain greater prominence later in the therapy. Her technique bore no resemblance to her previous, richly-coloured, and shaded painterly style. It was a rigid, simplistic, and lifeless cartoon, which was both distant and impersonal.

I asked her to introduce her family to me and to my greatest surprise, she stopped crying for just a second to talk to me for the first time. 'They are niiiiice . . .' she said, in a miserable tone of voice. The ambivalence between her picture and her comment was quite extreme, but I did not take it up at that point as I was more astonished by the fact that a dialogue had unexpectedly started between us. I felt it was the first major turning point of the therapy. However, our time for that week had run out at this point. Therefore, once more her personal statement, the therapeutic process, and the potential of an interpretation remained in undisturbed fusion within her picture, preserving its content for later unravelling.

The teacher and the blackboard of riddles *(Plate 16, bottom)*

Next week when we met in the waiting-room at our usual time, I felt for the first time some sense of recognition from her. It was also the session that Claire first decided to use paint and brushes. She started the picture from the middle of the usual white paper, where two large brown eyes in a bearded face stared at us for a considerable time. 'Who is he?' I asked.

'Mr B— my teacher. I am frightened of him,' was her answer. She then slowly expanded her picture, first on the right side, painting a lamp and a book shelf which contained an old-fashioned radio, a box of chalk, some books, plants, and a mug steaming with a hot drink. 'What was it? Coffee or tea?' I asked.

'Coffee,' she said.

'Do you like coffee?' I tried to start a conversation.

'No!' she exclaimed. And that was the end of our conversation for that day, but not the end of her painting activity.

A large-sized blackboard appeared on the left side of the picture, close to the dreaded teacher. The blackboard was covered with drawings, the space between them filled with illegible writing. Was the teacher just about to reveal the hidden sense behind it all to his class? What did the clock with 'time' written above it mean, I wondered? What was the significance of the rows of sums which did not add up? What of the two sets of clouds, one with rain and lightning, the other hovering above a little figure? He stood partly in sunshine but was just about to be soaked by the rain pouring from the other side of the cloud. Did the unfinished word 'Teach' written under his feet refer to Claire or to her teacher? Would I ever be able to understand the riddle of the abandoned steering wheel with arrows pointing in conflicting directions? My intuition suggested, that these symbols contained a concise formulation of her painful conflict at this time of her life, yet she would not disclose any further clues to the solution of the puzzle.

Her crying had moderated by the end of the session, but she was still sobbing when I said good bye. Before she left, I reminded her that the next week was going to be the last meeting before I was to go on holiday.

Living in an internal prison: Claire's nightmare world *(Plate 13, top)*

'You remember Claire, I will be away on holiday for the next three weeks,' I said, opening our session. She nodded, and started to paint without delay. Her picture took longer to finish than usual and this time it was she who asked me to come and look at it. The small cloud with rain and lightning – one of the previous week's symbols from the blackboard – had grown to giant proportions and had overtaken most of the picture's background. Huge rain drops seemed to fight a losing battle against the ferociously burning fire at the bottom. Amid raging flames a small, rectangular building stood, overshadowed by a huge, red-coloured, and grotesquely cross-eyed Devil. Moustache and beard surrounded his open mouth, which revealed the yawning gaps between his sharp, shark-like teeth. He held both his hands in a possessive and overbearing gesture on the flat roof of the building. The building had only one window which was separated by enormous metal bars from the outside world. Right behind it a tiny figure cried; tears – like rain drops – surrounded her head, and her outstretched arms begged to be rescued from what seemed to be a giant bubble. It was obvious that the tiny saw in her left hand was insufficient to free her from her prison. Without prompting, she started to explain her picture. 'It is me inside the egg, trying to cut myself free, but I am unable to get out . . . .'

It was difficult to believe that she had started to speak about herself. I felt that new possibilities could open up for us to explore and wondered whether her unexpected courage had anything to do with my departure and her fear of losing me. Her desperation was still almost tangible; she interrupted her own crying and sobbing only to utter a few words. Nevertheless, I had for the first time glimpsed the presence of a wish to grasp, formulate, and share the terror created by the persecutory figures of her mind. 'Do you feel, as if the outside world could turn into something terrible, like the Devil in your picture?'

She answered without delay or hesitation: 'I see the outside world like this, everybody looks like the Devil, I am frightened that they are going to hurt me!' It was clear that the boundaries between the internal and external world had long lost any relevance for her, and I realized how genuine were her reasons to cry.

The little girl who held up the globe in the loneliness of outer space
(Plate 13, bottom)

On return from my 3 weeks holiday I wondered what Claire would paint in our first session. I was pleased to see that some layers of her clothing were shed; she did not have her woollen cap on and the baggy pullover had disappeared. I could see more of her thin body, although she still had carefully hidden her legs in her trousers and was not to exchange them for skirts until her discharge from the ward.

When I arrived to greet her, she looked up at me and I saw for the first time her blue eyes, overshadowed by her upper eyelids. She sobbed at frequent intervals, but her mood seemed to have lifted slightly and altogether she was a bit more mobile.

The motif of black clouds, lightning, and rain – as in her previous painting

– was the main focus. It once again filled the background and appeared to echo and magnify her own tears. A tiny figure – which she identified as herself – stood on a huge, black and white, barren rock whilst trying to hold up a giant-sized globe with her bare hands and head. It seemed inevitable that she would be crushed by the weight of the globe, were she to fail to hold it up. Yet clearly it was an impossible task to fulfil, since the globe was so heavy that an indentation had formed in the rock under her feet. The figure was crying and her desperate pain seemed to have kept everything in and around her in unresolved, paralysed suspense. Before she gave me her picture at the end of the session, she said: 'That is how I feel' – and left.

The visit of the terrifying lady of darkness and flames *(Plate 14, top)*

Since Claire first allowed herself to translate her experiences into symbolic form, her fears of a persecutory and evil world slowly diminished. She cried less and had managed to come out from the shell of her isolation. Her little saw, which she felt would not be sufficient to release her from her captivity in the mysterious egg, had by now managed to cut through the iron bars of her solitude. Having escaped, she was overwhelmed by her feeling of total loneliness in a cold and empty universe, where her illusion of omnipotence made her believe that she had to sustain the weight of the whole world. However, by this time she had reached a point where she was able to confront her inner universe, an event more terrifying than anything she had experienced before.

Some years ago, when she first fell ill, defeated in her wish to recover, she recalled that uninvited, strange visitors would arrive at her bedside when twilight fell. 'I was not asleep, I know. But it was not quite like being awake . . .' she said.

The most regular of her apparitions were the 'terrible man' and the lady, who would appear from the darkness of an impenetrable wall, surrounded by flames. It was not a dream or a nightmare, she could not make any sense of it or get rid of it, so Claire decided that she could not share her experiences with anyone. Both these figures seemed so real, the threat to be hurt by them so inevitable, that Claire became quite convinced that they had the power to appear anywhere, inside or outside of her. The lady had a menacing, mocking grin on her face, which made it exceptionally difficult for Claire to put up with her uninvited presence. She felt more and more trapped in her confusing experiences and soon came to a total emotional impasse. Her next picture expressed her growing sense of hopelessness at this point in her illness.

Lost and alone in the maze *(Plate 14, bottom)*

There was an intense feeling of desolate sadness in my room when Claire decided to paint her journey through the green maze. The most obvious irregularity that I instantly noticed was that the maze had no entrance or exit to it and the avenues of the maze did not connect at all. In the middle of this conglomerate of disconnected patterns, locked in a rectangular cell, was Claire, crying despondently in a posture of total hopelessness. In an attempt to create a point of reference, she set up a signpost in her picture: 'Maze', and afterwards added: 'Lost and Alone'.

When I asked her to tell me something about how she felt before things started to go wrong, she painted a small yellow figure at the bottom right corner of the picture. The broad smile of the tiny, schematic figure reminded me of something which I could not immediately recollect. The outline was in the manner of simplistic, rigid cartoons and the smile was forced and unnatural. The almost manic optimism of the figure seemed to represent – as it so often happens at this stage of therapy – the overwhelming wish to believe in a state of perfect happiness. This 'paradise lost' was supposed to exist prior to the present conflict and turmoil. From this assumption evolved the fantasy that this imagined, 'pure' state should be restored in its totality, as the main aim and purpose of recovery. However, it seemed that the lifeless rigidity of the figure had expressed Claire's healthy doubts and strong ambivalence about how genuine and viable such an idea would be in reality.

At that point I suddenly remembered where I had first seen this somewhat simplistic, caricature-like style. It was Claire's portrait of her family. I thought that the family would soon constitute an important topic in our sessions, but I left it to Claire to chose the appropriate timing.

We returned to the trapped, little figure in the middle of the maze. I put the idea to her, that every maze has an exit, and although it seems often that one is hopelessly lost, in one's own time one discovers the way out of it. She shook her head in disbelief. I said to her:

Do you know of the mythological hero, Theseus? He did not only slay the monster minotaur in the Cretan Labyrinth, but also was able to find his way out of the maze. He had a magical thread given to him by a lady called Ariadne, so he was able to re-trace his own steps and so with her help he escaped.

She looked at me and shook her head in disbelief. I continued: 'I think you have a magical thread yourself.' Her expression became suspicious and her eyes narrowed as she turned to me and watched. I said: 'You have got this lovely, strong Claire underneath it all, yearning to find her way out. I have great admiration for her.' She looked at me with the utmost disgust as if I had made her touch a smelly and revolting object. She shook her head and her lips took the position of someone, who had just tasted the most repelling food and was about to spit it all out.

'Oh no! What have I said, Claire?' I looked at her and then I was suddenly overcome by an absurd and overwhelming desire to laugh. And as I laughed and laughed, to my greatest surprise, I saw her eyes slowly open in amazement and her lips struggle in a last attempt to suppress a smile. 'Don't laugh, for heaven's sake, just don't laugh' I said in a playful mock-offence. But her smile grew and grew and finally gave way to a spontaneous release of laughter.

There are rare moments, when a very complex process which has come to a stand-still may suddenly find a resolution through a single, seemingly inexplicable gesture. It would be tempting to conceptualize such a moment in order to be able to give a rational account of it. However, it seems to me that it is more important to recognize at such a time that the power of the symbolic gesture – like that of the pictorial image – lies in the fact that they both contain and harness the undiluted energies of the unconscious forces, and tap into powers which have the potential to destroy the ego as well as to resolve its conflicts.

The black dwarf departs *(Plate 17, top)*

Claire's next picture marked the end of an era. She sat down silently and painted a large black wall. It certainly seemed to have strong connections with the impenetrable wall from which the terrifying lady of the flames had appeared. However, this time the wall did not open up to reveal a nightmare lurking behind it and had lost its power of impenetrable silence. In it there was closed a white door, a small window, and a large, jagged gap, through which a cat-like, menacing black dwarf was making a hurried departure in order to escape from Claire's room.

'I used to see him, when I was very ill,' she said.

'It seems to me that you have defeated these terrifying creatures, so they have no choice but to leave now,' I commented.

'Maybe . . .' she said and got up from the desk in order to look around my room, as if she had never seen it before. She carefully examined all the available art material, then suddenly asked me: 'You have got some lino, haven't you? Can I use the last 20 minutes of the session to make a lino cut?'

I agreed. That was the beginning of a new pattern, which was to continue until her last session, when she was finally ready to print her lino and to reveal the contents of it to me. After the session I realized that she had left something on my desk. It was a little ball of red woollen thread, long enough to measure my room and to lead out of it. Was it Ariadne's thread, which she could discard now that she had defeated the monsters in the labyrinth of her unconscious mind?

The journey back to childhood *(Plate 17, bottom)*

A new period in Claire's development started with the picture of a train just about to enter a dark tunnel. It was painted with confident strokes using a largish brush. By now she had completely stopped crying and sobbing and the creative process was frequently disrupted by conversation. The painting of her picture did not take up the whole session any more, since she reserved the last 20 minutes for lino cutting.

Her next picture was a well-known landmark near the hospital. It was a big biscuit factory, the windows of which released huge quantities of thick, dark steam. The train taking her home had to pass by it a few minutes after leaving the station. 'It stinks . . .' she said with considerable disgust.

Having left the present behind, her pictorial journey rapidly took her back in time to where she was able to recall her early childhood. 'Do you know that I remember how I felt when I was just eight months old?' she asked.

I used to get desperate at night. Often I would get lost under my blanket and was terrified of not being able to get out and breathe. When I finally got out, I saw that I was imprisoned in my cot. It was awful.

She painted herself as a baby, covered with a colourful blanket, her head turned towards the unending rows of black prison bars of her cot (*Plate 15, top*).

She was just a few months older when her brother unexpectedly decided to play a nasty trick on her. Without any warning he pushed the pram over, trapping her under it, she screamed helplessly until mother eventually came to the rescue. 'Claire's tip up' was the title of the picture (*Plate 15, bottom*). A strange, crooked tree grew beside the pram, not dissimilar to the one she had painted behind the window in her first picture of the cat, the fish, the man, and the bird. She expressed for the first time in our therapy, anger toward her mother, who – she felt – had badly let her down.

Further incidents of conflict between Claire and her brother were to follow. Her next picture was an account of another confrontation:

I was still very small when we visited the War Museum. I climbed into a tank and as my parents went ahead, my brother sneaked back and locked the door behind me. I was terrified and I screamed for help.

she said, whilst she was finishing the last of the large brown letters: 'HELP'. She stopped for a moment, but then continued: 'Still, I adored and followed him everywhere. I wanted to be exactly like him. I could never show my anger to him when he had upset me.'

When Claire was 2 years old, her life changed drastically. Her younger sister was born and – as her next picture expressed so vividly – Claire was completely bewildered and desperately jealous. She painted herself standing above the cot, with only the back of her head visible, in what seemed to be the posture of a detached and frozen stare, whilst the new born baby slept peacefully, unaware of her visitor.

It was the second time that I thought I recognized elements recurring from her first picture. I felt as if I had just witnessed the return of an old theme: the cat, standing over the fish bowl, watching her prey in motionless silence. When she finished her painting and was just about to start to work on her lino, I asked her:

'Do you remember your first picture, Claire?'

'Oh yes, I do!' she replied.

'Do you know anybody who could be the cat or the fish?' I asked her. She took a long time to answer.

'I suppose I could be the fish sometimes, but I am also the cat,' she replied thoughtfully.

It was about this time that she wrote a number of cat stories. In one of these stories Claire described in first person the experiences of a tabby cat, who had to be taken to the vet where she was examined and inoculated against cat disease. In the next story we met the same cat, this time however, as the much admired first prize winner of a big cat-show.

Her last story was a very different one. It was the account of terrible crimes committed by a sinister, mysterious, dark cat. Alongside a river, leading to the abandoned Castle 'Bla-Bla', strange things started to happen. Every Tuesday night a burglary was committed in one of the big mansions. 'The next morning the police were called in, but all they found was a black kitten, no money,' as Claire described it in her story. As the incidents continued and the police found it more and more difficult to look after the growing number of black kittens, they decided to call in a Sherlock Holmes's look-alike, Inspector Piggy. It was time for taking serious measures, since 'The Cat' – as the police called the criminal – had committed his first murder. One Tuesday night a little girl heard an unusual noise and saw that a dark figure had crept into the house. Silently following the intruder she surprised him in the dining hall and as the man turned towards her, she screamed in horror at the 'sight of his terrible, mangled face'.

The next morning the police were called in and found the little girl stabbed, lying in a pool of blood but found only a black kitten, no money. Inspector Piggy decided to confront 'The Cat'. The last house at the riverside was Castle Bla-Bla. A long time ago two old ladies had lived there with a fabulous collection of jewellery, but now it was empty and haunted by malignant spirits. Inspector Piggy decided to hide in the Castle, but nobody called. Next morning on his return to the police station he heard that a cat with a mangled face had given himself up to the police as he had been terrified by the malignant spirits of Castle Bla-Bla.

Claire's self portrait and the art of how to become nothing
(Plates 18 and 19)

Claire was getting better every day, so the possibility of her returning home now seemed within her reach. I wondered what plans she might have for her future, so as she was just about to start her self-portrait, I asked her: 'What do you want to be, when you grow up Claire?'

Claire: Nothing!
Me: Nothing? Could you tell me more about how to become nothing?

She was silent for a while and then looked at me.

Claire: Well, first you sit down and don't talk to anyone. And then you just sit there and do nothing . . . and then you burn off your hair . . . after you burned your hair you paint your face and you don't wear nice clothes . . .
Me: How does it help you to be nothing?
Claire: I don't know . . . then you don't eat or drink, all you drink is salt-water and I tell you what happens afterwards —

I interrupted her:

Me: How long did you do it?
Claire: I haven't tried it yet, no, no, no, I haven't! I want to be a nothing when I am older!
Me: When will you start?
Claire: When I am older . . . (after a short silence) . . . and then when you've burned off your hair you cut your fingernails off . . .
Me: Your fingernails . . .
Claire: Yup.
Me: And what would you do then?
Claire: That's it. You then sit down and do nothing at all.
Me: Would you talk?
Claire: No.
Me: Would you move?
Claire: No.
Me: Would cry?
Claire: Yup.
Me: For how long?
Claire: I don't know, I would just cry and cry and cry . . .

At this point Claire suddenly changed the subject and started to talk about her self-portrait. She crossed out the first attempt just after painting the eyes. The second attempt ended in a similar fashion. 'They are all wrong. On the first one I looked cross-eyed, on the second one my eyes are much too big, and I don't have my eyes so wide open!'

For a while she was silently working on her third and final attempt of a self-portrait. When it was finished I realized that she had now dismissed herself in an almost irrevocable fashion. The girl with the blue eyes was crossed out with two large black brush strokes. The entire background was filled with the repetition of one, finite word: 'no, no, no, no . . .'. At the right bottom corner of the page she wrote the following comment: 'This picture has gone wrong because I look nothing like this and it looks like a person who has murdered someone and they are in the paper. By Claire, only.'

It was the first time that Claire allowed me to share her terrifying dilemma. The irrational guilt and overwhelming wish for self-annihilation were very powerful, but I also felt her hope that together we might still survive it at the end. I found myself feeling inexplicably confident as Claire picked up her paintings and asked: 'Can I throw it out now?'

'I would like to keep it' I answered.

Claire: It is rubbish.
Me: I would like to keep all three of them.
Claire: I hate it!
Me: You could feel very different about it within a short time.
Claire: I don't know . . . I don't know . . .

She repeated it several times and our session came to an end.

The queen says farewell and returns to school *(Plate 20, top)*

Claire's first trial-return to school was a unique event. She set out, accompanied by two trusted male members of the ward staff, but before the end of the short trip they had been arrested twice. The first time was a so-called 'citizen's arrest'; on the second occasion the police were called by a guard to deal with the commotion. She screamed and struggled so desperately – not wanting to return to school – that everybody on the train thought she must have been kidnapped. As she indignantly recalled the event to me in our next session, she found it difficult to hide some measure of satisfaction at being the central figure of such an event. 'Would you like to paint yourself as Queen Claire?' I asked her. She looked at me with a mischievous expression and drew herself sitting on a throne with her eyes closed, in the company of two cats. One of the cats was just an ordinary tabby cat, but the other one had an unusual, eccentric nature. She refused to drink anything from an ordinary cat bowl and preferred pure, fresh water directly from the dripping tap beside her in the picture.

In front of the Queen there was a mysterious egg, guarded by two gerbils. 'Is anything hatching in the egg?' I asked her.

'Yes, but I am not going to tell you ever, what it was!' she said with a contented smile, as she was leaving my room. A few months later, after she left the ward I got an invitation to attend her school's Christmas play. You might have guessed that the role of the Queen was played by none other than Claire.

The ship's final departure from the magical island *(Plate 20, bottom)*

Claire continued to make steady progress and tried to negotiate internally the conditions for her return to 'normal life'. One of her options she described in her story: 'The Elephant's Return to the Jungle'.

> I was living in the Zoo for a time, when they decided to close it and since I was too old to be sold, they thought the best thing was to send me back to the jungle. After a long, long journey the train finally stopped and I found myself in a hot, steaming country: Africa! Two coloured men in uniform appeared and opened up the door of my cage and said: 'Bye, baby', and closed the door behind me. I found myself outside, nervous, because I knew that I was far from human aid. If I failed, I could be driven away by wild elephants and I would die on my own.

She then described how she was edging her way day by day closer to the herd, remembering her early years living in the jungle with her mother.

> When I finally approached them they all stirred and one of them turned on me. It was a challenge to win my place in the herd. He charged at me, I hit him hard and I won my place in the herd. I had a happy life in the herd and I had two children. It was a better life than in the Zoo.

Claire's story about her return to the herd became a reality. In the autumn term she felt finally ready to rejoin her school. The headmaster tried to dissuade her from her plan. 'We cannot have you crying here' – he said. 'Here I am, and I am going to stay' said Claire in a fighting spirit.

As time passed by, Claire's lino-cut began to take shape. An island with lush palm trees appeared from the sea.

'It is my secret island, nobody knows how to get there,' said Claire.
'How do you travel?' I asked.
'By bird. You have to hire a bird, a miraculous bird!' said Claire.
'Where can you get hold of these birds?' I asked.
Whilst she was working on her lino, she disclosed some of her secrets to me.

> These birds are miraculous golden eagles, I have got twenty of them, each one is bigger than the Clinic! The young ones are only 500 years old, but by the time they grow up and die, they will be millions of years old. They live deep beneath the ocean, under the sea bed. When they feel that it is time to retire, they will settle in my island. If I want to go to my island, I just call one of them, and it will take me there.

Her dilemma seemed to be a deep and existential one. To leave the magical island of childhood, with its mythological horrors and miraculous golden eagles in exchange for happiness in the herd is an irrevocable decision. On the threshold of having to find her true identity, she had lost direction.

Just before her discharge from the ward she explained the symbols on the blackboard in one of her earliest pictures. The clock meant that time had stopped for her and the steering wheel represented her loss of direction. The sums did not add up because she could not make sense of them and the rain – her tears – could not extinguish the flames – her anger – which she needed a further year to fully own-up to and to resolve.

She finally printed her lino in which once more the fish, the man, and the bird were reunited. A ship left the island, heading towards the edge of the picture. 'I banned all three of them to the island, they can never get away without my permission,' she said. The cat was not on the island and I sometimes wondered whether she took him on board when she decided to leave her magical island behind. The influence of this shadowy figure – appearing sometimes as the man with the mangled face or the terrifying lady of darkness but also disguised as the harmless, domesticated tabby cat and exposed in its naked form as a dark, primordial, and destructive force – will have a crucial part to play in Claire's final quest for individuation.

I saw her for another year as an outpatient. When we last met, she took in to the clinic her costume for her role as the Queen and we all – Claire, her family, the consultant, and myself – posed for a photograph. Claire has now transferred to secondary school and is doing very well, according to the cards she sends me from time to time.

References

Dubowitz, V. and Hersov, L. (1976) 'Management of children with non-organic (hysterical) disorders of motor function', *Developmental Medicine and Child Neurology* (June) 18(3): 358–68.
Feldman, M.M. (1975) 'The psychoanalytical approach to neurotic problems', *Medicine* (2nd series) 12: 558–9.
Goodyer, I.M. (1985) 'Hysteria in childhood', *Hospital Update* (Feb.): 103–10.
Kendell, R.E. (1983) 'Hysteria', *Medicine*, Medical Education (International) Ltd, pp. 1614–17.
Reed, J.L. (1971) 'Hysteria', *British Journal of Hospital Medicine* (Feb.): 237–47.

Acknowledgements

I would like to thank Dr John Pearce, Consultant Child Psychiatrist, for inviting me to the Bloomfield Clinic and giving me the opportunity, freedom, and support to work with children who were in desperate need of help and yet who puzzled us all. I am most grateful to Dr Robert Jezzard, Consultant Child Psychiatrist, who generously provided me with an invaluable reading list of the relevant psychiatric literature. My thanks to Mr Peter Townsend who read the manuscript and kindly assisted me with some of my problems with English grammar. Mr Francis Wood most kindly gave me some of Claire's schoolwork which seemed to have direct links with her pictures in art therapy. Finally, I am deeply indebted to Dr Andrew Crowcroft, Consultant Child Psychiatrist, for his unwavering support and encouragement of my clinical and written work.

Chapter five

Control, uncontrol, order, and chaos: working with children with intestinal motility problems
Aleathea Lillitos

This chapter is empirical rather than theoretical, since I am still engaged in the work I describe, though not these actual cases. It is based on the clinical material and my understanding of it, of children referred for art therapy from the Children's Intestinal Motility Clinic, which is a specialist clinic for children with bowel disorders, within the Department of Paediatrics in a teaching hospital.

Although many of the disorders and diseases of the bowel have a straightforward aetiology (and some of the children do develop secondary psychological symptoms as a result of their illnesses), I will be focusing on the case material of children in whom the physical and psychological factors are not clearly delineated. I will examine the position of the child in relation to the authority of the parents, and to the assumed authority of the hospital, and I will discuss the ways in which the child may (consciously or unconsciously) use the physical symptoms as a means of expressing feelings around the issue of control – especially within the perimeters of an art therapy session.

Using two case studies, I will comment on the manner in which children engage in their art therapy sessions, and discuss how different behaviour – e.g. co-operative, withholding, controlled, or chaotic – can reveal, in the transference and counter-transference, the conflicts of both their inner and their external worlds. This behaviour also often replicates their physical symptoms of chronic constipation or faecal soiling, and may be analogous to the bowel movement that they (either in the present, or previously in infancy or early childhood) decided to give, or to withhold, from their parents. I will therefore refer to the symbolic meaning of faeces and discuss what they might represent to the individual child in relation to their image or non-image-making in the sessions. Being able to give and having to withhold from giving, or giving without meaning to, can be seen as an issue of control – and the ability to relinquish control. This in turn would seem to relate to the way in which children are able to make sense of the chaos of their inner and outer worlds, and to give this chaos some differentiation and form and, thus, be creative.

The children referred to the clinic (and from there perhaps to art therapy sessions) fall into two broad categories. First, there are those whose symptoms of chronic constipation (and its attendant problem of overflow faecal soiling or encopresis) are caused primarily by an organic disease such as Crohn's Disease or Hirschsprung's Disease, or are secondary to a spinal condition like spina bifida, which affects the nerve supply to the bowel and results in constipation. Second, there are those whose persistent symptoms, despite exhaustive tests, have no detectable physical origin. Literature on the subject is divided as to the cause of psychogenic constipation. But, put simply, the precipitating factors are likely to consist of various combinations of circumstances, constitutional disposition, and environmental, social, and emotional factors. For example, a child who unconsciously or consciously remembers the pain of passing a large or hard stool, and perhaps links this with fearful fantasies about the inside of her body, will be particularly prone to resisting defaecation. Furthermore, if this child is unable to articulate his fears and is misunderstood by his parents and punished for soiling or for being wilful, this resistance to defaecation will now also involve a conflict with her parents and she will probably become constipated.

Children with severe, long-standing constipation are likely to have, or to develop, other physical symptoms – such as abdominal distension and pain, vomiting, anorexia, failure to thrive, urinary tract infections and, in extreme cases, respiratory trouble. It is therefore important to begin by clearing the bowel before starting other treatments and then perhaps continue them in tandem. Methods for clearing the bowel vary according to the severity of the case – from stool softening medicines, or enemata, to rectal washouts, or manual evacuation of impacted faeces under anaesthetic. During treatment a child may undergo physical tests and examinations, and surgery may be necessary in some cases. This could be anal dilatation or, in extreme cases, colostomy. By their very nature, these treatments are intrusive and may be perceived by some children as a cruel punishment authorized by their parents, which may only succeed in making the child more rebellious, angry, fearful, and negative and the symptoms intractable.

Sometimes parents complain that their child is unaware of the soiling, which perhaps indicates how cut off from her body and its sensations the child has become. If the child soils frequently – which she[1] is likely to do, until the constipation has been cleared and the colon returned to its normal size – the mother may insist that it would be practical and preferable for the child to have a permanent (or temporary) colostomy, since the soiling is then immediately reduced and so, obviously, are the tensions.

A colostomy would seem to be the logical conclusive act, or final victory, in a long history of coercive bowel training and attempts to make the child conform. In this battle over treatment it is possible to see that the parent (usually mother) is symbiotically involved with the child's bowel and symptoms will sometimes be driven to the extreme of sabotaging less punitive treatments in order to gain what she appears to want – which is control over the child's bowel and, therefore, over the child.

The body symbolic

During the 'anal stage' (in Freud's theory of the three stages of psycho-sexual development (1905)), the anus and defaecation become the centre of the infant's self-awareness and are a source of pleasure. This is also a period of ego development in which control over the body and its sphincters (leading to an acceptable socialization of libidinous impulses) is one of the infant's major preoccupations.

> the contents of the bowel . . . have important meanings for the infant, they are clearly treated as part of the infant's body and represent his first 'gift'. By producing them, he can express his active compliance with his environment and, by withholding them, his disobedience.
>
> (Freud 1905:52)

The idea of faeces being the infant's first gift created from and within himself, and treated as part of his body, echoes the belief held by archaic and primitive clans that the nature of anything is inherent in all of its parts, even when the parts are separated from it. Thus, man treats as part of man's substance

> not only his blood, saliva, umbilical cord, sweat and other excreta, hair clippings, nail parings and the like but earth from his footprints, the remains of his food, his name, his portrait, his garments, ornaments, weapons and implements.
>
> (Hamilton-Grierson in Hastings 1913:198)

This archaic and perhaps contemporary though unconscious, notion suggests that if the self (or soul or ego) inhabits all of one's parts or property – whether it is attached to or detached from one – it may be used by oneself or others to benefit or endanger any other person with whom it is brought into contact. Conversely, whoever gains possession of a part of oneself could use it to their advantage against one.

> (Lillitos 1986:18)

Karl Abraham (1921) and Melanie Klein (1932) wrote of children's ambivalence towards their urethral and anal products. At first these may be an offering inspired by gratitude and love, signifying the child's willingness to co-operate but, later, they become vehicles of hostile impulses linked with the desire to corrode and destroy.

If it is felt that there is a spiritual bond between things which are a part of a person and the person himself, the obligation of reciprocity is understandable. Donor and recipient/counter-donor, united in the giving and receiving of parts of themselves, are able to surmount the boundaries of self and non-self, form relationships, enjoy concord and share gifts – not with a sense of loss or threat, but with a feeling of mutual gain.

(Lillitos 1986:18–19)

If the infant has not been helped to negotiate successfully the 'gift' – giving of the 'anal' phase, or if his or her gift (and, therefore, self) was rejected, or forced from him/her, faeces can cease to be a medium for reciprocal communication and become instead part of the child's relationship with itself.

Melanie Klein (1932) found that in the phantasy world of children mother is split into good and bad. The bad mother becomes the object of the child's phantasised attacks, who will demand back from the child the faeces he has stolen from her. In demanding cleanliness from the child, the mother becomes a terrifying figure, who not only insists on the child relinquishing his faeces but, in his imagination, she will tear them from him if they are not offered freely. Because of the child's own destructive phantasies projected on to the mother (or any external object), the child's fear is the anticipation of equally savage attacks inside himself (Lillitos ibid.).

If faeces are given as a gift to consolidate a relationship, it would follow that a symptom like constipation could be interpreted as withholding from a relationship and also as an expression of the child's anxiety about yielding to his own hostile impulses (through fear of retaliation). To 'give someone shit' is to be hostile and aggressive towards them and clearly giving faeces as a gift is inappropriate in latter life. Does the importance of this faecal gift become displaced on to other objects? And does the attitude towards giving or withholding, that the child developed in the anal stage, continue or change?

Most psychoanalytic theories agree that the object or activity symbolized (in dreams) is of a basic, instinctual, and biological nature. In Ernest Jones's paper, 'The Theory of Symbolism' (1916), he asserts that the symbol itself is conscious but represents, and so allows for a limited discharge of, that which is unconscious and must remain repressed. Freud (1908), Abraham (1917), Ferenczi (1913) and Jones (1916) have all written of the symbolic connection between gold and faeces.

Certain forms of mental activity such as joking are still able to make obstructed sources of pleasure accessible for a brief moment and thus show how much of the esteem in which human beings once held their faeces still remains preserved in the unconscious. The most important residue of this former esteem is, however, that all the interest which the child has had in faeces is transferred in the adult on to another material which he learns in life to set above almost everything else – gold.

(Freud 1908:187)

Excrement was supposed to contain the basic raw materials from which the alchemists were to make gold. What is most worthless is often associated with what is most valued: myths and fairy stories abound with examples for quests for lost treasure (which may be understood symbolically as the lost treasure of self) and, often, seemingly worthless fairy gifts turn to gold and *vice versa*. The unconscious displacement of the child's esteem for faeces into the adult esteem (or disgust) for money is largely to do with what money represents – autonomy, status, wealth, power and control.

(Lillitos 1986)

According to Karl Abraham, 'toilet training exposes the child's narcissism to its first severe test', but this 'injury' is compensated for by the child's sense of achievement and by the parents' praise. However:

Not all children succeed and there are certain over-compensations behind which is hidden that obstinate holding fast to the primitive right of self-determination often seen to manifest itself later in children (and adults) who are noted for their 'goodness', polite manners and obedience, but whose masked rebellious impulses are formed on the grounds of having been forced into submission since infancy.

(Abrahams 1921:373)

To control is to restrain and regulate: it also means to exercise authority. It seems clear that issues of control (self control, lack of self control, and being controlled by others) are operative in children suffering from psychogenic bowel dysfunctions.

Just as adults are controlled by society in various ways (some more subtle than others), so parents (or the child's first authority figures), police the child. Children, as they develop, have two main areas of control: one is their bowel and sphincters, and the second is control over their mouths and, more specifically, over their eating. These two areas are constipation and/or soiling, and anorexia and/or bulimia. As symptoms/illnesses they are the body's expression of a malfunctioning ability to take in and to empty out and, therefore, are the expression of unmet psychological needs and the child's control of these needs. We often hear of prisoners who use the two most powerful means of protest available to them in order to express their limited rights to self-determination. One method is to refuse food, and the second is to use their excrement to defile their environment. Both these forms of protest can be understood as the non-co-operation with, or undermining of, authority. It could be argued that children who are chronically constipated are attempting to establish that they are the ones in control of their bodies, and children who soil or who are incontinent may be expressing just how out of control they actually feel. Furthermore, because it undermines the parents' authority, a symptom like constipation can be seen by the parents as subversive, and faecal soiling as flagrant disobedience.

Case study: Carol

I was asked by the paediatric surgeon to see a child who had been an in-patient on the ward for about two weeks. She was described as being tense, unhappy, and withdrawn. Her symptoms of constipation and 'what looked like withholding' had begun when she was 3 years old and this coincided with her starting playschool, shortly after the birth of a fourth sibling who had usurped her position as the youngest child. Carol, who was now 9 years old, had come in to hospital to have another manual evacuation of faeces and, possibly, a temporary colostomy. However, she had resisted the doctor's examinations and refused the pre-medication injection, which prevented her going to theatre.

When I met Carol she stood by the window in the art therapy room, resting her distended tummy on the window-ledge in the attitude of an exhausted, pregnant mother. She rarely looked at me and only did so when she thought I was not looking at her. Carol's family were financially disadvantaged and it seemed as if nothing she wore had been bought specifically for her. It is logical to assume that such a deprived child would value her faeces highly since they belonged exclusively to her.

At the beginning of her therapy Carol spent two full sessions working silently on a clay model which she painted red and green and then proclaimed it was a 'throne surrounded by precious jewels'. 'Being on the throne' is a recognized euphemism for going to the lavatory and conveys the feeling that the act of defaecation is one of great importance and reflective of a person's power. Although Carol was referred to as being 'a shy and withdrawn child', I often experienced her as being manipulative and controlling, in that she came to therapy when she chose to and alternated between working and non-working (evacuative and retentive behaviour). It was clear that the 'precious jewels' were her idealized faeces which she used (unconsciously) as collateral bargaining for the love and attention of which she felt deprived.

Eventually – because of a mixture of her frozen, distrustful behaviour; the symbolic content of her pictures, (especially since she rarely spoke about them); and my feelings of powerlessness and oppression in the counter-transference – I began to consider seriously the possibility that she had been sexually abused. I tried to keep an open mind about what her images meant but, because she reproduced virtually the same image time after time, I thought she must be trying to tell me something important. These repetitive images were of houses (mostly depicting an external view) but, without exception, the features were abnormal in some way: doors were situated in odd places and were often very large in relation to the rest of the house; windows were irregularly placed; sometimes the roof fitted badly; and the chimney was always drawn at an angle and looked as if it were falling off. The houses were mostly isolated under a heavy, dark blue sky that often depicted night and day simultaneously, suggesting that there was never any relief from her problem. The colours she used – either by accident or design – were dark and muddy; the houses appeared unlived in, unloved, and desolate (*Plates 21* and *22*).

I then realized that in fact Carol *had* been abused – by the hospital, in undergoing numerous examinations and operations in an attempt to diagnose and cure her condition. And, like any other abused child, she had – to some extent – been unwittingly betrayed by someone she loved and trusted: her mother. Having been able to understand and, to some extent, work through this with Carol, she was able when re-admitted months later (and again threatened with a manual evacuation – unless she had a bowel movement before the operation date) to express her feelings quite directly. She took three different coloured pipe-cleaners and made a 'NO ENTRY' road-traffic sign. This sign is part of a system of laws in which disobedience could result in prosecution and a penalty and, by invoking it, Carol was obviously assuming control and prohibiting entry into her body. She opened her bowels normally and was discharged home (*Plate 24*).

In the art therapy sessions with her, I experienced through the counter-transference, all the feelings of rage, powerlessness, and de-personalization that properly belonged to Carol, until she was able to use her power to take control in a positive way, rather than divert it into symptoms. Through Carol I realized that art therapy, as part of the hospital culture, may well be perceived by the child as 'abuse' in the form of probing, since in many ways the efficacy of its effect on the psyche is analogous to an enema's effect on the bowel.

A hospital can be likened to the State, and the members of the multi-disciplinary hospital team to the family. As such, we are to some extent limited and regulated by the rules demanded by our roles within the hospital. Through the dynamics of this team, it is possible to recognize the way in which a child's symptoms or behaviour – played out in the hospital setting and affecting the relationships between team members – affects, to a greater extent, the parental and sibling relationships within the family. The following case material will perhaps illustrate this point.

Case study: David

David, aged 11, was referred for art therapy because of his chronic constipation, faecal overflow soiling and 'anti-social' behaviour at school. His parents arrived without him for the first session, explaining they wanted to speak with me alone first. His mother told me tearfully that she was 'at the end of her tether', but both parents focused their despair on David's failure at a school where he was threatened with expulsion. During that meeting, David's parents expressed the hope that the hospital could 'help' – by which they seemed to mean control and modify his behaviour, as well as cure his symptoms. They also wanted someone to intercede on their behalf with the school but, when I suggested that a paediatric social worker (as one member of the multi-disciplinary team) could liaise with the school, David's father thought this was a criticism of their home life and opposed it, saying that the only trouble at home was his son.

The child I eventually saw, arrived with his arm linked through his mother's, was small for his age and looked the archetypal angel, though he behaved in the first session – and often thereafter – in a manner which was the antithesis of this image. He was aggressive, abusive, and destructive but, behind this defensive behaviour, there could occasionally be glimpsed a vulnerable little boy who was desperate for help. Sometimes I would spend the same time as the length of David's session clearing up after him. Once, I emerged from the session feeling that I had barely survived the persecutory attack he had made on the toys, materials, and room. As I set about the task of clearing up, my overwhelming feeling of despair was superseded by one of intense anger which, surprisingly, was directed not at David but at the consultant paediatrician who had referred David to me. I realized I was experiencing the identical despair of being 'at the end of my tether' that David's mother had expressed. She apparently never had much help or support in caring for him, and her husband – like the paediatrician – was extremely busy and worked long hours in an 'important' job. Consequently, she was frequently left alone to cope with David's 'mess', as I felt I had been left alone by the paediatrician – thus mirroring the family dynamics.

The stereotyping of roles within the hospital replicates those in the family, and identifies, regardless of gender, mother/therapist as carer, and father/doctor as provider, authority figure, as protector or as abuser. Traditionally, it is the mother who intervenes or consoles if she considers the father's punishment of the child to be severe. But is the mother/therapist in a strong enough position to help the child who has been 'abused' by the father/doctor in a setting over which she had no control? And does this reflect what happens in a family in which the father actually abuses the child, and the mother – perhaps to keep the family together – silently colludes?

For the child whose illness manifests itself in physical symptoms the focus, in the first instance, is on their body. For the child who has a bowel problem, this focus is necessarily on the anus and the bottom, until the diagnosis of a physical malfunction of the colon or anus has been confirmed or excluded. But, even then, the constipated child will continue to have attention paid to this part of their anatomy. As discussed above, the pleasure an infant derives from its anus and defaecation in the anal stage is later repressed but, if a child is subjected to repeated anal attention, it is likely that conscious or unconscious sexual or pleasurable feelings will be aroused by this, accompanied by confusion, guilt, and loss of body boundaries. In order to tolerate this attention, the child must repress all these conflicting feelings. (In this, there are undeniable parallels with child sexual abuse. When the child's body is used by an adult for sexual gratification, this transgression of the child's body boundaries leads to the child losing the sense of 'self', becoming 'de-personalized' and switching off all feelings.)

As an art therapist in the hospital setting, not only do I mediate between the child/client and the father/doctor but also, simultaneously, I am aware of my position in the community/hospital and feel that my neighbours/hospital staff on the ward also perhaps expect me to control the child. This, in David's case, would have meant stopping him from shouting, swearing, and making liberal use of the materials to create a mess – which I did not. (I did, however, have certain boundaries concerning the physical safety of both therapist and client, and the avoidance of damage to the room or its fixtures.) However, in his sessions it often seemed that David wanted me to take control – perhaps so that he would not have to face up to the chaos inside himself. When playing with a toy aeroplane, David staged several crashes with his parents and grandparents on board: 'That's got rid of the fucking lot of them,' he said vehemently after the final crash. Then he immediately wanted me to play the part of the 'control tower' at the 'airport'. Instead of punishing him for expressing his violent fantasy, I understood this to be a plea for me to help him negotiate his own out-of-control feelings of destructive rage towards his family and to help him bring them (and therefore himself) safely to land.

In this particular case, it was important for David to realize that he could depend upon me and trust me to help him, by being with him in an uncritical manner, while he experienced feelings which were infantile and out of control. In this David expressed a need which is described in Winnicott's concept of 'holding' (1963) and being 'a good enough mother' (1960:145) and Bion's idea of 'containing' (1962:102–5). Martha Harris sums up Bion's concept succinctly:

> he talks of the infant's need for a mother who will receive the evacuation of his distress, consider it and respond appropriately. If this happens, the infant has an experience of being understood as well as of being comforted. He receives back the evacuated part of his personality in an improved condition together with an experience of an object which has been able to tolerate and to think about it. Thus introjecting what Bion called the mother's capacity for 'reverie', the infant begins to be more able to tolerate himself and to begin to apprehend himself and the world in terms of the *meaning* of things. The mother's failure to respond to his distress results in the introjection of an object which is hostile to understanding, together

with that frightened part of himself which is divested of meaning through not eliciting a response. This is then experienced as a 'nameless dread'.
(Harris 1970:36; author's emphasis)

Recurrent experiences of being 'contained' allow the child to internalize the process and eventually, with maturation, become more able to 'contain' his or her own anxieties. There were many indications in David's therapy that he had been emotionally deprived as an infant and probably never experienced either of his parents as 'containers'. One sign of this was pica (a perverted appetite or a craving for unsuitable food) which is likely to be associated with disturbed early relationships. He had in the past been hospitalized after eating something highly poisonous, at an age when he should have been able to discriminate, and in his art therapy sessions he often tried to eat or drink inappropriate substances, which caused me to intervene. (Perhaps he had an unsatisfied craving for love, or wanted to test whether I cared enough about him to look after him.)

In moments of extreme distress he would clamber across the table, stand on the window-ledge wrapped in the curtain and shout obscenities at the top of his voice. If I attempted to intervene too quickly to ease his – and my – distress, he found this frightening and would shout louder to try and drown my words and project his rage and anxiety on to me. During these moments of regression, I reflected that what he needed was to be held and comforted by me until he saw that I was able to survive the awfulness of his feelings and, therefore, he could come to see that they were manageable and tolerable. However he thwarted any 'holding' or comforting that might have helped him, in the same way that a baby screams, kicks, and protests about being picked up and held, if the comfort arrives too late. When David expressed his rage and his chaotic, out-of-control feelings, I felt he was determined to destroy me and the room before – as he phantasized – he himself was annihilated by me (or the person I represented in the transference).

Although I did not physically hold David, I was occasionally able to 'hold' him emotionally by using the silent spaces and a carefully considered choice of words and tone of voice. (At his age the comfort of being physically held had arrived too late and could have been misinterpreted as sexual.) In this way, perhaps, I managed to give his 'nameless dread' a meaningful and bearable form which he was eventually able to accept back as part of himself, rather than projecting it on to me. Sometimes, his feelings were so over-whelming that he would run from the room and disappear before I could stop him. Gradually, as he perceived that running away did not help, he stayed in the room and devised symbolic ways of expressing his need to be 'contained'. On one occasion he filled two pots with water and, with the two mouths facing, bound them together using a whole roll of masking-tape, to make a completely enclosed bundle the size of a baby. In another session, he used string to tie himself to his chair and then tied the chair to the table leg near me.

These binding activities seemed to be both an expression of David's difficulty to differentiate between what belonged inside him and what belonged inside another (symbolized by the flow of water between the two pots), and a powerful statement about his need for all the unintegrated fragments of his inner self to be bound together and 'contained' in a way which they had not been in his infancy. Watching David as he shook the wrapped pots so violently, I wondered if he was unconsciously re-enacting being shaken as an infant. As the water seeped through the masking-tape, it was easy to speculate that David felt his psyche was as uncontained as fluid without boundaries, and that his insides were uncontainable and seeped out – like the water from the pots – as faecal soiling or, in early childhood, as urinary incontinence.

A continuous stream of undifferentiated experiences and sensations flow through the infant's mind and body. Before it develops the faculty to contain, integrate, and process these into understanding, the infant relies on the primary carer (mother) to fulfil this function for it and, in so doing, to hold or wrap the unintegrated parts of its personality together. 'This containing object is experienced concretely as a skin' (Bick 1968:484–6). If the infant has not experienced being held by an attentive mother, because she has been unable to perform this function, the infant attempts to do this for itself and dependence on the mother is replaced by a 'pseudo-independence' and the development of a 'second-skin'.

In David's first session, he told me about a 'horror' film he had seen on video which included violent scenes he described in detail, and sexual scenes which he alluded to. While talking he casually interjected that he had 'a bowel problem', as if this too was part of the horror. He asked me if he could swear, in order to tell me about the film and I told him he could, if he felt this was necessary. Interestingly, the words he used most frequently were 'holy shit' and 'arse-hole'. It felt as if all the words, images, and feelings that had been 'festering' inside him for a long while were expelled uncontrolledly – like diarrhoea – and he was not only getting the film out of his system, but also his feelings about his 'problem'. He seemed to perceive that art therapy might be a space for decontaminating himself and evacuating his feelings. In other words, he was getting rid of the 'shit' – albeit 'holy' – from inside himself. Eventually, he produced a painting of a 'horrible face' in this first session. He had very little control over the paint – or the form the painting took – and described the face as 'like jelly'. Indeed, it had no structured boundary and spread messily across the page, with the eyes being the only recognizable feature (*Plate 25*). Subsequently, this image seemed indicative of David's own sense of himself as having no boundaries, unless he was contained in the way in which jelly has to be contained, so that it sets into a defined shape.

David expressed feelings of being out-of-control and uncontainable when he talked about things happening to him by accident with a different outcome from his intention. This seemed to be how he also viewed his soiling, which happened suddenly and could be seen symbolically in the art therapy sessions. For example, he was unaware most of the time of the 'mess' he was making in the process of working but, if he accidently spilt some paint, he would apologize and want to clear it up immediately. However, his attempts to clear up increased his frustration since he was not very efficient and resulted in a larger mess. When this happened he abandoned the attempt to control himself and evacuated his feelings in a frenzy of undirected activity. His attempts to control himself in the sessions mirrored his physical symptoms. During the last session before a break in therapy, he suddenly stopped playing and decided to make something out of a huge cardboard box. He gathered several bottles of paint to squirt at the box, and said, urgently, 'Quick, put down the cloths' (large sheets which we used to cover the floor if he wanted to flick paint). It seemed as if he wanted to evacuate his feelings before the holiday and recognized that the paint might make a 'mess'. Perhaps his soiling was to him, also a sudden, explosive mess expressing his inability to contain things inside himself after the effort of holding in or trying to be 'good', (as he had been at the beginning of the session).

In another session just prior to a break, he arrived with a partially deflated balloon he had found on the ward. He pummelled and kicked it and attempted to burst it by stamping on it. Finally, he pierced it with the scissors and it gradually deflated. He then sat staring out of the window and told me plaintively, 'it's going to rain now', as if he felt as let down (because I was going away) as the balloon. Later, perhaps to escape these feelings, he began painting patterns. He squeezed paint on to the paper, covered it with another sheet then used the water pot as a rolling pin across them. Inevitably, the paint oozed out over the table, but he did not notice. When he did, he asked 'why does it always happen to me?' and 'how did it happen?', which shows his bewilderment about soiling. David felt that everything he did turned to 'shit' and, as he seemed to have few genuine feelings of worth, perhaps that he too was 'shit' – or the rejected aspect of his parents' relationship.

As he continued to make the print, he asked me what it would look like but answered himself by saying 'shit'. However, as he peeled off the top sheet he expressed surprise and delight that instead of 'shit' it looked like a 'rainbow'. He used more and more paint which, mixed together, resembled faeces, then smeared it over his hands and arms. He revealed that it was a sensual experience by rubbing the paint vigorously across the apron over his genitals. Then, in order to make another print, he sat on the papers making a large brown stain on the seat of his trousers which then looked as if he had literally soiled himself. Although he had been using the word 'shit' liberally throughout the session, he referred to this stain as being 'like "do-do"', indicating his regressed state by the use of this childish term for faeces.

It seems that not only does the bottom fall out of David's world when he fails in the intentions of his actions – at school, at home, in his art therapy sessions – but also, more significantly, the world falls out of his bottom in that what is inside him (and his self) is uncontainable. He is unable to contain an image of good parents, or himself. As I said above, his experiences as an infant were probably 'uncontained' and consequently 'unprocessed' by him, so all of his subsequent experiences and emotions rush through and out of him, without differentiation, and are all expected to be 'shitty' – worthless – and, literally, shit. Hanna Segal writes:

> When this symbolic relation to faeces and other body products has been established, a projection can occur on to substances in the external world such as paint, clay etc., which can then be used for sublimation.
> When this stage of development has been achieved, it is, of course, not irreversible. If the anxieties are too strong regression to paranoid schizoid position can occur at any stage in the individual's development and projective identification may be resorted to as a defence against anxiety. The symbols which have been developed and have been functioning as symbols in sublimation revert to concrete symbolic equations.
>
> (Segal 1986:56)

David was eventually able to sublimate his feelings and to find symbolic equivalents for them, and rather than attempting to 'destroy' me or the room he showed concern about 'mess' and made attempts at reparation which indicated that he had reached 'the depressive position' (Klein 1935). Our relationship worked through his regressed infantile stages until he was emotionally old enough to express concern, to work through the Oedipal jealousy he felt towards his father who locked him out of a more intimate relationship with his mother, and a family relationship with them both. He no longer had to express symptoms of being out of control and was able to master his aggression, take control, and let go enough to be creative.

Carol, on the other hand, was a girl who needed her symptom both as a means of expressing how empty and deprived she actually felt, and as a powerful means of gaining attention from her family, especially her mother. Playing squiggles with her in her sessions enabled her to take all the space and attention she needed, expressing this by using larger and larger sheets of paper until we had a piece 6 metres' square on the wall. Her constant representations of food expressed the emotional and physical feeding of which she felt in need. Later, she was able to work on her own again, but without being distant or cutting me off. She was able to use the materials freely, to splash about with the paint, to sing and to tell me that she had fallen in love with a boy at school. This is the converse of David: she was able to let go and, in letting go, was able to be creative. He had to hold on before he could be creative. David is an example of a boy who was 'uncontained' and deprived as an infant and with whom it was important to work within tight boundaries. Carol was a girl who exerted a great deal of control, both over her bowels and during her art therapy sessions and, therefore had to learn to let go.

Creativity – control and release

In this last section I want to look briefly at the concepts of control and letting-go of control (rather than being out-of-control) and the relationship between this and creativity.

In the beginning of the process of a creative act there is necessarily a period which seems chaotic and formless, like the 'void' before the creation of the world. During this period the creator has to negotiate the anxiety about their ability to hold together all the unintegrated parts (perhaps there are parallels here with the task of the therapist in 'holding' the unintegrated parts of the client's personality). It would seem that creativity (that is, giving a form to that which is without form and is chaotic) has as its prototype certain of our biological functions – principally perhaps conception, pregnancy, and birth of a child – but also the process of defaecation. There is, of course, a vast difference in the form, function, and end result of these two examples (though David may have felt more like the waste product of his parents' sexual relationship, than a creative result of it). In terms of the link between creativity and defaecation, examination of the profound resistance I experienced to writing these pages would be instructive since, in many ways, it mirrors the physical symptoms and problems of chronic constipation/overflow soiling of the clients referred for art therapy and, perhaps, apprehends their physical origins.

After many attempts to begin writing, and days and days of being unable to produce anything at all, I had the following dream: I was strolling through the dark, narrow, streets of a foreign city when I saw a dustbin overflowing with interesting objects, which I stopped to examine. I delved into the refuse, which consisted mostly of scraps of cloth but, in amongst them, I was surprised to find delicate Christmas tree baubles whose coloured glass surfaces shone in the street light. I picked them out carefully and gathered them up in my arms. As I was doing this, an elderly tramp came towards me and began shouting. I was suffused with a strong feeling of disappointment as I realized that the baubles were not the genuine treasure that I had imagined them to be, just before I awoke. On waking, I understood this dream to be of relevance to this chapter since it is about both the feelings I had in writing it, and the subject matter itself.

In the case of writing and, specifically, theoretical writing there is much preparation to be done. This often involves reading, thinking, and discussing ideas. I propose that the first phase can be likened to the 'oral stage' in Freud's concept of the three stages of psycho-sexual development (Freud

1905), since it involves 'drinking in', 'spitting out' or in realizing that you have 'bitten off more than you can chew'. During this phase the ideas are being 'chewed over', as it were, and are without form. (Being unable to 'stomach' them might cause the creator to spit them out and reject them, implying an inability to contain them until it is possible to give them form – because of conflict or unbearable tension. Some of these ideas are 'digested' and what is good is 'absorbed'. During this process there is a period of chaos through which the creator has to work and it is vital that she is able to contain the anxiety inherent in this period in holding the non-integrated parts that will form the whole.

Later comes the point at which the creative act takes form – a painting, a piece of writing, etc. – and becomes external to the creator. Perhaps the thing created was not fully formed and came out in a sudden rush, or perhaps something blocked the process and, although the ideas were formed inside, the creator had difficulty in externalizing the ideas and giving them concrete form. However, once the formed 'art' is outside the creator, it is recognized as separate from them though containing elements of her. These formed ideas give rise to relationships and intercourse and are perhaps like the 'genital stage' of creativity, as the previous stage – of undifferentiated chaos – was the 'anal stage'.

In these stages of development are the prototypes for the maturation of creative acts, as well as physical and emotional maturation. In my dream, the dark, foreign, narrow streets suggest the alimentary canal, at the end of which is the dustbin, or rectum, full of faeces. However, the dustbin also conveys the idea of being full-up with improperly digested ideas since it is full-up with scraps of cloth which are the symbolic representation of the material foraged through (books, journals, etc.) before I began to write and the work that had been done with the clients which is referred to as 'case material'. These scraps were too small to make a garment but could be sewn together as words and ideas to make an article. This suggests that, although my efforts had been unproductive, I felt unconsciously that there was something of worth inside me, as the child in the anal stage feels that its faeces are gift-worthy. Alas, just before I awoke, I realized that the treasure in the dustbin is only faeces. My inability to let go of what was inside me, for fear that it might be rubbish, was what produced the 'creative constipation', and mirrored Carol's inability to let go of her stools because she unconsciously attached a great deal of worth to what she had to recognize as excrement. The fact that faeces are not treasure in the external world, is one of the devastating realities to be negotiated by the infant during the anal stage.

Letting of of all the excited mess, faeces, vomit, saliva, noise, flatus – no one differentiated from the other, a state of blissful transcending of boundaries, which to the conscious ego would be madness. The dread is of a wish to return to that state of infancy in which there was no discrimination between the orgiastic giving of the body products and the products themselves. I suggest that it is this original lack of discrimination which is partly responsible for the later idealisation of the body products; and the disillusion is then experienced when the real qualities of the intended love gift come to be perceived. I find clinical evidence which seems to show that particularly in poets and artists who are inhibited in their work, there has been a catastrophic disillusion in the original discovery that their faeces are not as lively, as beautiful, as boundless, as the body feelings they had in the giving of them.   (Milner 1957:150)

Art – and more specifically art therapy – with its emphasis on visual images, has the potential to stimulate the deepest levels of the psyche by facilitating psychic projections into material things. It is possible through symbolism, if only fleetingly, to apprehend distant reverberations of feelings that one is unable to name, and to recognize in them a link with one's present feelings and thus, if only momentarily, understand them even without being able to speak of them. Metaphorically, it feels as if being an art therapist in this setting is akin to being a mother waiting for her toddler to produce a stool in the pot (rather than withholding, soiling, or being encopretic). Although I am hopeful that the constipated children I treat may eventually be able to produce real stools regularly, I also hope that art therapy – by providing the opportunity to relinquish control – may facilitate the release of what the blocked stool represents, whilst being held and contained. It is essential to wait patiently, without probing and without overt or covert threats until this can be given freely. At which point, the child is able to release his or her ability to be creative, and to give form to thoughts and feelings from within. Having what is inside oneself acknowledged and accepted by another, enables one to use one's capabilities, to form relationships, to be creative and to make something in and of one's life, which had previously been struggling to achieve shape.

If faeces represent internal treasure and elements of taking control of one's own internal and external reality, I feel that my work as an art therapist is to help the children find and take control of their feelings, to help them externalize their treasure and feel that they themselves have intrinsic worth.

© 1990 Aleathea Lillitos

Note

1 The subject referred to throughout this chapter is a female child.

References

Abraham, K. (1917) 'The spending of money in anxiety states', *The Selected Papers of Karl Abraham*, London: The Hogarth Press and The Institute of Psycho-Analysis (1927).

Abraham, K. (1919) 'A particular form of neurotic resistance against the psycho-analytic method', *The Selected Papers of Karl Abraham*, London: The Hogarth Press and The Institute of Psycho-Analysis (1927).

Abraham, K. (1921) 'Contributions to the theory of the anal character', *The Selected Papers of Karl Abraham*, London: The Hogarth Press and The Institute of Psycho-Analysis (1927).

Bick, E. (1968) 'The experience of the skin in early object relations', *The International Journal of Psycho-Analysis* 49.

Bion, W. (1962) *Learning From Experience*, London: William Heinemann Medical Books Ltd.

Ferenczi, S. (1913) 'The ontogenesis of symbols', in S. Ferenczi *First Contributions to Psycho-Analysis* (1952), London: The Hogarth Press.

Freud, S. (1905) '*Drei zur sexual theorie*', Leipzig and Vienna (1949 edn). Published as 'Three essays on the theory of sexuality', *Infantile Sexuality*, London: The Hogarth Press and The Institute of Psycho-Analysis.

Freud, S. (1908) 'Dreams in folklore: faeces symbolism and related dream actions', *Standard Edition* VII, The Hogarth Press and The Institute of Psycho-Analysis.

Harris, M. (1970) 'Some notes on maternal containment in "Good enough" mothering', *Journal of Child Psychotherapy* 4.

Hastings, J. (ed.) (1913) *Encyclopaedia of Religion and Ethics. Vol. VI*, Edinburgh: T. and T. Clark.

Jones, E. (1916) *The Theory of Symbolism in Ernest Jones' Papers on Psycho-Analysis*, 2nd edn, London: Ballière Tindall & Cox (1918).

Klein, M. (1932) *The Psycho-Analysis of Children*, London: The Hogarth Press and The Institute of Psycho-Analysis.

Klein, M. (1975) *A Contribution to the Psychogenesis of Manic-depressive States, in Love, Guilt and Reparation and Other Works, 1912–1945*, London: The Hogarth Press and The Institute of Psycho-Analysis.

Lillitos, A. (1986) 'The giving of gifts', Goldsmith's College Postgraduate dissertation.

Milner, M. (1957) *On Not Being Able to Paint*, London: Heinemann.

Segal, H. (1986) *The Work of Hanna Segal: A Kleinian Approach to Clinical Practice, Delusion and Artistic Creativity and Other Psycho-analytical Essays*, London: Free Association Books and Maresfield Library.

Winnicott, D. (1960) 'True and false self', in John D. Sutherland (ed.) *The Maturational Processes and the Facilitating Environment, Studies in the Theory of Emotional Development*, The International Library, London: The Hogarth Press and The Institute of Psycho-Analysis.

Winnicott, D. (1963) 'The development of the capacity for concern', *The Maturational Processes and the Facilitating Environment*, London: The Hogarth Press and The Institute of Psycho-Analysis.

Acknowledgements

I acknowledge my indebtedness to my clients who continue to teach me, to my colleagues at the hospital – particularly Graham Clayden, Consultant Paediatrician – and to Malachi and Angela for their support and help. Special thanks to Kay McCormick, without whom this would never have been completed.

Chapter six

Working with cases of child sexual abuse
Carol Sagar

Introduction

During the 1980s there has been a rapid increase in the number of cases of sexual abuse seen in child and family psychiatry, the social services, and by other agencies concerned with child welfare. Public awareness of the resulting physical and psychological damage in children and adults has increased. The media has brought information and reporting regarding sexual abuse into homes and family life in such a way that it cannot be ignored. There has been a change in public consciousness, which has brought the subject into open discussion and recognition.

During the last 20 years organizations involved with the care and protection of children have formulated various systems for dealing with child abuse. Area review committees have been set up as policy-making bodies for the management of child abuse cases. In 1980 the Department of Health and Social Security issued the 'Child Abuse: Central Register Systems', for the recording of non-accidental injuries to children, amongst which sexual abuse is included. In the area of the country in which I work the Area Review Committee has delegated responsibility to the Director of Social Services, to maintain a central register of child abuse cases. This Director has also to ensure that case conferences are held where appropriate and that all notified cases are periodically reviewed.

Health authorities and social services as well as the police, have needed to devise ways in which to handle sexual abuse cases. For example a police detective constable experienced in this work will interview the child with a social worker present, also family members if the child wishes. Anatomically correct dolls may be used at this interview to help the child relate what has happened with a minimum of words being necessary. The abuser will only be approached by the police if the child is willing to make a formal complaint against him or her following this disclosure. For the child to have told a parent or therapist, but not to tell the police detective, is not sufficient grounds for proceedings to be started against an abuser.

Every county has had to construct its own procedures, communication channels, and liaison between the various agencies concerned with dealing with sexual abuse cases.

Referrals of sexual abuse to the appropriate Area Social Services officer will therefore result in the Area Officer convening a case conference. However due to the need for more flexibility and sensitivity in such cases a Core Group has been formed to operate within each Health Authority boundary to discuss and monitor each case and make plans as to the best way to proceed initially.

(Child Abuse 1985)

'The relevant Area Social Services officer will maintain responsibility for each case and must at all times be approached in the first instance' (ibid.). The Area Officer is responsible for consulting a member of the Core Group who will communicate with the other Core Group members. The Core Group decides upon the course of action to be taken together with the Area Social Services officer. In the Core Group are: (1) a consultant psychiatrist from the Department of Child and Family Psychiatry, (2) a police officer, and (3) a social worker appropriate to the area concerned. Communications and co-ordination between workers are the essence for effective intervention. DHSS document LASSL (76) 2 states regarding abuse, 'The safety of the child must in all circumstances be of paramount importance and must over-ride all other considerations' (ibid.). This is essential in sexual abuse cases.

The criteria for registration of cases on the Sexual Abuse Register are:

Children under the age of 17 years subject to
1. illegal or other sexual activity between parent or custodian and child within the family context (including adoptive and step relationships);
2. failure of caretakers to protect children from illegal or otherwise inappropriate sexual activity.

(Ibid.)

However, these criteria are being re-examined in the light of some difficulties presented by a recent case.

Coming into therapy

Sometimes a referral is made to art therapy specifically because a child is emotionally disturbed as a result of recent sexual abuse. Sometimes sexual abuse took place months or even years previously but recent disclosure brings a family to the Child and Family Centre when the abused child may be referred to art or play therapy. Almost inevitably work is being done with the family concurrently with individual therapy for the abused child. Every case will be investigated and responded to according to the specific situation and needs of the abused person and their family or family substitutes. In cases where abuse and/or disclosure have been recent there is likely to have been a case conference before referral to art or play therapy. At the case conference an initial course of action will have been decided upon for the abused and the family.

Sexual abuse may be the cause of physical, psychological, and behavioural problems for the child which can be manifested at home and at school. Such difficulties include aggressive behaviour; behaviour problems reflecting lack of recognition of boundaries; lack of concentration. Truanting, nightmares, phobias, and depression are other indications of the anxiety that these children experience. Enuresis, soiling, irritation, and infections of the urinary tract can be physical expressions of the feeling of having bad contents which need to be got rid of, as well as expressions of anger, irritation, and unhappiness caused by extreme and inappropriate over-stimulation of the genitals. For each case circumstantial indications are important. An abused child's development in every aspect can be disturbed so that any symptom of disturbance can be shown, and frequently many are shown at the same time.

For children referred to art therapy it is not unusual, after some months or a year of regular sessions, for disclosure of past sexual abuse to arise. In the Child and Family Centre therapists from various disciplines recognize that sexual abuse that was never suspected, identified, or disclosed is often likely to have been the cause of emotional disturbance which did not become resolved during therapy. Due to development of awareness amongst therapists, with regard to sexual abuse, more cases are now identified, and abused people feel more likely to be believed, thus they have more confidence in making disclosures.

The disclosure of recent sexual abuse usually has traumatic repercussions depending on the nature of the abuse and relationship between abused and abuser. It is important for the therapist to know of the history and background of disturbing events. Initial disbelief within the family may be followed by denial by the abuser leading to family disputes, anxiety, anger, guilt, and blaming. The child is likely to have been physically examined in order to discover any damage caused by the abuse, as well as to verify that abuse has taken place. Even when carefully and sensitively done this may be felt by the child to be as abusive as the initial abuse. The child is likely to have been required to talk about what happened to parents, a police woman, a social worker, and possibly to a therapist assessing the child's therapeutic needs. The abuser, who may be a parent, could be in, or at risk of going to, prison. There may have been the break-up of the family with the child or children being taken into care. All of these possibilities, as well as attempts to adapt to changes, are liable to be potent sources of fear, anger, shame, and self-blame, in spite of the relief of stopping the abuse. Some or all of these feelings are likely to have been there before the disclosure, the pressure of them may have led to it; they are likely to be exacerbated as a result of the disclosure and reactions of others. Therefore the sexually-abused child coming into therapy is likely to be defending him or herself against some overwhelming emotional feelings, including the experience of loss relating to the disclosure and its consequences. Although needing to share these feelings in the safe, confidential therapy situation the child may feel intimidated from doing so by anxiety, guilt feelings, and general confusion.

Art and play therapies are particularly appropriate for this group of children as they can work with their feelings and experience them directly in the handling of materials used in the therapies. The process and results express clearly the confusion and damage which abused children suffer and reflect how they find ways in their work to bring about repair, change, and growth from within.

Sometimes the art therapy process involves drawings and paintings which show explicit situations in which the abuse has taken place, or the abuser is shown as the child felt him (or her) to be. Often the way in which most satisfaction seems to be found in using art materials is by making a messy mixture which is then spread on any surface. Messy packages may be formed and given to the therapist to keep. Containers and packages of the mixture may have to be kept for a long time until the child emerges from the ·compulsive need to handle and examine the internal chaotic feelings where 'good' and 'bad' are indistinguishable. The messy package may represent the secret which the child has had to hold, often over a long time, which is now passed into the therapist's keeping. At some point later the package and the containers of mess will be asked for by the child who may decide they can be disposed of – usually thrown away – or who may not yet be ready to let go of them. Later the child may begin to use the materials to represent and express present phantasies and the current relationship with external reality.

The secret map and the secret letter *(Figure 6.1)*

This drawing was produced in the fifteenth therapy session with a girl of 6 years of age. The previous sessions had been largely spent working with the messy feelings as outlined above. In session 15 the secret was explored in the form of a secret letter to a friend and a secret map. There was also a character drawn upside-down. This feeling of things being turned on their head by the abuse is recurrent in art therapy with abused children. Contradictions abound as the child tries to work her way through the anxieties of keeping a secret, and the need to share it, to keep the loved privileged feelings but let go of the abused ones. The secret letter was shown to me but I was told it was not for me. The secret map looks very much like a vagina leading into the internal space where the dots were said to represent 'things to find'. Finding some sense of herself and her own boundaries seemed to be functions of the map, as well as expressing her anxiety about invasion of those boundaries

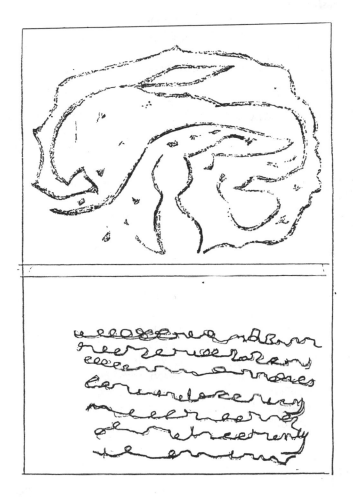

Figure 6.1 The secret map and the secret letter

and what may have been put inside her. She shared phantasies at other times that she had been made pregnant. Further details of this therapy are discussed below, under the heading 'Working with the secret internal situation'.

Patterns

The most widely-recognized pattern arising from sexual abuse in childhood is that of becoming an adult abuser, this pattern is also seen as a result of physical abuse. It is increasingly becoming clear that abuse breeds abuse. It is also noticed that being abused sexually and/or physically can lead to entrenchment in the victim role. A child who has been abused already is more likely to be abused again.

It is easy for those working with abused children to feel empathy and strong compassion for the abused child; it is not difficult to feel fierce anger towards the abuser; but it is helpful to remember the small abused child in the abuser which is repressed, and to remember that, without effective therapy, the abused child is a potential abuser. If we ignore one side or the other in an abuse relationship we are ignoring half of the dynamics in the child's inner world and a significant drive behind the child's responses and behaviour. It was remarked in a discussion with a play therapist[1] that after learning to say 'No' and being taught that a child has ownership and authority over his or her body – these lessons coming, as it were, from outside – the child continues to remain vulnerable when in situations which render him or her liable to abuse, even when in the company of a 'safe' adult. The boundaries need to be reconstructed working from within in order for them to be reliable and automatically protect the child. To be effective, these boundaries need to be built on the ground of the healing work with the deeply damaged inner parts of the self. In the art therapy work we can see how this deep damage is experienced and expressed, as well as how repair is attempted symbolically with the art and play materials.

I have already briefly mentioned the need to find a way to handle the mixed, confused, and messy feelings which can dominate the inner world of the abused child. A later stage followed in one child's art therapy process in which she seemed to find a way to symbolically repair feelings of internal damage through working on a clay body. Before treatment ended a representation of her internal reproductive organs was made very precisely and accurately. Many sessions of straightforward anatomical study preceded this work of putting her understanding into form. It was vital for her to feel that she knew what her internal organs looked and felt like. She seemed to want to restore her body to the state it was prior to the abuse and at the same time restore her relationship with it.

As for any child coming into therapy the abused child comes with the whole experience of life up until that moment, with more or less well-established patterns of relating to her or himself and the world. How deeply the abuse will have affected the development of those patterns is likely to depend on the age when the abuse began, the time over which it has been consistently repeated, or if it was once or a few times. It depends on with whom the abuse occurred, for example, whether within or outside the family; where it occurred, whether in or out of the home; and the extent to which the abuse was painful and frightening. Tilman Furniss (1987), during a workshop on child sexual abuse, stated that the more long term the abuse, the earlier the onset, the more close the relationship and depending whether the abuse takes place in the child's own home or not, the more severe the damaging effects will be.

One instance of sexual abuse is enough for a potential pattern of relating to oneself and the world to be laid down, further occurrences of abuse feed that potential. When abuse is consistently repeated from a very early age over the whole or a large part of childhood it is inevitable that the whole of that person's development will be in reaction to the abuse. Some adults who have disclosed sexual abuse in therapy can be understood as having lived their whole lives in largely unconscious reaction, at times towards and at times against their abuser and the abuse suffered in childhood. This can be seen to have motivated most of their adult decisions and limited or biased their capacities in every aspect of their lives, intellectual, emotional, and sexual. One adult patient wrote:

Eventually you grow out of this self-hatred stage and start to make yourself forget that anything happened. . . . The only problem being [that] in doing this you actually become devoid of any real feeling or real sensations. Most of the time you are and feel like an outsider in whatever is going on around you. . . . All of the younger part of your life has been spent in *hiding* – hurt – hatred – love – anger – anything at all that makes you appear real.

Anyway you do very well through your teenage years just being a little hard case, all bravado and show, because inside you cry and cry, why do people not see this? Eventually your feelings are gone completely and life is an act. You will fit into any situation – go along with what everyone wants and generally feel that life is too long . . . you just don't know how to be. I guess you feel afraid that you may really be the person your father hated after all.[2]

Art and play therapy with children give the opportunity to interrupt and change the patterns on which unsatisfactory systems of relating with others are based before they become too fixed. Some of the patterns unless changed through therapy, tend to become automatic responses. Although these patterns are described sequentially and as if they occurred in an ordered separate way, it should be remembered that in the experience of the child there is an intense onslaught on body, mind, and emotional feelings. The emergence of these patterns results from the chaos and confusion in which everything is happening at the same time, in which the person concerned is traumatized, at worst, on every level.

The addictive pattern

In the workshop already referred to, Tilman Furniss drew attention to the syndrome of addiction in the abuser. He spoke of the child as the drug, the compulsion to repeat the abusive behaviour, the psychological dependency of the abuser on the child, and the denial of this dependency. It looks as though this addictive element with its feelings of dependency also features for the child who has the experience of long-term repeated abuse.

An adult in therapy felt that the nightmares which had brought her father to her room, where abuse then followed, were 'unconscious calling'. She felt that she had wanted the love, attention, and caring which came expressed as non-painful abuse. Her father's repeated question, 'Why do you make me do it?' seems to reflect and reinforce this patient's feeling that she drew the abuse to her. It also reflects the power being projected into the child. For this patient the defence of projective identification was strongly developed and was used to thrust out sexual feelings. These could become introjected and identified with by others who were then perceived as sexually-abusive by the patient. It looks as if her father used projective identification towards her in this way during her infancy and childhood, so that she felt and identified with his desire and he always felt that she wanted his sexual approaches and was making him abuse her. Indeed, in therapy she has felt open enough to share her feelings of wanting his love in whatever form it came, and feeling that he was nice at these times, gentle, and loving. It was not painful and she loved him. Difficult feelings developed later especially when the abuse became painful, then her distress manifested in nearly all the behaviours mentioned where 'Coming into therapy' is discussed. This patient remembers feeling in a constant state of sexual arousal throughout her childhood which persisted until the time of her father's death. The strength of the bonds forged by the abuse tends to lead to repeated unconscious searching for abusive relationships after the primary one has discontinued.

In adult life in both physically and sexually-abused people the partner chosen is noticeably likely to be physically or sexually abusive to the adult partner or to their children. A 10-year-old abused boy enjoyed games of being tied up by others more powerful than himself. In this way he put himself in the helpless victim role. Describing the game in therapy gave us the opportunity to focus on his rather unconscious identity with this role. In his drawings of powerful machinery he gave the other side of the picture – the phantasy of himself in control of the power, or the drive. In play therapy sadistic, angry attacks were made upon the therapist in phantasy by an 8-year-old abused girl who wanted to cover the therapist with the messy mixed-up paint which she had made. She needed to know if the therapist could protect herself from the anger and messy feelings. She was playing out her transference feelings towards her mother from whom she felt she had stolen the adult partner. She blamed the mother for a lack of protection, of the mother herself from the child, and of the child from the abuser.

Confusion arising from the breaking and loss of boundaries

Generational and relationship boundaries are broken through sexual abuse. This is an area which may be explored in therapy using the anatomically correct dolls. In art therapy with young sexually-abused children, I may have these dolls in the room. A child may decide to play with them, in which case I see my role as non-directive observation, accepting and reflecting back the feelings and/or confusion expressed.

A 5-year-old girl who had been abused by her father played out all kinds of sexual combinations between the male and female dolls, e.g. father and grandmother, grandfather and mother, mother and father, brother and sister, father and daughter, mother and son. She seemed completely confused, the game becoming quite frantic. The dolls were also required to change clothes as if in an attempt to disguise, for example, the mother as grandmother for the grandfather to partner. It looked as if the child could make no sense of it in her own mind – would change in *appearances* be enough to convince herself or me that it was acceptable? All the combinations made this little girl equally anxious.

The game with the dolls ended repeatedly with them being put to bed, laid side by side making sure that the mother was between the daughter and the father, the grandmother being given the position of authority as the head of the family. In the game the mother was given the role of protecting the daughter, which in reality she had been unable to do through necessary absence. In her games the child seemed to be trying to structure the family in its boundaries and hierarchy as she wished it to be for her own safety needs. The influence of other family members, especially that collusive aspect which mothers can unconsciously or half-consciously adopt, is important and, although passive, actively colludes with the abuse. Sexual abuse is most usefully treated as part of family pathology rather than as an isolated problem between the abused and the abuser as the latter attitude tends to reinforce the unreality and secrecy which is characteristic of the abuse itself. Tilman Furniss (Workshop 1987) has said that, 'The core element of therapy is to establish some reality.' He spoke of how the syndromes of secrecy and addiction, with the internal denial of the abuse, interfere with the establishment of reality.

The *body boundaries* of what is 'good touching' have been broken so that oversensualized and oversexualized behaviour is common in young sexually-abused children. Approaches may be made to men generally in a sexual way, with the child wanting to touch the man's genital area, sit on his knee and wriggle around, or frequently undressing at inappropriate times. Some children regress to wetting, some become soilers. The confusion of body boundaries, of what is appropriate to allow inside, keep inside or put or keep outside, is expressed by these feelings of lack of control over the body and wanting to get rid of something from inside. The overwhelming feelings of being full of mess inside which have somehow to be dealt with are expressed in art therapy through the materials used. A 12-year-old girl made a very large painting within the outline made by drawing around her body whose insides were represented by thick black paint. The painting was rolled up so that the paint, when dry, made it impossible to unroll the paper. This was trusted to the care of the therapist for some time before being undone. Another figure in clay was shown with its abdomen swollen and cut about

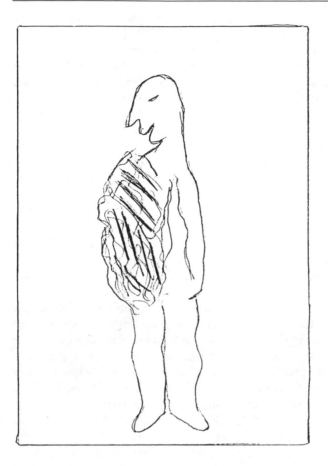

Figure 6.2 Clay figure with abdomen swollen and cut about

(*Figure 6.2*). Frequent masturbation or preoccupation with the child's own genitals whether in public or private may occur. The child may be seen sensually caressing his or her own body with a dreamy, absorbed feeling. This was repeated every session over a period of weeks by a 5-year-old. The clay, made wet and smooth, represented the body and was stroked, smoothed, wetted again, and gradually spread onto her arms as if the clay and her body had become one and the same. This sensual activity seemed to take the little girl back into the feelings and sensations of the occasions of the abuse which had been similarly sensual, gentle, and non-penetrative. She was no longer in contact with me or aware of being in the play room or of my presence, to me she felt as if fascinated, spellbound. I felt as if she excluded me completely from this experience, as if I could not intrude, I did not exist for her. The transference may be understood in that her feelings towards her

Plate 21 Carol: House with sun and moon

Plate 22 Carol: House and garage

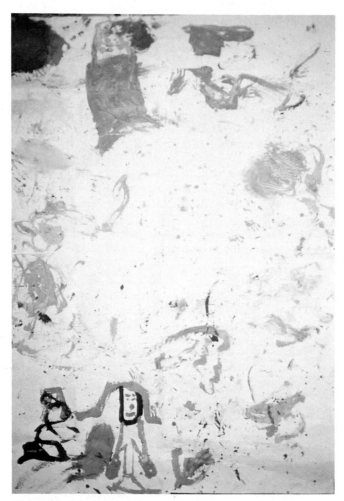

Plate 23

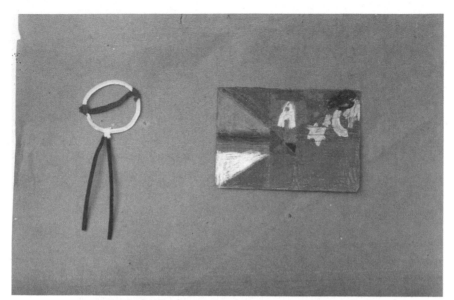

Plate 24 Carol: No entry

Plate 25 David: An horrific face

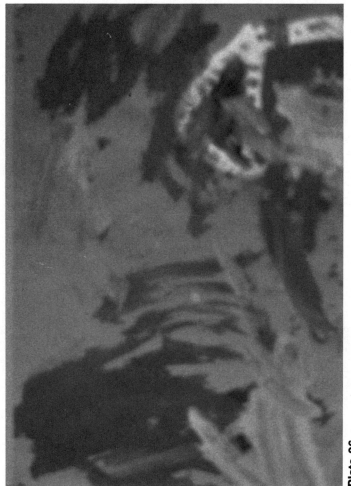

Plate 26

mother were transferred to me in the therapeutic relationship; in the counter-transference I felt absent as her mother had been absent during the incidents of abuse, I felt shut out, just as her mother had been shut out from any knowledge of the incidents for several years before the disclosure.

Premature genital sexualization can lead in adulthood to relating primarily with others through phantasies of sexual powerfulness which predominate over other feelings in relationships. A child who has been abused consistently in infancy grows up experiencing himself or herself as sexually powerful and discovers that the sexuality can be used as a means of manipulation. Although not consciously sought after, a child soon realizes the manipulative value of his or her own sexuality and the power of hiding the secret. Conflicting feelings arising from early abuse are split off and projected on to the other who is used to play a role in sexual, and sometimes sadistic, phantasy. The other is then perceived divested of the wholeness of their personality. When the other introjects and identifies with the projection of sexual and/or sadistic feeling and responds with it, they are then experienced by the abused person as abusive, and the abused person feels treated as a sexual object. In unconscious phantasy, projective identification, filling the other with the overwhelming feelings, is a strong defence which denies both body and mind boundaries. The other is made a container for the split-off feelings and experiences them. The other becomes, for the abused person, an inner sexual object and loses their outer reality. This pattern is played out in therapy with the therapist who needs to be very clear in understanding what is happening in order to respond in ways which will facilitate change in the pattern. Tilman Furniss (1987) described how therapists can become drawn into the sexualization and how sexually-abused children can be hostile towards both male and female therapists.

Secrecy

The secrecy involved between abuser and abused is a bond joining them which separates their life experience, especially that of the child, from the outside world, physically, emotionally, and psychologically. The child may be intimidated by warnings about the reactions of the mother if told, or of the break-up of the family or by threats of injury and violence. There may not be verbal warnings but a clear understanding nonetheless not to tell – 'this is our special secret'. Children keep the secret for fear of being disbelieved, also because they feel somehow it is their fault and that they are bad. At a certain point some children manage to deny within themselves that there has been any abuse in what has been called 'the child sexual abuse accommodation syndrome' (Roland Summit 1983). This is an attempt to make a threatening environment or figure non-threatening. It is an attempt to find a way of survival in long-term abuse.

The relationship between abused and abuser can be highly ambivalent.

Often there is a wish to protect the abuser in spite of the fear and anger felt against him/her: 'a father really hurts you mentally because you love him regardless', wrote one adult survivor abused throughout childhood (see note 2). Adults may be keeping the secret years after those who abused them have disappeared from their lives or died. A kind of magical thinking can persist long after childhood which tells the abused person that the threats can still be carried out. The internalized punishing and threatening parent is still alive.

Case illustration

A 10-year-old boy was seen in therapy for 18 months. During this time disturbing influences upon his development such as his parent's divorce, as well as the divorce following his mother's second marriage, formed the material with which we worked. He had a huge anger which caused trouble for him at home and at school. Sexual feelings began to predominate in his sand tray work. For example, the boy built a castle with a moat around it, he was most interested in making the doors and windows by pushing film container cylinders through the sand walls. While this was happening he was telling me sexual stories and jokes which led to relating these to his penetrative activity in his play. At first in the session he found it difficult to talk about his sexual phantasies but then he could not stop. He felt, and expressed verbally, embarrassment, excitement, and curiosity. The building of the castle was preceded by the building of an underground house. This expression of underground or repressed feelings seemed to have surfaced both in the castle protected by its moat and in the stories and his intrusive questions. Characteristic of the castle was some difficulty regarding entrances and exits. What could be allowed in and out was an issue which reflected his concern about what he could repeat of adult conversation, what he took in from the television, what he could let out when he spoke, or what he felt must be contained. He seemed to be questioning the appropriateness of boundaries, testing what he could say to me imagining I might become angry with him. He was anxious about sexuality which he said was sometimes funny but could be serious, 'sex is to have some fun, but you could have children, that would be serious', he said.

The whole family attended for sessions in which they worked together using the art materials on a large sheet of paper about 6 feet by 3 feet. From the individual work I felt the changes needed to take place within the family dynamics rather than this being the boy's problem. The first drawing could have been aptly named 'the birds and the bees'. This was the focus for the family. Unsurprisingly the boy claimed the largest share of the paper space, his familiarity with the art room and confidence in using it, as well as the therapeutic relationship with me, underlay this. Being seen up until now as the identified patient by the family was another factor giving him permission to claim more space and attention. He drew a man looking over a wall with a magnifying glass as if he were aware of the need to look closely beyond the defences, perhaps searching for clues – what was happening in the family? He drew insects, birds, a space vehicle, and space man, a large crescent moon, and a monkey with many legs or penises. A small face peeped over the wall. The right side of the paper was shared by mother, little sister, and step-father. As well as flowers, flowery shapes, and insects, the mother placed, to the right of a tree drawn by the step-father, a black spider holding a flowery shape which dwarfed a very small woman and large sperm-like creature. Another very small figure appeared lower down beside a big flower. This seemed to be the male counterpart of the small woman. The mother suggested that they all move around the paper so that each person could draw anywhere but only the boy acted upon this, elaborating on a large caterpillar, another many-legged creature under the flowers where his mother was working (*Figure 6.3*).

Looking at and discussing what was happening in the drawing, how it had felt to work in this way together, and how members of the family felt treated by the others helped them become more in touch with their feelings and with each other. A lack of proportion in the use of space was remarked which led to reflections on the share of time, space, and attention available to and from different family members. The mother became aware of her own anxiety regarding her femininity. I understood the black spider image to be symbolic of her negative feminine aspect which she could later relate to consciously, seeing it at work in her relationships with men. The whole figures, which were so small, seemed overpowered by masculine and feminine sexual symbols drawn disproportionately large, for example, the flower shapes, the spider, the sperm shape, the monkey, the phallic shape from which bees emerged and by the general 'birds and bees' theme of the overall work. There is a small owl in the tree which the boy drew in the centre of the work. This owl may be seen as his awareness of the therapy/wisdom/insight-gaining aspect of the work. There is a hole in the trunk of this tree which, if seen as the boy's family tree, may be seen as the part that is missing – his father. A tree was also drawn by the step-father and may represent the new family situation which the boy had some difficulty accepting.

A symbol does not stand for one aspect, feeling, or experience only, there are always many possible levels of interpretation, however sexual issues were those that were most clearly calling for attention in this family. After three family art therapy sessions, involvement in a sexual incident brought another family member in for individual therapy. At this point the mother realized that severely-damaging sexual abuse, which she had suffered herself in childhood, was likely to be the cause of the disturbed and disturbing behaviour of the two children. Compassion for her children was aroused with memories of her past which surfaced when the sexual incident took place leading to acceptance of her own need for disclosure and help. During several treatments for depression, the disclosure of abuse had never arisen. She now came for art therapy

Figure 6.3 Family art therapy session

sessions on her own. This relieved the treatment needs of the children. They had presented as the indicated patients but their acting-out could now be seen to speak more for their mother's repressed, distressed feelings than their own.

Tilman Furniss (1987) has described the 'entrance ritual' which lets the child know abuse is about to take place and the 'exit ritual' which closes the abuse, in long-standing abuse relationships. The ritualization takes the abusive activity out of the level of the rest of a child's life. These rituals may consist of a few words, gestures, or an instruction. For example: 'It's time for your bath now, go up and run the water', or 'I'll be up soon to say good night'. These seemingly harmless words and phrases may have another significance to the child who has been initiated into understanding their ritualistic undertones. They come to be understood, to isolate, and encapsulate the abuse in some kind of out-of-time mode which carries the nature of secrecy, and in which the parent/authority role, as it takes place the rest of the time is suspended (Tilman Furniss 1988).

Mrs K. knew when she was a child that she was about to be abused when her mother left the house and her step-father took her into the sitting-room where he turned on the television. This was the entrance ritual which took place on the same day of the week and at the same time. The exit ritual was that of being put to bed before the mother returned (*Figure 6.4*).

During art therapy sessions the scene of the entrance ritual was drawn as Mrs K. explained to herself and me what had happened and how it had felt.

Figure 6.4 Entrance ritual

A small child sat on the floor in front of the television. Step-father sat on the settee. The clock said 7 o'clock. She described the small child's feelings of helpless, anxious awareness of the inevitable invitation to sit on his knee. She remembered the fear and discomfort of the sexual touching which followed. She became in touch with her repressed and denied feelings. As a child she had felt more helpless than angry, but later despairing and angry feelings had been strong.

An ill or absent mother was unaware of leaving a space in which the sexual activities could take place. This pattern is frequently revealed when incidents of abuse are described. Some reliable absence of the mother, or of her attention, may provide an opportunity for her partner to satisfy, maladaptively, his own unmet sexual and emotional needs, as well as a need to feel powerful, by abusing the child who may also be vulnerable because of unmet emotional needs, at the same time as being helpless in terms of age and physical smallness.

Mrs K. saw thoroughly for the first time how the abuse had destructively affected all her relationships with males, including that with her own son. She saw how protective she had always been, and still felt, towards her abuser, even while recognizing her anger and resentment towards him. During her adulthood he continued to be verbally intrusive, with regard to her sexuality, which distressed her deeply. Psychologically the abuse relationship was perpetuated.

It's because you know the person and they are in your home. It's frightening and it hurts

said Mrs K.

I don't know how the Social Services did not get him put in prison when they knew. I hate what he did but not him, you can do nothing to stop it. I just see him as a weak old man now.

This was her conscious view in the present, yet her fear regarding the threats he had made to prevent her from disclosure had remained as strong, unconsciously, as it had been in her childhood.

It is as if having the secret stands for feeling loved or hated and becomes part of a false sense of identity which the long-term abused person acquires. Abused children can become expert at keeping secrets which can create a life pattern so that false impressions are continually created. A habit is formed of selecting what to leave out to create a misleading picture, or, less often, lies are told. A skill, like that of the illusionist, is developed in making things appear to be other than they are. In play therapy, games of magic were played out by a 7-year-old in which a repeated play was to make disappear objects which I then had to find.

An object from the room was shown to me then buried in the sand tray while I closed my eyes as demanded by Celia. The object on one occasion was a purse, an object which it may be appropriate to see as symbolizing the female genitals. I was then invited to open my eyes, look at the sand tray which now had a flat and undisturbed look, then say where I thought the object was buried. Laughter and satisfaction followed when my answer was wrong. When I was right the game was repeated with more attention to smoothing the surface of the sand. Whether or not it was possible to hide things from her mother was an anxiety to Celia. She had been able to hide the sexual abuse incidents for several years. In the sand tray game she seemed both to want to hide things successfully but at the same time to want the therapist/mother to know. If mother had known about the abuse but not prevented or exposed it then perhaps she did not care what happened to her child? It was a possible logic. It might feel worse if mother had known but not cared than if she had not known. 'Did Mummy know what happened to my genitals even if she did not see?', seems to have been her question.

The child sexual abuse accommodation syndrome has the effect for the child of 'making it all disappear'. The adult patient who could make 'herself forget that anything happened' (see p. 95) remembered the magic set of her childhood games revolving around getting things to disappear. Magic games are not unusual for all children but the emphasis which abused children place on them may be significant.

Another of Celia's questions regarding secrecy which was relevant to the absence of her mother at the times of her abuse was 'Can you see what I am doing when you are in another place?' She tried to establish how much I could know of what she did when I could not see her. She explored the one-way mirror of the playroom. I would go behind it then she would dance or move the toys. When I came back she would want to know what I had seen, although she could not see me. Then she would go into the observation room to experience knowing what I was doing when I could not see her. She seemed to have a feeling that even when she could not see her mother, her mother would be able to see her. The internalized inner mother was not experienced as separate from the external mother, any more than Mrs K. was able to differentiate between the internalized threats of her step-father and his present intentions and capacities in her adulthood. Celia asked me whether her mother knew what we were doing in the session while her mother had gone to the shops. She said on different occasions that she both wanted and did not want her mother to be able to see her. She finally managed to ask me directly whether her mother knew what she was doing while they were apart. It seemed likely that during the confidential play therapy situation what she had felt during the abuse incidents was repeated. She was working in the therapy with those feelings, playing them out with the materials and the dolls. She was symbolically representing the damage and confusion which had occurred and trying to find ways to repair them. She was trying to understand whether her mother could have known and prevented the abuse.

Abused children are frequently more angry with their mothers than with the abuser. Celia's behaviour with her mother: refusing to listen to her, angrily shouting at mother if she had not brought something for her at the end of the session, refusing to go to bed, telling her mother she could not tell her what to do, as well as experiences when they were out together, e.g. 'you don't care what happens to me, you don't care if I get run over', when being difficult or frightened about crossing the road, as well as regular nightmares in which wild animals and spiders were attacking or about to attack her, all testified to the anger, contempt, and at times hatred towards the mother whose protection Celia had needed in her mother's absence. She played games of dressing-up as an adult woman who was seductive and powerful, but made her face up with face paints as a sad clown. She drew the spiders from her dreams, this negative mother symbol terrified her, at the same time as she sought refuge from them in her mother's bed at night. These kinds of contradictions abound in work with the sexually-abused. Family work is essential for restoring a basis of appropriate boundaries and confidence in them for each member of the family in relation to each other. Anger and hatred for the mother come into the therapy work of abused children more often than negative feelings towards the abuser where the abuse has not been physically painful. The adult patient, already quoted, had a protective and parenting role towards her mother consciously; none other than loving feelings surfaced until, in adult therapy, painful realizations of the collusion of the mother, in facilitating the abuse by the father, came into focus with all the energy of repressed angry feelings.

The way of life whereby the right hand must not know what the left hand is doing becomes generalized. This is not an easily-changed pattern. In therapy with a teenager a wish to change appointment times or an explanation of lateness were usually expressed so confusingly that it was only much later that I could see how the patient perceived herself as controlling and manipulating the time and me. This kind of controlling attitude towards adults and parents seems to arise out of a need to compensate for the lack of control over their bodies that abuse has caused such teenagers to experience. There is some demonstration in these attempts to control, of an opinion of the stupidity of adults and those in authority. This is hardly surprising when the abused person is aware how blatant the abuse has been for years, and yet those who could have recognized and done something to change it did not speak or act. It is not difficult to understand the lack of trust shown by long-term sexually-abused people when we see how they have lived with a feeling of being false all their lives. The inevitable assumption is that others are equally false and have as little connection with reality and openness as the abused person. Adults may be perceived as not caring as well as stupid.

Nobody really cares about you, that is what you find in this life, so why care about yourself [writes a patient]. You get defensive and guard anything that is actually yours or you think is yours, what you are doing or anything that belongs really to you inside, with your life. These few possessions belong to the person inside of yourself and must not be shown to anyone or they will take them away.

Not only does this feeling describe hiding things, keeping them secret, but it also portrays a feeling of being stolen from, which is the counterpart of the stealing which is another typical sexual-abuse reaction pattern.

Feeling special

One result of having a secret is feeling special. 'We shall be the only ones in the world to know, you are my special little girl/boy' and similar phrases are seductive. To have something which others do not, and to be special to a parent or loved adult, to feel exceptionally loved and close can make it easy to keep the secret for a small child who has not been penetratively or painfully abused and who does not receive normal parent/child physical affection in the course of everyday life.

Behaviour motivated by the wish to feel special may become a pattern. In his sessions, a boy of 9 years old who had been abused by a trusted adult showed, in his art therapy work, the importance to him of feeling special. He drew the exceptional places he had lived in, the place where the disclosure took place. He drew in detail many huge modern container lorries and trucks. He would tell me as he drew 'There are only two of these in the world', 'This is the only one of this model'. He would explain the mechanical and spatial details which made these trucks special. He painted very big paintings of farm machinery saying how it worked and how he had driven a tractor, in spite of being too young. In the abuse relationship specialness was the positive reward the boy had experienced. The negative effects of it had brought about the disclosure, which had isolated him further. His behaviour involved persistently testing all the boundaries at home and at school because his high level of anxiety and insecurity required him to find out how safe or not he was. The family's feelings of guilt and concern to repair the damage, led to a relaxing of boundaries, giving the boy what he seemed to *want* rather than understanding his *need* for a safe holding situation to contain his feelings of vulnerability and phantasies of what his abuser might do if he knew of the disclosure. The boy felt unprotected and too powerful in the family. An accident at home causing the loss of the use of a foot, immobilized him. This gave him some weeks of close attention from his parents, in this way his immediate needs were met.

Apart from an initial large free painting, the art therapy work mainly consisted of coloured drawings of neat, clean, large, new container lorries. This 9 year old, who particularly liked trucks and lorries, told me of their unusual features and functioning. They were usually extra large: the cars he talked about were extra fast and, generally, it seemed that he associated with people who were older than he was, special in some way, and with whom he seemed to be inappropriately included. Thus he was telling me that specialness was the most important quality for him and that boundaries which would keep him safe were often broken. He never showed me what was in the container lorries but their external appearance gave some clue that painful feelings in the father/son relationship were being kept inside. A clean, perfect exterior denied the confused, angry, messy feelings expressed in the initial painting and, perhaps, contained in the lorries (see *Figure 6.5*).

Figure 6.5 Container lorry – what is inside?

Case illustration of working with the secret internal situation

Sexually-abused children use art materials symbolically to express feelings of being full of mess inside, of being messed-up, and of trying to find some way to control and handle the mess or poison. These messy feelings may be expressed by play with paint, sand, clay, and water.

In the case of a 6-year-old abused girl, Fay, the inner reality of dark, confused feelings was hidden by her clean neat appearance. These chaotic mixed feelings had to be externalized, handled, given form, shared with, and accepted by, the art therapist. This process took many months with other issues arising from the abuse being dealt with in play, drawings, and clay work. However, work with paint seemed to inevitably lead to a black, sticky,

Figure 6.6 The inner messy, messed up feelings handled and given expression and containment

slimy mixture in quantities large enough to fill buckets and washing-up bowls. This mixture is a reflection of the chaotic, overpowering, confused feelings by which the sexually-abused child feels entirely swamped. This messy stuff, by being wrapped up in layers of paper and being rolled into a ball, was given a holding form which was given to me to look after. I also took care of the containers of the mixture. For this child there was confusion as to whether this black or brown messy substance was really foul and poisonous or whether it was good food which she and I should share together. Sometimes lumps of this mixture looked like excreta which, again, I was asked to look after. The questions being asked seemed to be, 'Is this good food or is this bad food?', 'Is this a good product or is this a bad product?' (see *Figure 6.6*).

In *Images of Art Therapy*, Joy Schaverien (1987:75) has written about 'the scapegoat and the talisman', she points out how 'scapegoating, the ritualized disposal of unwanted or evil aspects via transference to objects or people is a universal process which can be found in practice in slightly different manifestations in many diverse cultures'. She describes rituals in which painful feelings, physical and/or psychological, are transferred to animate and inanimate objects. The talisman carrying the transferred feeling, through its disposal, purifies the tribe or individual.

This 6-year-old girl invested these dark, wet, slimy packages with her feelings of inner chaos, mess, confusion, and anxiety. She repeatedly asked, when making the mess of paint, clay, sand, and water, whether she or I would get into trouble, whether somebody would be angry. She expected retribution of some kind for these expressions of feeling. She was also able to say by the seventh session that she felt she was very bad, that she felt she was a bad person inside. This badness seems also to have been transferred into the packages and containers of substance which I was asked to look after. During the first nine sessions six precious (or shameful) objects were made; both feelings were expressed about them. They were kept, then discarded in the following sessions when a new one would be made. By the ninth session the ability to let go of the feelings and transform them had increased so that many of the different kinds of dark, wet, stored mixtures were thrown away, while new cleaner kinds of mixture were to be kept for next time, e.g. dry sand, sand and water as well as the clay/sand/paint mixture.

The creation and disposal of the packages and the mixtures enveloped in them demonstrates clearly the process which Joy Schaverien was exploring. They had the quality of the talisman. In this case, their disposal followed by the re-creation of new ones indicates an ambivalence in relation to the mixture of feelings which was continually reflected in the child's handling of these packages. There had been some good feelings of being loved in the abuse as well as the bad ones. One aspect of art therapy is the work of cleansing and purification. The child seeks for rituals which will perform these functions. Apart from trying to deal with the internal chaos and uncontainable messy feelings, this child used the materials to play out operations on a clay body. These operations had to be done urgently to avoid death. Over time, operations were performed upon several centres of the body, starting with the lower abdomen moving up to the stomach, heart, throat, and brain. This child felt the need to purify and repair her body and mind fundamentally, and one cannot help but be impressed by her creative rituals and the integrity with which she worked through them.

Example (Figure 6.7)

By the time of the sixth session, the theme of the work had become established as 'operations'. Three operations had already been performed on a clay abdomen to remove bad, poisonous stuff which if left in the body of the 'little girl', as it was identified by Fay, would cause death. The operations were performed with urgency. First, paint, paper, clay, sand, and water were squelched together into a ball. The previous session's work was then examined. It was the same kind of mixture which had been painted bright red and which had related to the pain and alarm of the emergency abdominal operation for which it had represented the body. This 'body' was used, the red messy colour was 'bad stuff', said Fay. A new green heart was placed on top of the body. The heart gave a clue as to the attempted repair of her feelings and emotional damage. Several times Fay said that the 'bad red stuff will be given to the doctor'. She also reminded me that this was 'pretend'. It was

Figure 6.7 An operation to remove the bad stuff

important that we both recognized that it was not a real body, but the clay stood for a body, it was as if it were a body. Fay had spoken of her anxiety about being seen as 'mad' so her concern for reality was significant.

Fay expressed feelings of both liking and not liking what she called the squelchy feelings. This kind of play, she said, was not allowed at home. The squelchy feelings seemed close to her abuse experience as she had described it. It may explain her fear of retribution resulting from making a mess in the session. After the disclosure, upheaval, which may have felt like retribution, occurred in the family.

The operation was a heart transplant I was told. She painted gloves on her hands 'so as not to get the germs'. The bad stuff was felt by her as contaminating. The new heart was tenderly treated as she worked with fine paint brushes. The heart had to be put in with great urgency before the patient died. The heart, generally recognized as the seat of feelings, or generator of feelings, if damaged or absent, would feel like death emotionally. Fay told me 'if your heart did not work you would die'.

At the end of the operation, for which I was the assistant, passing tools and equipment, Fay said the solid masses of paint, paper, etc. should be thrown away. It felt important to me that she should do this herself although she asked me to. This disposal of the talisman, the work invested in with such urgent intensity, was the completion of the ritual which she had created and performed. Her wanting me to enact the disposal made me wonder whether she had some doubts about being able to do it herself. However, I also wondered if the doubts may be mine as she had made a beautiful and careful piece of work which felt to me to have taken place on a deep, creative level of experience – the level of healing and transformation through the art therapy process.

The new heart was implanted with what Fay described as 'good stuff' and 'confidence'. She seemed to be letting me know that she could get the bad stuff out and put good stuff in and become confident. Confidence in the family is lost when sexual abuse occurs. All the family relationships become focal points of mistrust. Siblings are watched warily by the parent who has not known about the abuse. Anxiety as to whether, and in whom, one can feel confidence is a prime question. For Fay the restitution of confidence in herself as a feeling person with good contents was vital to repairing the emotional damage. Schaverien writes, 'a ritual transference' such as those briefly mentioned here

> assumes a faith, a belief that an object can become empowered. A belief of this nature involves magical investment in the thing, which effects a transformation of the mere thing into a talisman. This has considerable implications for the practice of art therapy. When art therapy is fully affective there is a transference of attributes and states to an object which, subsequently empowered, become a talisman. Once an object is experienced as a talisman any act of resolution in relation to it becomes significant and might be seen as an act of disposal.
>
> (Schaverien 1987:75)

During the 'operation', Fay was transferring attributes of herself, as she felt herself to be, to the clay body. It was full of bad stuff, poisonous, it was damaged in the area of feelings. In her work on the body, she was removing the bad stuff and poison and creating a new possibility for positive feelings and confidence in them and in herself. The power of her investment was such that she could feel enough inner transformation to let go of the outer symbolic object at the end of the ritual.

One of the main problems that children suffer as a result of sexual abuse is the loss of ability to differentiate between good and bad feelings. In the abuse experienced the child may well have felt special and loved by a trusted, loved adult. At the same time the child's emotional, physical, and psychological boundaries have been assaulted and broken leaving hurt, angry, anxious, and hating feelings. The child does not want to throw away the love but wants to purify herself from the strong, negative, impure feelings; letting go of one feels like letting go of both. To be effective, therapy needs to tease apart the mixture and give a value equally to positive and negative experiences. In the unconscious world there is always the opposite aspect to the conscious one. In the abuser's unconscious are the abused feelings; in the abused person's unconscious are the abusive feelings and impulses.

Conclusion

Using play and art materials, because of their tactile, physical nature which relates directly to sensation and emotional feeling, is arguably the most useful therapy for children who have been sexually abused. In this chapter I have discussed both children in art therapy and the child inside the adult. The experience of being or having been abused and manifestations of resulting feelings and defences, in relationship with the therapist and in the art work, are different in the adolescent. By then, in long-term abuse, the false identify has developed and functions as if that were the real person. Depending on how early, consistent, and painful was the abuse, and on the relationship with the abuser, more or less reality will remain in the adaptation, and relationship to the self and the world, of the abused person. The quotes from adult patients whose memories of childhood abuse were particularly strong give examples of the shutting-off and confusion of feelings which are not easily expressed verbally by a child in therapy, and show the stage of fragmentation, splitting, and projective identification at which emotional development is arrested in severe abuse.

The sexually-abused child's experience is based upon invasion of every kind of boundary: upon love which is partly felt as hatred and pain; upon secrecy which is bound up in lies; upon dishonesty with oneself and to others, and in creating false impressions and presenting false appearances. The stealing of the father's penis and the mother's partner may reflect in theft of material objects. The appropriation of characteristics of others in dress, speech, behaviour, and thought arises from feelings of envy and attempts to find a way to be. Oedipal phantasies become realities, a confusing specialness is created for the child who knows and experiences too much too soon. From the child who looks good and feels bad, looks clean and feels dirty and full of mess, seems open and is full of deceit, appears always to be what he or she is not, it is no surprise to find the drawing of a house upside down with a ship in a storm above, which was produced by a child in therapy. The contempt, anger, hatred, and envy felt towards adult authority figures, especially towards the parent who could not, or did not, protect the child, cannot surprise us either.

It is easy to feel for the abused child. We recognize less easily in ourselves our own abusive aspects. It seems to me essential to be in touch with both these parts of our own nature so that we can work positively towards healing, repair, and growth in both aspects of our patients and ourselves.

In art therapy, because the main area of exploration and expression is the materials, tangible records of the opening-up of the chaotic, swampy inner world are created. Transference on to the materials as well as the therapist takes place. A symbolic experience of the rebuilding and re-orientation of the self so that a person can appear to be what and who they are and feel loved and accepted as such is the aim of a sexually-abused child in therapy. For this to happen, however, work with the whole family situation is essential. Without this, reverberations of unresolved issues which often underlie the sexual abuse are likely to continue to be expressed in some way by a member or members of the family. Where children have lost a parent or been taken into care because of the abuse, their perception of the new situation will need a space to be received. 'Who am I really?', 'What has happened inside me and in my outer world?' These questions can be explored in art therapy and answers may be discovered, then changed through growth so that the upside-down house can be felt to be the right way up again, even though it may never feel as it did before.

© 1990 Carol Sagar

Notes

1 Elizabeth Smith, Child and Family Therapist, Bethel Child and Family Centre.
2 Adult patient who wishes to remain anonymous.

References

Child Abuse: Guidance Procedures in the County of Norfolk (1985), 4th edn, Norfolk County Council Social Services Department, pp. 5–7.
Furniss, T. (1987) 'Integrated treatment approach to child sexual abuse', workshop at the Annual Conference of the Association for Child Psychology, 4 July, St Bartholomew's Hospital.
Furniss, T. (1988) *Surviving Child Sexual Abuse*, London: Routledge.
Schaverien, J. (1987) 'The scapegoat and the talisman: transference in art therapy', in T. Dalley, C. Case, J. Schaverien, F. Weir, D. Halliday, P. Nowell Hall and D. Waller *Images of Art Therapy: New Developments in Theory and Practice*, London: Tavistock.
Summit, R. (1983) 'The child sexual abuse accommodation syndrome', *Child Abuse and Neglect* 7: 177–94.

Chapter seven

A family centre: a structural family therapy approach
Sarah Deco

The work described and discussed in this chapter took place at the Greyhound Family Centre. The Centre itself has been in operation in West London since 1978. The Centre at one time combined day-care for under 5s with family centre work. For the past 3½ years however, it has worked only with families; children and parents together. The Centre's brief is to work with families who have children, or at least one child under 5 years old. A large proportion of the families referred have children who are on care or supervision orders, or who are likely to be placed on an order unless the quality of relationships within the family improves. This means that families are often frightened and resentful when they arrive and expecting to be blamed and criticized. Staff therefore have the dual and often seemingly incompatible roles of making parents feel supported while at the same time making clear and realistic plans for the protection and well-being of the children.

The Centre runs a sessional and an intensive programme. The intensive programme involves families attending for 4 days per week, from 10 a.m. to 3.30 p.m. During this time there are periods for children and parents to be separate and also times for families to be together. The sessional programme is designed for families who either do not need the concentrated experience of the intensive programme or who it is felt need to ease into this kind of intensive work more gradually. The emphasis and focus throughout, however, is on the family system as a whole. The aim is to try and make sense of the way the family functions and the unspoken rules by which it organizes itself.

The philosophy behind this style of work is based on the application of cybernetic and systems theories to human behaviour. The systems approach arose out of an 'epistemological revolution' which began to manifest itself around the 1950s. New ideas were developing not only in the field of therapy and the study of human behaviour, but also were part of a larger epistemological shift, involving changes in the way scientists in the fields of physics, biology, and mathematics viewed the world; and developments in the cognitive sciences which emerged from computer technology. This view sees human life as taking place 'within a vast hierarchy of interacting systems from the small molecular systems to the largest system of the universe "the family" being merely an arbitrary defined system of which we are members'. (David Campbell *et al.* n.d.)

Lynn Hoffman (1981) describes the central concept of this 'new epistemology' as that of 'circularity'. Rather than a single agent acting on an object and producing an effect, the concept of circularity sees object and agent being mutually influential. To give an example, to say the 'dog bites the man', is a linear description of an event. But the dog of course will be influenced in its behaviour by the signals it receives from the man, and the man in turn will modify his behaviour in relation to the signals he receives from the dog. Viewed in this way,

> The therapist can no longer be seen as 'impacting' on the client or family through personality craft or technique. The therapist is not an agent and the client is not a subject, both are part of a larger field in which therapist, family, and any number of other elements act and react upon each other in unpredictable ways.

> (Hoffman 1981:8)

Or to put it another way, for therapists to think systemically, they have to 'free themselves from the linguistic and cultural conditioning that makes them believe they are capable of thinking in terms of "things" so that they may rediscover "the deeper truth that we still only think in terms of relationships"' (Ruesch and Bateson 1951:173).

One of the first to write about the application of these new ideas to problems such as schizophrenia was Gregory Bateson and his colleagues who were involved in a research project at Stanford University in the mid 1950s which was set up to look into schizophrenia and what light if any, the study of family interactions could throw on to the aetiology of this 'condition'. In the paper, 'Towards a theory of schizophrenia' (Bateson *et al.* 1956:173), Bateson and his colleagues describe the necessary conditions for '"The double bind", a situation in which no matter what a person does he cannot win'. They describe various modes in human communication, for example, signals which identify behaviour as play, non-play, fantasy, sacrament, etc., as of a higher 'logical type'[1] than the messages they classify. They postulated that people exhibiting 'schizophrenic' behaviour had difficulty in differentiating between different logical types.

The habitual mode of communication within families with a schizophrenic member was thought to be one where the child was subjected to two inescapable and contradictory messages, the one of the higher logical type contradicting the command of the lower logical type. This is what constitutes 'double bind', for example a mother who is feeling bothered by a child, but instead of saying 'go away I am sick of you' says 'go to bed; you're very tired and I want you to get your sleep'. On the one hand the command 'go to bed, you're tired', indicates concern for the child, whereas on the other, the non-verbal behaviour of the mother which is of a higher 'logical type', indicates her anger and annoyance. This kind of thing is of course common in all families, and will be well known to exasperated parents. What distinguishes the families of those schizophrenics that Bateson and his colleagues studied was the intensity of these 'binds' and the fact that the child had no means of escape from a stressful situation.

Three main 'schools' have developed, based on systemic ideas, the Milan or Systemic approach which focuses primarily on patterns of communication, Strategic Family Therapy, where 'the clinician actively designs interventions to fit the problem' (Hoffman 1981:271), and Structural Family Therapy, which concentrates on the organization of the family in terms of its boundaries and hierarchy. The work of the Greyhound Centre is based primarily on the Structural Method as developed by Salvador Minuchin and I will therefore describe this in more detail.

Minuchin's style of work arose out of his studies of poor and 'under organized' families in America. The problems that these families had were very similar in kind to those of most of the families that attend Greyhound and other similar Family Centres and so his method of working is very appropriate for this client group. Minuchin has a normative model for a family that is functioning well. According to him, an appropriately organized family will have clearly marked boundaries, and a sibling sub-system that is organized hierarchically, so that children are given tasks and privileges consonant with sex and age as determined by the family's culture. From a structural point of view, therapy consists of helping a family redesign its organization until it accords more closely with this 'norm'. In order to do this the therapist adopts the role of an 'active intruder', who begins to restructure relationships within the family as soon as he enters it. The therapist takes note of whom he speaks to, who is allowed to speak, whom he challenges, which persons he brings together, etc. He 'functions very much like the director of a play. By directing certain members to talk with one another, he is testing his hunches about the way in which the family functions. 'The family therapist is guided in this initial exploration, by his idea of an effectively functioning family. He is looking for the qualities of differentiation, delineation of boundaries, and flexibility' (Minuchin 1977:211).

The intensive programme at Greyhound provides a setting within which families can recreate their own family system and be helped to understand and change it, where necessary. For example, if a family operates by scapegoating one member of the family, then they are very likely to look for scapegoats within the group at the Centre, or become scapegoats themselves. Another example is of family members who, used in their own family of origin to helping and supporting their parents, may well take this role in relation to the staff in the Centre.

The resource of 'the team' is used to full effect, allowing the therapist to enter into the family system, share the experiences of the family, and then return to the team to gain a more objective view and a larger perspective of the system as a whole. The therapist is able to experience the pressure coming from within the family and also learn something of the pressure brought to bear on the family by the situation, both social and economic in which family members find themselves.

Often the emotions felt by the family will be extremely intense, they experience great hopelessness and despair and this can communicate itself to the therapist as an overwhelming sense of being 'stuck'. This is where the external viewpoints of the rest of the team can provide the key to unlocking the restrictions of the family system. Armed with a more holistic viewpoint the therapist can then re-enter the family system and begin to help the family change it from within. In some cases, however, the changes that families make are not fast enough or extensive enough to ensure the safety or normal development of the children within their care. In these cases the staff at the Centre work with families towards finding a suitable placement and making the best possible transition between their family and their new carers, be they adoptive or foster parents, an institution, or members of the extended family. It is against this background then, that therapeutic work takes place and therefore the sense of guilt, impotence, distrust, and anger that families feel needs to be acknowledged, before any work can take place.

Art therapy and families

The development of the use of art with families has been somewhat less well documented than the development of family therapy theory, and its pioneers have adopted 'systemic' ideas to a greater or lesser extent. Hannah Kwiatkowska (1979) explored this area for a number of years in her work at the National Institute of Mental Health in Bethesda, Maryland, USA. She developed a system of Family Art Evaluation, which makes use of various 'procedures', e.g. 'the joint family scribble' to elicit information about the family dynamics and a method of research to evaluate the success of treatment through art. Her work has been very influential in the development of art with families and she amassed a large and invaluable body of knowledge on this subject. But although she uses some systemic ideas her methods are basically an adaptation of the psychoanalytic ideas based on linear rather than than circular causality. For example, there is still a primary emphasis on the perceptions of one individual in the family, and often an emphasis on one member needing to 'change' rather than seeing all members as contributing to the family's problems. Kwiatkowska also relies heavily on the family gaining insight into their situation, whereas a systemic family therapist would claim that insight was not an essential part of promoting change.

There has been a great deal of work based on Kwiatkowska's model by, for example, Rubin and Magnussen (1974), Sherr and Hicks (1978), and Wadeson (1973). However

none of the family art techniques advocated by any of these writers departs significantly from techniques used for years with individuals and groups. Moreover, the objectives of family art therapy as described in the literature appear to be essentially those of individual and group art therapy expanded to embrace the rich interactions of family life.

(Sobol 1982:43)

Barbara Sobol has tried to combine art therapy with strategic family therapy and successfully manages to combine art activities with strategic moves. For example, with the Jackson family she sets a task of asking Laurette, the daughter, to give a painting lesson to her father, whom Sobol asks to 'pretend to be naive about painting and follow her (Laurette's) instructions'. She then asks the son, Luke, to paint by himself, without his sister's support, and Mrs Jackson to observe from a few feet away. In organizing the family in this way she is 'beginning to draw lines of separation that emphasises the reality of the divorce and Mrs Jackson's position as an outsider' (Sobol 1982:48). The therapist here is helping to delineate boundaries appropriate to this family's situation (i.e. divorce, where custody of the children is with the father). She is also challenging both the 'enmeshment' of the two siblings and the excessively authoritarian stance of the father.

Another attempt to combine systemic ideas with art therapy, is described by Hugh Jenkins and Mike Donnelly (1983), who associate art therapy with other non-verbal techniques such as family sculpting and geneograms. They identify these techniques as 'client centred activities', rather than 'therapist orientated activities' (1983:3). They describe client-orientated activities as emphasizing the family members' 'inherent ability to initiate the therapeutic material drawing on their own creativity and resources', whereas therapist-orientated activities are those in which the therapist initiates and remains 'central in focusing attention on the family, or on some part of it' (ibid.). The idea of drawing on family members' 'inherent ability to initiate therapeutic material' is an attractive one, particularly to art therapists who are trained to nurture creativity and take a basically non-directive stance. I am not sure, however, whether this approach, used in its pure form, can enable a family 'stuck' in a destructive system to mobilize enough creativity to 'free' themselves and whether it will inevitably fall to the therapist and therapeutic team with their 'external viewpoint' to provide the means to do this.

Jenkins and Donnelly also discuss the importance of reconciling 'the language of treatment with the language of distress'. They describe how 'impasses in therapy may result from the therapist failing to recognize the language or idiom of the client' (1983:1). Adapting one's methods and style of communication to suit the client is of course very important. I feel that it is, however, misleading to suggest that a family would feel that painting or sculpting is more 'their' language than the use of words. Words are, after all for most of us, our usual means of communication. It is, however, an important part of 'engaging' with a family to begin to speak their language. This would be true, whether one was using drawing as a 'language' or words. Perhaps the success of these non-verbal techniques is as much because the therapists find the information about the family easier to 'read' in this form, than because the family finds it easier to communicate in this medium. The characteristics of a system are inherent in a family's behaviour whether the family is talking, painting, or watching TV and it is therefore appropriate for the therapist to choose any of these activities to use with a family, if by using them he gains a clear enough understanding of family dynamics to be able to help the family change them.

In Jenkins's and Donnelly's paper there is again emphasis on the discussion of the picture at the end of the session. I feel that it is important in adapting art therapy to a systems approach, that the focus is laid on 'process' and interactions and one should not need to rely on discussion and for 'insights' into the meaning of the pictures. The objective after all is not to come to a new articulated understanding, but rather to bring about 'change in the family structure whether or not the family is aware of it' (Sobol 1982:43).

At Greyhound, art therapy had to, of course, be shaped by its context and be adapted to a family therapy, systems-based, point of view. This meant developing a way of working which focused more on 'process' than on 'content', that is, more on sequences of events that take place during the production of an image rather than the symbol chosen or the style and manner of representation. Family therapy works primarily with the 'here and now' and attempts to give families an experience in the here and now of a different way of relating to each other. This does not necessarily involve any examination, understanding, or analysis of the families' past experiences by the families themselves. For art therapy, this means less emphasis on finished products and their symbolic content and related associations and more on the actual process of production, that is: the family interactions that take place during the production of an image, including such subtle signs and signals as facial expression, body language, tone of voice, etc. Also, the context within which the therapy takes place, the relationship with the therapist, the expectations of both therapists and family as to the possible outcome of therapy, and arrangement of the physical space, e.g. who is sitting close to whom, who is left out by the seating arrangements. All these will have an effect on the pictures produced.

During the years I worked at Greyhound I tried a variety of ways of introducing the use of art. One of the major difficulties I encountered was the parents' resistance. This is of course very often the case, but the special circumstances of Greyhound exacerbated this. First, the nursery associations of a centre designed primarily with under 5s in mind, made parents feel they were being asked to do something 'childish'. Second, the level of distrust that families came with meant that they were highly suspicious of any 'secret' information that pictures revealed being conveyed to the courts or social workers and somehow used against them. We tried to employ a variety of strategies to get round this problem. One was to ask parents to help their children draw or paint, by painting with them. Another was to ask parents to use art to explain something to their children, and another was to set up a large group picture as a play activity for a group of families.

These strategies certainly did get parents and children involved in art work. The problem was, however, how to move on from there. There was still resistance to thinking about the symbols involved from the family members. Seen as part of the Centre's system, however, the resistance was also in part due to the fact that art therapy with a psychodynamic emphasis did not fit very happily into the programme at Greyhound. Therefore rather than the resistance coming just from the parents, it emanated from the system as a whole. Families were also resistant to our attempts to focus on what we saw as 'process', because for families as disorganized as these, the very fact of having completed a painting session without a major mishap was felt to be a major achievement. Paint and its 'messiness' causes a lot of anxiety to families whose control over their feelings and what they feel to be their own internal 'mess' is very precarious. This is also reflected in the precarious control, if any, parents have over their children, and painting often brings out in these parents the most aggressively heavy-handed attempts at control. Also the families often had a limited and stereotyped vocabulary in art and therefore quickly became bored.

Another way of using art, which seemed more appropriate to the family therapy situation was simply to have art materials available, and to allow parents or children to use them or not as they felt appropriate in family sessions. This also gave the therapist the opportunity to suggest, at a moment when the family may have been struggling with words that they explain or clarify something to a child or another adult, with the use of the art materials available. This informality seemed to be more productive than a structured art therapy session.

Pictures produced by children are influenced and largely formed by the child's family situation and also by the context of therapy. They are formed by 'the characteristics of the System'. The rules of this system, within which family members operate, are demonstrated time and time again by sequences of interactions between them; almost like a sequence of dance steps in which an action from one member provokes a reaction in another and that action provokes a response in another member of the family and so on and so on, in a habitual pattern or 'sequence' of interactions.

Problems, dysfunctions or symptoms in the family can be understood by considering them as a difficulty in dealing with certain underlying issues. These 'underlying issues' can often be clearly seen if one focuses on small pieces of sequential behaviour. For example, take a situation where a parent begins to talk reluctantly about a bereavement he has experienced. The child begins then to throw toys and be very disruptive, diverting attention away from the parent. This could be seen as the child's attempt to 'protect' the parent from experiencing too much discomfort, by creating a distraction. Thus the parent is not able to grieve properly and the child does not have the experience of seeing an adult deal with grief. Parents when they are distressed are very often less good at meeting their child's needs, and so the child may feel it to be in his or her best interests to prevent the parents from becoming overly upset. The parents may have learnt from their own families of origin to be frightened of being overwhelmed by grief, and the danger thereby of losing control, and may unconsciously welcome the child's interruption. So the child's difficult or dysfunctional behaviour is very often the visible tip of an iceberg which reaches back into the whole family's unresolved emotional themes.

The case examples I am going to give focus on the areas of 'separation' and 'control'. These are, of course, both fundamental issues that all families have to deal with; but the problems that these 'tasks' of separation and control throw up, are perhaps at their most intense in families with small children. To give an example: a young mother of 24, let us call her Jackie, and her 9-month-old son Andrew, were referred to the Centre by her social worker. The social worker was worried about Jackie's 'suspicious and paranoid feelings' as a result of which she felt Andrew was very passive, under stimulated, and had a history of minor illnesses which required short hospital admissions.

In the first interview Jackie, Andrew, Jackie's social worker, and a female therapist were present. Two other members of the team observed the session behind the screen. Jackie placed Andrew on the floor with some toys, he sat motionless, staring blankly into space. Any attempt on the part of Jackie or the social worker to change this had little effect. It seemed very unusual for a child of Andrew's age to show no concern or distress at his mother's obvious anxiety, or at being in strange surroundings.

During this initial assessment period, the role of the team is primarily to observe such areas as level of attachment between mother and child, and the amount and quality of interaction. The team then begins to develop a 'working hypothesis' on which to base the interventions that follow. This working hypothesis is constantly revised as more information comes to light. As therapy progresses the team will also be noting how the therapist in the room with the family becomes absorbed into the family system, and from their external viewpoint the team will give guidance to the therapist about how she can intervene in the system to bring about change. This may involve facilitating discussion between two members of a family by making sure there are no interruptions from other family members. It may involve the 'reframing' of what the family has previously considered a weakness into something that can be considered a strength, or it can simply involve the support of a parent in dealing with a child's tantrum. The number of interventions that may be used are of course too numerous to be listed here, but they will generally be designed to clarify the family structure and develop definite but flexible boundaries within the family.

To return to Jackie and Andrew. During the following weeks we had the opportunity to observe how they behaved together; we were able to watch what happened at meal times, during play sessions, etc.[2] We also learnt something of Jackie's own family history, and we saw how she dealt with relationships with others at the Centre. It soon became clear that Jackie was extremely anxious about separating from Andrew; her own traumatic separation from her parents when she left the West Indies, the breakdown in her relationship with Andrew's father, and her increasing isolation had made it very difficult indeed for her to tolerate any separation between herself and her son. He himself had given up expressing his own needs for separateness, because any expression of separateness was denied and not tolerated by his mother. Indeed any slight sign of difference that Andrew showed, was felt by Jackie to mean that Andrew was unwell. She re-interpreted Andrew's normal attempts at separation as 'illness'. In fact she interpreted any expression of feeling by Andrew as a sign that he was ill or overtired. In this way Jackie also denied that Andrew may have had feelings, both good and bad, towards her.

Andrew became caught up in a terrible dilemma, which he attempted to solve by developing the ability to fall asleep almost instantaneously when the tension between the conflicting demands of his mother's anxiety and his own growing need to become an individual became too great. The crunch finally came when Andrew, although having the balance and co-ordination necessary in order to be able to walk, continued to crawl. This continued for nearly 4 months. In the end, however, the natural drive of a toddler towards gaining new experiences and learning new skills won out. At last Jackie's increasing confidence and ability to express her own feelings allowed her to tolerate this new expression of separateness in her son.

Jackie who had become very isolated over the previous few years was given lots of support from the staff and other families at the Centre. She was given the opportunity to develop peer relationships, test out boundaries, and feel contained enough to begin to express her feelings, particularly in relation to separation. She was subsequently able to allow Andrew to begin to express his own feelings. In this way Jackie was helped to enable Andrew to learn new skills, showing her that although Andrew was growing up, he needed her at every stage of this process to help him move on. A big breakthrough came when Jackie, during a play session, spontaneously chose painting as an activity for Andrew. Jackie had previously avoided painting as an activity as she said she found the 'mess' too much. Andrew was very tentative with the paint and they were both obviously anxious throughout the session. They both survived the experience however, and even Jackie seemed to find it on the whole pleasurable. Jackie's decision to use paint seemed to be a statement that she was willing to try and take control of her own anxiety in order to allow Andrew to express his own individuality. She was very proud of his picture and took it home to put on his bedroom wall. Jackie found that she was gradually more able to allow Andrew to explore and that she could also be firmer with him when necessary and also more loving towards him. Andrew responded by becoming a much more responsive and rewarding child.

In this example the underlying issue was one of separation. Jackie's paranoid feelings, which so worried her social worker and almost resulted in Jackie being identified as psychiatrically ill, were it seemed, linked to her anger with her family whom she felt had neglected and ill-treated her. We noticed that these 'paranoid symptoms' became more marked in times of stress, for example, when her social worker went on holiday, but quickly subsided if the underlying difficulties were addressed and if Jackie was brought back to concentrating on the practicalities of her work with Andrew.

Another area which often causes difficulties in families is that of control. That is, the parents' ability to exercise control over their children, in such a way that the children feel safe and contained, and the parents feel confident and relaxed in their role as 'parent'. This is particularly important in families with small children and often particularly problematic. Parents in their teens or early twenties may be in conflict with their own parents over issues of control and this makes taking a parental role with their own children even more difficult. When parents do not have a basic level of control over their children, the children, in their eyes, seem to be extremely powerful. Parents may feel quite persecuted by their children and devise more and more harsh punishments in an attempt to control them. Therefore in these situations, it is important for the parents to feel supported by staff members. This sometimes puts staff in the difficult position of appearing initially to accept quite harsh treatment of the children by the parents, in order not to further undermine the parents' confidence. Gradually, as trust builds up in the relationship between staff and parents, suggestions can be made as to how to approach areas such as control in a different way, without resorting to physical punishments or threats.

Plate 26 was produced by a mother and child, where the problem was one of control and the mother's feelings of having her authority constantly undermined. In this family mother and grandmother exhibited extreme rivalry, in structural terms, the 'generational boundaries' were blurred. Here as with many of the families that attend Greyhound the father played a very peripheral role and was unwilling to take part in family sessions. The toddler and her mother behaved like rivalrous siblings and the family system kept the mother as the incompetent one who always needed her own mother to step in and take control. Grandmother saw her daughter's inability to choose a supportive mate as a further indication of her incompetence. The toddler over-ran all of her mother's images who seemed unable to prevent her pictures being 'swallowed up'. Witnessing the production of this particular image was rather like seeing the mother's picture being consumed by a forest fire.

The task here was to strengthen the generational boundaries and help the mother exercise control over her daughter and begin to feel competent, and that her own self, and her own images, mattered. The way we went about this was to support the mother in drawing up very firm boundaries for her child. For example, we asked the mother to restrict her daughter to one side of the paper only and her own painting to the other side. There was of course a struggle and many tantrums, but with support the mother was able to complete the task and, after a few weeks of working in this way, was able to strengthen her authority with her child and gradually develop more confidence. Work with mother and grandmother began to clarify the issues between them and meant that the toddler daughter was not so caught up in the rivalry between them. She was therefore more able to respond to her mother's growing firmness, and became less confused about who was her primary carer.

To explore this issue further, I would like to describe some work that was undertaken with, a family – let us call them the Price family. The family consists of:

Mrs Cathy Price
Mr Price (who was moving out of the family at the time of referral and had left by the time this piece of work I am about to describe took place).
Mandy 6 years old
William 3 years old
Jack 18 months old

When she first came to the Centre, Mrs Price had a perpetual snarl on her face, her mouth pulled down in an intimidating grimace. The Centre rang to the sound of her voice shouting threats at the children. Mandy, though lively and bright, was extremely demanding and aggressive, while William was very withdrawn and delayed in his development. Jack, although not apparently unhappy, did not show appropriate signs of distress, for a baby of his age. The whole family was very dirty and smelly. This had led to Mandy being ostracised by her peers at school.

The first stage of work involved clarifying the situation between the parents who eventually decided to part permanently and get divorced. The family therapy session I am about to describe took place roughly mid-way through the family's attendance at the Centre. The importance of the session is that it showed the underlying difficulty the mother had in taking control of her children. This problem had in the past been obscured by the fraught relationship between the parents, and Mrs Price had of course a very difficult task in trying to manage three small children single-handedly. At this stage neither the staff at the Centre nor Mrs Price herself knew whether the task would prove too much for her.

A large sheet of paper and some paints were set out on the floor by the two therapists. Mrs Price sat some distance away from the paper with the baby, Jack, on her lap. Mandy began to paint a figure (*Plate 23*), but did not complete it. Instead she began to splash paint on to the paper (and on to everything else). William copied her (as he usually did). Mandy looked at her mother in a challenging way, her mother told her to stop splashing and threatened various punishments if she did not. Mrs Price, however, made no attempt to move. Mandy and William continued to wander aimlessly around the paper. The splashing became wilder, while they giggled conspiratorially. Meanwhile, Mrs Price tried to engage the therapists in conversation. She said, 'this painting business is a distraction away from the main issue'.

The main issue, however, Mrs Price's great difficulty in providing containment and control for her children, was clearly being played out in front of everybody. The atmosphere in the room became more tense and chaotic. Mandy began to paint her hands. Mrs Price said, 'If you do that I'll smack you'. At this point, Mandy walked determinedly to the other side of the picture and placed her 'hand prints' on the incomplete figure she had begun earlier, so that it now had large green hands. Mandy identified this figure as Patricia, one of the therapists. This was an interesting response to her mother's threat to smack her. She had given hands to Patricia, because she felt perhaps that Patricia was the only one at that point who would be able to provide the control and containment that she needed, or because 'Patricia's hands' would not be used to smack her. It was also a good example of how the family system maintained the mother as incompetent, previously in relation to Mr Price, and perhaps now in relation to Patricia the therapist, who the children now related to as 'the parent'.

The children's comment about the picture at the end of the session was that it was 'a mess'. Mrs Price said, 'it shows mess, confusion and anger'. Mandy and William rushed out of the room at the end of the session leaving Mrs Price calling frantically after them as she started to clear up the mess. Meanwhile the baby, who she had put on the floor, began to scream.

The message of this session was clear. The first task for the family was for Mrs Price to gain control over the children. During the early part of a family's stay at the Centre the focus of family sessions is to elicit information about the family system, though 'the therapist may transform certain aspects of family functioning even as he learns about them' (Kobak and Waters

1984:92). Once a working hypothesis has been agreed upon by the team then the role of the therapist becomes one of facilitating change in structure. 'The transformation of structure [being] defined as changes in the position of family members *vis-à-vis* each other.' (Minuchin 1974:111)

At this point a more individually-orientated therapist, may have wanted to try and discover what lay behind Mrs Price's apparent inability to take control of her children. Was she simply unaware of how to do it? Or did this way of behaving have some meaning in terms of her own past experiences? Structural family therapy is, however, 'a therapy of action. The tool of this therapy is to modify the present, not to explore and interpret the past'. Therefore the next task was to give Mrs Price some instruction in how to persevere with the children, some help in making her tone of voice authoritative rather than just angry, and for the therapist to stay with her and support her while she set basic practical boundaries for her children in the next session. I do not want to give the impression that the underlying reasons for behaviour are disregarded in this way of working, but they are not the central focus. Practical and directive help in taking charge of the children is important, given that children grow very fast and changes need to take place in keeping with their urgent needs. Directive and structured programmes of work concentrating on the children's needs, often brings the parents' difficulties more clearly into focus, and the confidence parents gain in learning new parenting skills often enables them to make changes in other areas of their lives.

The family continued to attend the Centre regularly in spite of many ups and downs. Mrs Price's confidence gradually increased with support from staff and other families. A structured programme was devised for Mrs Price to help William with his speech and in other areas where he was thought to be under stimulated. She was also given help in finding ways of managing all three children at once. The confidence of having succeeded in a task led on to other successes as she was helped to manage 'messy' activities such as painting, in small quantities and fix limits that she was able to maintain.

The Price family, some 3 months later

Mrs Price sat talking to the therapists. She was relaxed and had plenty to say. The children sat quite close together engrossed in their play with crayons and paper and construction toys. The therapist said to Mrs Price 'in previous sessions you spent a lot of time putting the toys away as if always preparing to leave or wanting to get away, but today you arranged the furniture in the doll's house' (as if in preparation for play). Mrs Price had obviously gained great pleasure from arranging the doll's house and, it seemed, had moved from a state where she was desperately trying to create and maintain some kind of order and control, to one where she could begin 'play' herself and arrange the toys creatively. The children were now more able to articulate their thoughts and express in their pictures their feelings and concerns. For example, Mandy's picture produced at this session, with its depiction of a lady with a veil, who is swimming under water (or drowning?) and her rather spikey smile, seemed to be a clear reference to her confused feelings about her father's forthcoming marriage, which she was able to articulate now that the family had emerged from under the oppressive weight of its chaos and confusion. As Sobol (1982) says, in relation to the Jackson family, 'As the family hierarchy began to realign, a foundation was laid for productive self-exploration in art.'

The deceptively simple and basic changes that this family made, brought about an impressive transformation. Mrs Price's care of herself and the children improved dramatically. Mandy became calmer and was able to show sadness as well as anger. William and Jack both became very much individuals in their own right, asserting their needs in a way which would previously have been hard to imagine. Mrs Price lost her habitual 'snarl' and her need to shout continuously and therefore became much more approachable to her peers. This added to her growing confidence and she left the Centre with a sense of herself as competent and able to manage her own life and her children.

Conclusion

I decided to describe these examples of families where control and separation were difficult issues partly because they are very common and fundamental difficulties but also because, it seems to me, that art therapists working with very young children and disorganized and chaotic families, perhaps need to extend the traditional view of their role and area of work. The medium of art provides an alternative and very often more effective language than words for expressing such abstract ideas as: distance/closeness between individuals; boundaries; enclosure; exclusion; and relative size/importance. It therefore provides a metaphorical language for describing the organization of family structure.

The use of art can provide a setting where families can 'rehearse' new ways of relating to each other. For example, the mother and child who produced *Plate 25* were using the paper as their 'battleground'. Once the mother could take control of her 'territory' in this metaphorical language, then other boundaries in their lives became easier to define. To do this, however, it is necessary to be more directive than is usual for an art therapist. He or she has to initially make an assessment of the 'angle of deviance between (the structural norm) and the family that comes in the door' (Hoffman 1981:263) and devise art activities for the family that will through action and experience begin to help them redefine their structure.

In the majority of the families seen at Greyhound, the degree of chaos is such that it overshadows any attempt that may be made by an individual child to express his feelings creatively. The very basic needs for control and separation in the relationship between parent and child need to be met to some extent, at least, before the children and parents can enter the world of creative expression. Art therapists working in this area need, I think, therefore, to be prepared to get involved in the stages that precede creative self-expression – to find ways to help the family reach a point where the children are contained enough, and the parents confident enough for creative 'play' of any kind to take place. Given this kind of help, parents often show remarkable sensitivity to their children's need to play and are able to nurture their children's creativity. Given that the brief of the Centre is to help families change their structure enough to enable them to be 'good enough' parents to their children, then at this point the Centre has achieved its aim.

© 1990 Sarah Deco

Notes

1 Bateson and his colleagues took as the basis of their theory Russel's 'Theory of Logical Types' (*Principia Mathematica*, Cambridge University Press 1910).

> The central thesis of this theory is that there is a discontinuity between a class and its members. The class cannot be a member of itself nor can one of the members be the class, since the term used for the class is of a different level of abstraction – a different logical type – from terms used for members.
>
> (Bateson *et al.* 1973:174)

2 As part of the programme at Greyhound, families attend 'play sessions', every morning. These include up to ten families at a time. The aim is for parents to provide toys and activities (including art activities) appropriate to their child's age and developmental needs. The role of staff members here is to help the parents help their children. These sessions provide opportunities for parents to deal with helping their children share, take turns, and communicate with other adults and children. It also provides parents with an opportunity to share skills and support each other.

3 The development of this 'external viewpoint' is aided by the use of the one-way screen. This technique requires two rooms separated by a wall in which there is a one-way screen, mirrored and opaque on one side and transparent on the other. The family are interviewed by the therapist and interact together on one side of the screen, while 'the team' observes them on the other. This gives the therapeutic team the opportunity to observe the family and the therapist while remaining unseen and unheard in the other room. This technique is used as a regular part of the programme at Greyhound as is video equipment to record family therapy sessions.

References

Bateson, G., Jackson, D., Haley, J. and Weakland, J.H. (1973) 'Towards a theory of schizophrenia', *Steps to an Ecology of Mind*, London: Paladin.

Campbell, D., Draper, R., Pollard, D., and Reder, P. (n.d.) *Working with the Milan Method*, London: Institute of Family Therapy.

Hoffman, L. (1981) *Foundations of Family Therapy*, New York: Basic Books.

Jenkins, H. and Donnelly, M. (1983) 'The therapist's responsibility: a systemic approach to mobilising family creativity', *Journal of Family Therapy* 5: 1–20.

Kobak, R. and Waters, D. (1984) 'Family therapy as a rite of passage, play's the thing', *Family Process* 23: 89–100.

Kwiatkowska, H.Y. (1978) *Family Therapy and Evaluation Through Art*, USA: Charles C. Thomas.

Landgarten, H. (1975) 'Group art therapy for mothers and daughters', *American Journal of Art Therapy* 14: 121–6.

Minuchin, S. (1977) *Families and Family Therapy*, London: Tavistock.

Rubin, J.A. and Magnussen, M.G. (1974) 'A family art evaluation', *Family Process* 13: 185–200.

Ruesch, J. and Bateson, G. (1951) *Communication: The Social Matrix of Society*, New York: Norton.

Sherr, C. and Hicks, H. (1978) 'Family drawings as a diagnostic and therapeutic technique', *Family Process* 12: 439.

Sobol, B. (1982) 'Art therapy and strategic family therapy', *American Journal of Art Therapy* 21: 43–51.

Wadeson, H.S. (1973) 'The fluid family in multi-family art therapy', *American Journal of Art Therapy* 12: 115–18.

Plate 27 House

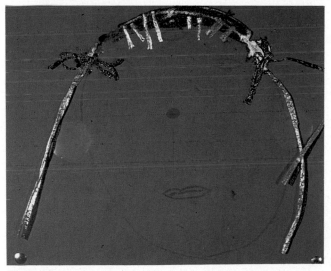

Plate 28 Dark Lady from Egypt or India

Plate 29 Mountain peaks

Plate 30 The Queen of Hearts

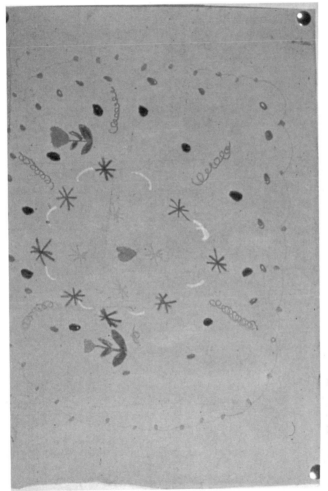

Plate 31 Heart pattern

Plate 32 Father Christmas

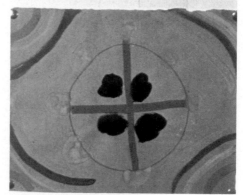

Plate 33 Top: Self-portrait
Bottom: Pattern

Chapter eight

Reflections and shadows: an exploration of the world of the rejected girl

Caroline Case

The function of art therapy in the Assessment Centre

In this chapter I would like to begin by looking at the major functions of art therapy in an Assessment Centre.

An initial function was to provide one part of a multi-disciplinary assessment by working with the child in the art and play therapy room. This took place in individual sessions; in a mixed 'family' age group; in a peer group; or in the natural family group if at the Centre with siblings. One could see how children were able to respond to a non-directive structure (Axline 1947; Rubin 1978; Stott and Males 1984); if they could make representations of their inner world, work symbolically, and had capacity for insight. Recommendations could be made for further therapy and a report passed on to the child's future permanent placement. In the material produced it was possible to see which of many past traumas and/or factors in the present situation were affecting the child and for them to express their preoccupations and feelings.

The second function was to work with the immediate breakdown, the experience of events that had precipitated the child being taken into care; to give the child a space in which to explore the feelings of fear, anger and loss, and probably most of all, rejection. The child had the sense of becoming uncontainable, beyond parental control or unwanted at home. It was very painful to explore these losses, to let oneself feel unwanted or rejected with the accompanying fantasies and fears. For instance, many children would feel guilty and responsible that they had 'caused' a break-up of the family or that they were quite simply 'bad'. They needed repeated opportunities to talk about their situation although it was often too overwhelming to put into words immediately. Art and play gave opportunities for these confused feelings about their sudden transition to be expressed and perhaps eventually verbalized. The paintings and models had a concrete form that brought intense relief. Previously formless worries or anxieties could be externalized and worked with instead of being trapped inside and experienced as a blank loss of feeling, emptiness, or a rush of conflicting emotions.

The third function was to have longer-term therapy with the more disturbed children who were going to be difficult to place. After assessment, the problem was often to match the recommendations with what was available either in the borough or nationally. So an 'ideal recommendation' might need to be mitigated by any number of factors; e.g. ease of parental access, maintenance of a child's education, or lack of places of the kind wanted. The difficulty was facing the fact that the older the child and the more disturbed, the harder they would be to place, especially if a number of previous placements had broken down. Children therefore might stay from a year to 18 months, giving them an added feeling of being dumped like a piece of rubbish at the Centre while other children came and went.

In the context about which I am writing art therapy was set within the education unit and therefore could be seen to have a further function in relation to both the teachers and the classroom. One of the dynamics of being part of a multi-disciplinary team is the awareness of everyone's role and function, to respect their value and difference. This is difficult when roles are given a differing status by society or by an institution, which might be reflected intrinsically by different pay and working conditions; hierarchy of decision-making; and influence on policy.

It was to our advantage as a small team working together in the unit that the art therapist was a qualified teacher with experience of working in the classroom and therefore knew the strains and stresses of this work. Employment on a teacher's post gave equality of conditions of service although experience of working with the children diverged. The post had to be rationalized within the system and so a sacrifice was made. The teachers had larger numbers in order for the art therapist to be able to work with individuals and groups. Despite an occasional pull to merge roles at times of illness or absence (a rare point where ambivalence – through need – was expressed), the necessity of keeping to the separate role of therapist was respected. Children, knowing that there was a place for them to be able to express their worries, concerns, 'badness', and mess, were able to contain their more disruptive behaviour and extreme feelings to the therapy sessions and thus allow attention and concentration (although sometimes obviously limited) to be brought to remedial and school work.

As a way of understanding the different aspects of our roles the experience of working in art therapy groups was offered to the teaching staff and residential social workers. This gave the staff the opportunity to have what the children experienced in some way; to share aspects of their personal lives; and to share their feelings about working with the children. It also brought an inner understanding to attempts to develop opportunities for art therapy with the children, leading to further support and feedback of the work; as well as being a rare opportunity for residential social workers and teachers to have personal sharing together. Art therapy in the education unit could be seen therefore to foster further opportunities for learning in the classroom. Giving the children a 'space apart' helped them to develop some opportunity to reflect on feelings which in turn greatly aided their capacity for reflection in the classroom context. Being able to see the child in two contexts we could share our perceptions, monitor splitting, and discuss the feelings that the children aroused in us, often disturbing, as they re-enacted old hurts. A small staff group was able to be both united under the often relentless attacks from children previously rejected and also tolerant of each other's idiosyncrasies as people trying to care for the children, respecting each other's strengths and weaknesses.

Merging, containment, and separation

In the Assessment Centre a very large part of the work of the staff consisted in receiving children into care. These were often severely emotionally deprived, having experienced frequent changes, inconsistency, and rejection from parental figures. Many of the families were often caught in a vicious cycle of deprivation where the parents too may have had experience of being abandoned, taken into care, breakdown of placements in children's homes or foster homes in their own childhood. Before trying to explore and understand the world of the rejected child there follows a brief sketch of what the reader will need to know of early development in order to make sense of the chapter. For a fuller account the reader is referred to Bion (1959, 1962), Klein (1940, 1957, 1975), Winnicott (1965, 1971).

Consistent contact in a human relationship is seen as a necessary condition for ego development to take place in the baby. The maternal figure, through nurturance and empathy, needs to provide a structure, a containment, and a sense of boundaries for the baby. The mother enters a period of 'primary maternal pre-occupation' where her own early experiences as a helpless infant are called upon to enable her to identify with the baby's needs. During this time the infant needs to have a good experience of merging with, having needs met by, and being understood by the mother. The role of the father or other supportive figures could be seen, at this time, to be as a protector of the mother's vulnerability as she exposes herself to the infantile feelings of anxiety and helplessness. The father can provide a protective 'skin' around the mother and child merger, helping to hold the mother's anxieties about her new-born infant.

The function of the mother at this time has been described by Bion (1962) as a 'container'. The mother needs to be able to receive into herself a chaotic input of feelings and sensations, mainly painful ones; to be able to understand the reason for the baby's discomfort, give it a meaning, and minister to the child's needs. The mother therefore uses her empathy, or a reverie of feelings and thoughts about the baby, informed by her own experience of helplessness as an infant, in order to metabolize in herself what the child is not yet able to process. 'Mother gives meaning to the meaningless'. The child has the repeated experience of having a space in someone's mind and of being understood. Through this model, the child is enabled to develop his own capacity to think and eventually develop a space in his own mind, which could be seen as a prerequisite for all future learning.

While the mother is feeling and thinking for the baby, sifting his anxieties and fears, she creates for him a sense of psychological well-being, allowing the development of an illusory sense of omnipotence by fulfilling his needs. The child's identity is further established by the mother's process of mirroring, reflecting back to him her perception as she responds to the impression the baby gives her, and also reflections from other people the baby encounters. 'The mind's mirror is cast in the matrix of human relationships' (Pines 1982:3). The baby is coming to a sort of halfway stage of fusion and separation, of differentiation from the mother but needs to be able to maintain an image of the mother in her absence in order to become independent. To mediate this transition from fusion to separation the child may choose an object to which he attaches particular importance, a transitional object (Winnicott 1971). 'This object can give a child a safe mid-ground in which to practise relating to the world outside without having to risk completely giving up fantasied control' (Ernst 1987:87). The ability to play and to use objects representationally is the beginning of a range of creative responses that the child and adult will be able to develop and where ambivalent feelings about merging and separation will be explored symbolically throughout life.

However 'good enough' the mothering the baby has received, he must experience frustrations as needs are not met or he experiences overwhelming anxiety at times of separation. All infants will therefore develop defence mechanisms against experiencing their helplessness at different stages. In order to be able to move out from the original merger with mother, both mother and child have to be able to let go, or lose this early stage of contentment to gain the next stage where both will have a different relationship. All development must have an element of loss.

A mother may not be able to perform these early functions for a child to a good enough degree if she herself has experienced deprivation as a young child. In the above description it can be seen that the 'primary maternal preoccupation' depends on the mother's ability to be in touch with early fears and anxieties. These may be frighteningly overwhelming for a mother who has experienced no containment or loving reflection from a mother herself. The child's anxieties may be felt as persecutory or the child may receive her projections of early unmet needs, reinforcing his sense of boundlessness. The mother may have had a baby to 'have someone who will constantly love her', only to find that the demands of the baby make her long to abandon him. Mother and child will become entangled in a circle of demands for each other and rejection as they cannot be met.

Rejected boys, rejected girls

Children who have been severely emotionally deprived and who have frequently experienced rejection are likely both to have lacked early experiences of consistent mothering so that their development has been impaired and to have developed extreme defences against dependence and overwhelming anxiety. It is difficult to write of 'general characteristics' of rejected children without a feeling of doing a disservice to the individual suffering encountered at the Assessment Centre, but an attempt follows to describe some of the features of early deprivation.

Children are likely to have been affected both in their capacity to establish trusting and secure relationships and in their capacity to think and to learn (Britton 1978; Holmes 1977). Children at the Centre lacked a model of having a 'space in mind' and the capacity to symbolize, or bear the tension and anxieties of 'not knowing' involved in learning, so felt at a loss unless they were doing simple repetitive work with a known outcome which made them feel safe. Children who seemed to lack any kind of boundary or containing function themselves would have difficulty holding thoughts and feelings; a sense that everything 'fell through' or 'went in one ear and out the other' (Henry 1983).

Those working with these children are likely to feel forcefully what it is like to be shut out, left, discarded, and abandoned. One tries to make a relationship only to encounter swings of mood, denial of affection, and an attempt to control by blackmailing behaviour. The children enact the full force of their feelings of resentment and hate against parental figures on to the staff who are at present trying to communicate with them. They are of course repeating a pattern that they have internalized, although it might often feel as if they are taking revenge. There is a compulsion to live out an old pattern; familiarity is preferable to the unknown. Treating a member of staff abominably, forcing them to retaliate, confirms the child's sense of being 'bad' and fills the staff member with despair that no progress is possible; they 'cannot get anywhere with this child'.

There are two further ways that the workers may feel for the child. Some of the children seem to have acquired a 'thick skin', or a stiff body musculature from which all feeling and physical contact is distanced. They can recount horrific episodes in their lives with apparently no emotional content while the worker feels the pain, guilt, and despair that this can happen in our society. This 'second skin' is a denial of pain, a kind of pseudo-containment developed through lack of early holding (Bick 1968). The second kind of feeling is a result of the bombardment of abuse, physical and verbal, the acting-out of anger and destruction. The worker then feels inadequate and hopeless, a sense of failure, of frightening aggression evacuated on to them; the child left empty and exhausted at the end.

Discussion of gender difference in the behaviour of emotionally disturbed children is a complex area because it inevitably involves an idea of innate capacities as well as social conditioning and expectation. Here, the outlining of some stereotypes may be useful to try to distinguish a broad difference; of course, exceptions immediately spring to mind. One is more likely to see in boys the outwardly defended child, thick musculature, an untouchable quality, mentally or physically; who, if touched by feeling would erupt into aggressive defences of physical and verbal abuse. They might attempt to keep an unemotional, neutral, flat relationship, getting by, with an air of bravado. Children like this might repetitively draw castles or other fortified objects, football heroes or aggressive masculine figures from film or TV. They may have a delinquent background, a sense of anger and hate projected on to others or there might be glue-sniffing amongst some children, giving them a relief from pain and release into a dreamworld.

In contrast, one is more likely to see in girls the undersize, pathetic, or appealing waif-like child with poor eating habits. One has a sense here of pale imitations of life that seem to know somewhere that they have missed something. There is sometimes the development of a false coping self; a child may have taken on the role of 'little mother' to younger siblings or the whole family. A sense of clinging or relating to surface qualities in people can make them unrewarding to work with because of the lack of depth in the relationship. This can show in similar ways through incessant, inconsequential chattering which tries to keep everything 'nice', and thereby preventing work together with the therapist from progressing on the real problems facing them.

Another female presentation is the unbounded, formless girl who drifts through activities, unable to begin or finish work, as if there were no containment for any thought, purpose, or feeling. These girls are likely to get by by doing superficially 'nice' pictures and may be unnoticed as having problems at school or in other situations because they are not naughty or acting-out, they just appear whiny and 'a bit of a nuisance'. In adolescence, problems might be expressed through early pregnancy, 'to have someone who will always love me', or abortions, evacuation of a 'bad self' by being a 'bad girl'. However, several examples of little boys who had become 'mothers' to their families and girls who exhibit acting-out behaviour come to mind which counteract this stereotype.

There is an interesting thread here. To some extent the boys' form of expressing their early experiences can be understood by the absence of fathers or often unknown fathers who tend in fantasy to be destructive figures with whom the boys are often unconsciously identified – pictures of Dracula, werewolves, aliens, etc. Their differing gender from their mother also aids an establishment of 'otherness' and a rejection of all 'femaleness' from their modes of relating. The energetic output and aggression also enable them to deny the underlying depression. The difference in gender noted above has been discussed by other writers (Wolkind and Rutter 1973; Wolkind 1977;

Wolkind *et al.* 1977) and in this form:

> It could be that girls react rather differently from boys to the lack of a
> mother's holding arms and caring preoccupations when they are very tiny
> . . . may lead to an impairment of the capacity to take in, grasp and hold
> on to thoughts, feelings, memories and experience. . . .
>
> (Boston and Szur 1983:24)

What if we reverse this quotation and imagine mothers reacting rather
differently with girl children than with boys? So the question is a general
one, not just addressing rejected children but considering how mothers
'mother' girl children.

Mothers and daughters; a feminist perspective

Writings which are a result of work done at the Women's Therapy Centre
in London have challenged the notion of a neutral 'baby' developing outside
culture. They have addressed themselves to considerations of gender
difference within a patriarchal society. 'We see the unconscious as the intra-
psychic reflection of our present child-rearing and gender relations' (Eichenbaum and Orbach 1982:15). In their work with women at the Centre they
have been exploring the effects of patriarchy and the inferior position of
women in our society on mother–daughter relations. Mothers and daughters
share gender identity, social role, and social expectations. Put simply, they
suggest that within a patriarchal system, women limit their capacity to 'act
in the world' but take on the social roles of wife and mother within the
home. The care and response to other people's needs are seen to be a
woman's province.

During the period of 'primary maternal pre-occupation' the mother will
bring both a positive and a negative self-image to the relationship. They
suggest that a negative self-image, a woman's 'well of unmet needs' is likely
to be painfully activated with ambivalent feelings on the birth of a daughter.
At this time of merging with the baby, mother is likely to identify strongly,
she 'sees herself', because mother and daughter have a shared gender. A
mother may see her daughter as an extension of herself and unconsciously
project some of the feelings she has about herself on to her daughter, positive
and negative. Eichenbaum and Orbach (1982, 1987) posit the development of
a push–pull relationship between mother and daughter. Mother will push her
daughter's neediness away because it reinvokes her own 'unmet needs' while
caring for others. She will also pull her to stay within the boundaries that
she inhabits, to protect her vulnerability, also a projection of her own, and
because of her own sense of atrophy within the home will resent her young
daughter's explorations outside the boundaries she sets for them both.

Mother will thus be able to merge with the baby and also at times be unable to separate through strong identification and projection of parts of the self on to the baby girl At other times she will not be able to connect with the baby girl but will unconsciously reject the image of herself that makes demands on her, painfully activating her own unmet needs and vulnerability. There is then no protection of 'otherness' that a baby boy might bring. The baby girl protects herself from this push–pull relationship by denying her needs. She feels as if she is 'insatiable', generating a sense of self-dislike and greed. The baby girl has known a 'giving mother' as well as a deeply disappointing mother so the sense of potential satisfaction continues to frustrate as it is not fulfilled. It is difficult to feel and express anger to those who disappoint for fear of further rejection and abandonment. The needy part of the baby girl is cut off from the self and repressed, leaving a sense of futility and hopelessness. The hidden part is felt to be destructive, devouring, and bad. To protect this part that demands, the baby can appear not to want anything from mother, developing a coping inauthentic self which protects the feelings of need and yearning.

Unlike a baby boy, a baby girl may never have had an illusory sense of omnipotence, self-esteem, and fulfilment of met needs. She will therefore find it much harder to separate, not ever having fully merged. She separates by denying her needs and gradually taking on the role of caring for others, filling her needs vicariously. A mother may have tried to fulfil her own unmet needs by having a baby so that her daughter's attempts at separation will arouse her ambivalence and sense of further loss. A baby needs to have feelings mirrored. Through experience of mother's ambivalence the baby will learn to 'read' mother's face, learn to predict her moods, learn to care for *her*; instead of there being an exchange and sense of enrichment for the baby. My own observation has been that daughters, particularly of emotionally deprived mothers, learn to mother them. Mother needs empathy in the early stage of merging but later needs to be objective, understanding baby's need to separate with encouragement at her own pace. This is difficult for an unbounded mother who has not separated herself to achieve, as the closeness with the baby may be the only one she has experienced.

Ernst (1987) sees women as lacking a sense of 'inner separation', i.e. women can be living a separate identity but still not be psychologically separate from their mother. She criticizes Winnicott's concept, of 'primary maternal preoccupation' as a 'disease model' and with reference to Chodorow puts forward the idea of women's identification with others as a central feature of women's personality (Chodorow 1978; Ernst 1987). She suggests that Winnicott does not recognize the importance of the mother's own gender or gender difference in relation to boy and girl babies, and fails to see that women's psychological structure is reinforced by their economic and social experience. There is a relative absence of adult separate identities for women. Mother's identification with a baby boy is tempered by a sense of difference and 'otherness' which is reinforced by father's presence as a model for the baby boy with whom to identify. Equally important is the presence of the father to the baby girl in developing a sense of separation.

Children who have experienced inconsistent and inadequate parenting are likely to have mothers who have had a lack of nurturance and emotional sustenance in their own lives and are frequently one-parent families experiencing social and economic deprivation. Daughters may be likely to evoke their own history of emotional life that will most unconsciously upset them. They are likely to play out their hurts and ambivalences on their daughters, rejecting their infantile needs and demanding themselves to be mothered. I would suggest that daughters then develop a 'little old lady' persona, becoming the 'little mother' often to their own mother and their younger siblings, a destiny especially likely for the eldest girl. In therapy these children often immediately present with flat, unemotional, almost tired voices, clean, thin, and well-behaved. They present as perfect little girls doing 'nice' pictures. This passive presentation of rejected and unmet needs is less likely to be explored because if workers are also working with the opposite presentation of angry, abusive, acting-out boys, they can almost be a relief to encounter.

Reflections and shadows

In the feminist approach at the Women's Therapy Centre some debate has centred on the need to experience a good merger with the therapist (Eichenbaum and Orbach 1987) or to aid the separation process (Ernst 1987) for women clients. Experience with children suggests that they need to experience what they have never fully had before separation can be negotiated. In working with rejected boys and rejected girls, a difference which reflects the therapist's gender emerges. Rejected boys frequently bring a distrust of women, a sense of their 'otherness', which needs to be expressed and explored, acted out, through the relationship with a female therapist. They may also take a 'male role' to protect the female therapist. Rejected girls, if they can form relationships, are more likely to merge, expressing a desire for 'no difference' between us, exploring images of women through identification with the female therapist before a separate identity can be painfully formed. Adult women, too, may refer unconsciously to 'our painting' or 'the painting that we did last week', actually painted by them alone, a fusion of images of client and therapist.

While thinking and writing about rejected girls and Ruth in particular, Tennyson's *Lady of Shalott* has run through my mind like a leitmotif.

> And moving through a mirror clear
> That hangs before her all the year
> Shadows of the world appear.

In the poem, Launcelot is seen as the object of beauty. The Lady of Shalott seems to represent, locked away in the tower, receiving only reflections of the world, the unconscious feminine element of the Age of Chivalry, that which was not allowed voice or image openly at the time. To come to consciousness, to reality, into the world is premature death, and indeed her beauty can only be 'seen' passively at death. She is the unconscious, making and weaving shadow images. In therapy, the mirroring that we do of the unconscious attempts to catch these shadowy images, in the tapestry of painting and to give them life in the conscious world. It seems that if they come to life and light too soon, then the mirror will crack, but that also a shadow-life is lived if the attempt is not made. The acceptance of shadows from the past means a working through of loss, depression, and merger towards separation.

Case study: Ruth

Ruth's case-notes suggested a typical background of rejection, experience of frequent change, ambivalence, being 'in and out' of care, and periods of abandonment. Ruth was the first child of a mother who had experienced difficulties giving birth. At age 9, after being in a children's home for a year, she returned to live with her mother and new step-father, brothers, and step-brothers. She began to run away, acting out a need to be held and contained or perhaps a search for a new beginning. As her mother was unable to cope with her behaviour, she again came into care, arriving at the Assessment Centre. She presented as a small, shrunken 9-year-old with rather superficially 'adult' speech, having had the role of 'little mother' to her siblings, and as 'companion' to her mother. Her mother had been able to state her perception of the main problem which was that she had always felt 'unable to love her children', particularly Ruth, the only girl. A cycle had been set up; of ambivalence whereby she abandoned them into care, felt relief, then guilt and love, would re-set up home, repeating a pattern that she herself had experienced as a child.

The context of practice has been described elsewhere (Case 1987) but I would like to add a note here about the boundaries of the sessions. At the Centre it became an acknowledged structure that children could 'ask for a session' in a crisis and also request to share a session with a particular child or children, sometimes forming a group for an agreed number of sessions. This arrangement seemed to reflect the residential setting and the needs of this group of children and was rarely abused. I found that I was able to work for instance with the symbolic significance of the chosen partner for a particular session(s) although there has not always been room in this chapter to go into this aspect in detail.

The 'heartland of the self'

During the first weeks in art therapy Ruth made tentative explorations in the sessions, remaining almost hidden from sight in the group of children attending together. She chose to play with the doll's house, a perpetual re-arranging of furniture and making of beds, a 'being lost in housework', a busy-ness that does not allow a moment's expression of feeling or unwelcome thought. It reflected her 'mother's helper' role in the family and a need to put the 'house of the self' in order. She also made brief use of the blackboard, sometimes chalking 'queens' before leaving, always to the same design, just a face and crown, almost sneaked on to the board, as if it broke with her neatness and controlled housekeeping.

Her first statement on paper was a pattern with a heart at the centre (*Plate 31*). A small red heart is surrounded by even numbers of red/yellow stars, then blue stars/white curves. There is a sense of wholeness in the middle which has a clear shape through the regularity and balance of parts. In the next layer outwards, two red flowers mirror each other across the circle and the patterning begins to get confused, losing balance. On the right side the flower is held firmly in a myriad of tiny shapes and marks. On the left there is a bare gap between the flower and the outer boundary, composed of delicate red dots. The two flowers confuse the main design of fours and eights. The heart both stands protected at the middle with layers to get through to reach it, but also lost, hard to find, as if at the centre of a maze. It has both a feel of potential wholeness, experience of some unity of self or distinctness, and also being like a collection of fragmented pieces.

The depiction of the heart recalls symbolic other uses of this image such as calling attention to a desire to express innermost fantasy. The form of the circle pattern reminds me of games of hide-and-seek, with echoes of Ruth running away and wanting to be found, the treasure at the middle of a puzzle. Seeing a heart on its own, out of the body, suggests a vulnerability, exposed for all to see, the nakedness of love and need, 'wearing a heart on your sleeve'. The heart is a major vital organ, through which physical pain can be felt at moments of deep feeling. It is also the way we express our love openly, hearts entwined, Valentines. In therapy it can often be used as a sign to point the way, to show a 'broken heart'. It can appear apparently like a piece of graffiti, an overused metaphor, a disguise, or signpost to catch the therapist's attention. If used in this way, apparently a banal image, there is safety in that if one draws attention to it too precipitately the client can withdraw saying 'it's *only* graffiti' – the importance can be denied. So I think it is often both a stereotyped description and a cry to the therapist. The therapist needs to discover what this particular heart is saying, to try to understand the heart's ache.

In this first picture the vulnerable heart is shown, but 'it's just a pattern'. The two flowers catch each eye as you focus on the paper, blurring the heart at the middle. It was a big move to have committed herself to paper.

> Psycho-social transitions are the times when we reassess our picture of the world and our means of being a part of it. They are experienced as impinging on us but their effects include major changes in the *heartland of the self*. At such times we are uniquely open to both help and harm. We need protection, reassurance, time to recoup, help in developing blueprints for the future.
>
> (Parkes 1976:13; author's emphasis)

Breaking taboos

Ruth naturally grouped with two girls at the Centre, as if they shared a similar world view. Jill, aged 7, recently orphaned, had the flattened depression of intense bereavement. Susie, aged 9, had a similar background to Ruth's. She was a pretty child, but almost two-dimensional; it felt impossible to know what she might want, all choices, all decisions, all people felt the same to her. Attempts to work with her felt as if they passed through a transparency and I was unable to make more than surface contact in the short time that we worked together. Experience of working with girls who have been rejected and who control their inside messy feelings is that sometimes they need an invitation to play, permission that it is alright to behave like a child, not a little adult. Being in an art and play therapy room with others playing is not enough. They will watch in the role of mother and may confide to me comments on another child playing, as two adults together. In the work that followed Susie sometimes took this role, as if going through the motions of play, whereas Ruth was able to make contact through regression with representations of early experience.

One afternoon we made a long strip of paper across the floor with the idea that they might work together or separately. Lots of liquid paint, and powder paint and finger paints were available. Jill began, using water and powder paint to make a mixture, then making finger-prints on and around one section. Ruth and Susie neatly painted colours with brushes, both very slowly, watching Jill all the time. Jill had nearly finished when Ruth realized that she had spots of paint on her knees and went to wash them. At the sink she said in a 'good' voice, 'Oh dear, it's all over. I must rub it off', actually rubbing the paint all over her legs. She was getting excited. We removed her shoes and socks. She started playing in the 'mud' on the painting. Gradually her clothes were removed, when it seemed appropriate, so as to protect them and not to interfere with the flow of the play. Jill followed and then Susie, soon all were covered in paint. Jill and Susie were more tentative but it was important to Ruth that she should be completely covered, laughing and laughing, finally rolling over and over along the disintegrating painting. When finally covered, she said in flat even voice, 'My mother would like to see me like this'.

The painting/play reached a natural end and we began to clear up, washing at the sink enough to be able to go over to the house to have baths. At the last moment before leaving, it seemed as if Ruth could not bear to leave the mess made, it was suddenly too soon, a dreadful moment of parting. As they bathed Ruth began to talk of her mother for the first time, expressing a worry that she would not be able to visit at the weekend. She told us of her mother telling her off once for cutting her hair, an association of this incident and the messy afternoon as two bad naughty things. All three were anxious to come again, Ruth saying that she would like to make a mess again. Her face had altered, bright-eyed, full of life. She said it was 'the best time' she had ever had, as she stood freshly dressed in clean clothes after the bath.

What had started off as an invitation to finger-paint, to explore something beneath these masks, ended in a complete mess, of paintings which disintegrated and had to be thrown away. The linking in Ruth's mind to other bad naughty incidents in her life suggested a breaking of taboos about girls not ever being messy with the accompanying guilt and glee. 'Our pollution behaviour is the reaction which condemns any object or idea likely to confuse or contradict cherished classifications' (Douglas 1984:36). In our society we seem to have an external system of ordering and stereotyping where innocent, pure, clean, little girls become messy, menstruating, emotional, women after puberty and messy, grubby, little boys become clean, logically-thinking men after puberty, presumably a reflection of our patterns of sexuality. One anomalous role is that of the artist, the bohemian, at home with disorder. Traditionally, the male is more acceptable in this role, as a female artist challenges notions of devotion to children, a woman's sphere of creativity. Entering the unruly world of the imagination and the unconscious can allow a wordless exploration. Words are about finalizing an order, or can be, about classification, putting an order to symptoms, the unknown. Art can be a way of exploring pre-conceptual experiencing. It is more at home with the unformed.

Artists, men and women, explore the interstices in our structuring of society. Putting words to experience in art therapy is always a delicate affair, naming can be painful. Bringing experience out of the play between imagination and reality and setting it firmly in the present, it can bring the pain home. It can also limit exploration as well as extending it.

There can be thoughts which have never been put into words. Once words have been framed the thought is changed and limited by the very words selected. So the speech has created something, a thought which might not have been the same.

(Douglas 1984:64)

The messy sessions that followed with Ruth were to be largely wordless. Douglas again, referring to dirt: 'In its last phase then, dirt shows itself as an apt symbol of creative formlessness' (1984:160). To make the messy child she felt inside real on the outside was both to break a social norm about little girls and also to break with what she had learnt to hide from her mother. In being an 'adult' with mother she kept her safe from seeing the neediness inside and her mother from identifying her own unmet needs, i.e. 'I'm not able to love my children because I've never been loved myself'. Ruth's first flat statement, an intensity of repressed emotion, almost like a riddle, 'My mother would like to see me like this', is both saying that her mother would not like to, but also that Ruth would like her to see her like this. In the session rather than making an 'embodied image', her own body had *become* the image, following her attraction to Jill's mixture.

The following session Ruth was keen to do some more messy paintings with Susie and Jill but all three felt a social pressure from the other children, particularly expressed by Jill's older brother. 'It's wrong to make a mess'. Disorder is experienced as destructive, as it is to patterns, but it also has potentiality. There was disapproval about this activity possibly because it awakened chaotic feelings or because 'their' art therapy room/therapist might be despoiled in some way. There is a difference here between working in a residential setting and children coming to a centre for therapy, because there is a culture and the children will have a standard of acceptable behaviour invisibly negotiated. Messiness is disturbing, 'it symbolises both danger and power' (Douglas 1984:94).

The three therefore set up their own rules and procedure on this occasion, after discussion. They would have a long strip of paper on the floor as before, two sections of paper each, but would not get messy themselves. A long strip of six quite messy but self-contained paintings resulted with very individual characteristics. Susie worked in a sandy, muddy brown covering the paper evenly, both sections split nearly completely across, one with a dark circle imprinted. They have an even, washed-out quality, feeling torn, split, and discarded. Jill worked with the clearest sense of form emerging from darkness, black background with a star drawn by finger, like a spark of consciousness at the centre. Her sadness, through bereavement, was of a different quality from the neediness and emptiness of the other two girls. Ruth worked mixing all colours, to all black, then started on top again, all colours, mixed in to all black, sprinkling powder paint on directly. They ended as black circular swirls with traces of colour, all contained in the picture frames.

'Not open yet'

In a clean session Ruth began a tight pattern in felt-tips of tiny flowers, then leaving it as if in some old style, not needed any longer, took a fresh sheet of paper and painted a large purple flower, adding red/purple handprints around it. She said of it, 'It's not open yet'. Turning to the blackboard she began chalking 'queens' as she had often before and began a flood of questions to me about myself. 'Did I live at the Centre, too?', 'Where did I live?', 'Was I naughty, bad too, to be sent here?', etc. She ended by saying that she would like to go home, then, that 'it didn't matter'. These questions were both about discerning difference and about exploring my structures of support. Also did I accept a naughty bad side? She then chalked a 'queen' on a piece of grey paper, the same colours and schema as all her previous blackboard images. There was a sense of the possibility of her renewed growth. She had transferred some of the fluidity of the messy sessions and been able to apply it to a finished image of the flower and handprints. She had also moved from the impermanence of the blackboard to paper, and the queen was a ruling image, perhaps of consciousness, perhaps also reflecting our relationship which had been acknowledged through the questions, attempting to 'see' clearly what we were about together. She was able to express, though quickly deny, a wish to go home.

The third messy session took place with Ruth working in a group of children, she alone wanting to be messy. She painted all black, round and round, using her hands, then adding powder colours 'all colours', alternating. Talking to me and herself as she did so, round and round like a spiral, 'getting blacker, getting blacker – going bright – going bright, all colours', she got fairly messy herself but could be cleaned up at the sink. She really enjoyed this rhythmical interchange, moving in and out, messy, until the paper practically disintegrated. Left to reach its own natural ending it was clear that the purpose of this was in the process of experiencing, not in the final product or in her own state of being messy which was incidental. This physical experience with paint and paper, rhythmically being joined to the painting, I have also witnessed with adults in art therapy who have made connections to difficult birth experience and the re-living of sensations of being inside contractions.

Cinderella, slime and hide-and-seek

It became clearer that these sessions had taken on a particular significance for Ruth who began to beg to be allowed to come into the therapy room at other times saying, 'I must be messy'. As it was disturbing to children wanting to work cleanly and no one else wanted to share this experience, the fourth and fifth sessions were individual ones. I suggested that a swimsuit might make it less necessary to worry about clothes, so she came in, changed, but then stood saying she felt lonely 'on her own'. She started a painting, all black, all colours, all black alternating. Next she decided to paint her face, all different colours in turn and then made a paint paste. She smothered this over her face, crying like a baby, like a baby being fed, sort of slobbering. This was very intense, and then it suddenly eased as she discovered movement on the paper paint floor and started sliding. There was a need to make it slimy, to find the right consistency. A lot of experimentation ended with a flood before it was time to end and have a bath.

The fifth session began with her dressed in all her clothes because she thought she might like to have a clean one after all. It soon turned into a messy session. She put paints on the floor and painted blue paper black, poured on water, sprinkled colours on. She said, 'it was too slow' and used her hands to spread it all over, off on to the floor. Shoes and socks gradually came off and some clothes. Possibly the taking off of the clothes, rather than beginning in a swimsuit, allowed her time to be involved, to regress gradually. Much sliding followed. The exact consistency was very important, a certain amount of movement for fingers and feet, more water, more paint. She wanted my hands to be painted too, feeling this was very funny, a blurring of boundaries as I became symbolically messy. She said that some marks on the paper reminded her of a painting her brother who is 4 years old would do, so I was wondering if we had reached this stage of development. Talk turned to fairy stories, how much she liked them. I read them on request during sessions and her favourite was Cinderella. She said how she had never heard them before, never had them read to her.

She asked if she could put her handprints on the wall and chose a spot. All the time we both had to keep our hands slimy, that is 'wet look', they must not be allowed to dry. She repeated how she 'had to be messy'. She said she wanted to play a trick on me, I must not look. She then hid herself in the room while I shut my eyes and I had to find her. I looked and looked and really thought she might have gone out of the room, perhaps out of the window. I finally found her in the cupboard where the tins of powder paint were kept, in a very small space, perhaps 18 inches to 2 feet high, on a shelf. The was repeated and repeated with lots of laughter on her being found. Finally she tore up the blue paper painting and scattered the torn fragments all over the room. We cleared up and it was time for a bath.

Each session refers back to the one before in form and content but also new developments emerge. Within the structure from messy art therapy room to bath and clean change, there is an exploration of emotions and body/ psychic experience. The role of the therapist is to contain a structure around the movements made, trying to support emerging forms and to reflect on the process that is happening. The hide-and-seek play expresses a need to be lost and found, with echoes of her running away before coming into care. It feels as if this is a successful experience as the room and therapist are able to contain the torn fragments at the end of the session without anxiety. She is content to leave them with me, a chaos of parts. She seemed to be semi-aware of herself emerging, very confident about the messy sessions despite some disapproval from children at the Centre. She wanted stories, Cinderella particularly, to be told, perhaps in reassurance of a positive outcome. It felt as if she was gaining bright eyes, a sense of a living self.

When working with children there is quite often an association of different mediums to bodily products, perhaps particularly clay to shit. There were different levels to Ruth's slime-making. It was both a breaking of taboos about what little girls are allowed to be, 'a social image' which allowed her internal messiness to be expressed, but also a re-enactment of early experiences partly ritualized through the structure of the sessions. There is also a way in which psychic experience was felt or expressed through matter, i.e. the need to find the exact consistency of material sensations around her. There is a difference between the making of slimy paintings and covering oneself in slime, both originally made from a mixture of black and all colours. It seems as if the latter is 'becoming the slime' and giving life to it. Movement is important here, to be able to slide in it, to be at one with it.

James Hillman discusses mud and diarrhoea in *The Dream and the Underworld*. He talks of them in terms of a description of the underworld 'as a realm of mushy or fecal matter' (Hillman 1979:183). Comparing the labyrinthine tract of the bowels to an interiorized underworld, Ruth is able to enter the underworld of unconscious feelings through immersion in slime. 'An underworld that has come to sudden and irrepressible life' (ibid.: 184) is compelling; 'I have to be messy'. The making of mud mixtures is very powerful, as if water and earth hold the secret of nature from which life will come. Other amateur alchemists in the art therapy room make primeval mixtures but usually in jars. For instance, it is not uncommon for them to go around the room collecting a tiny piece of each substance they find in a jar, to fill it with water and to place in on a window-sill, waiting for the sun to activate 'the life within'. Ruth seemed to be facing the other way, looking for the secrets of life inside her slime-covered self rather than being a scientist in charge of an experiment. She was an artist experimenting with forms of internal products, however crude at this stage.

'The mirror crack'd from side to side
"the curse is come upon me" cried
the Lady of Shalott'
                    (Tennyson)

By request, Ruth, Susie, and Jill came for an afternoon 'messy session'. All in swimsuits, they put paint and paper on the floor and mixed it up. Paper was laid on it and some work began. Jill, then later Susie, soon came out, washing their feet. Ruth put red paint on as lipstick and asked for a mirror. Looking at her reflection, she somehow slipped, fell, and broke it. She was extremely upset and kept repeating over again, 'Seven years' bad luck', a superstitious belief generally thought to originate from the idea of a man's soul being reflected in a mirror. She sat playing dejectedly with paint on her toes.

It was hard to offer a useful intervention because of the complexity of meanings around this broken self-image. Ruth responded on a conscious level to the superstition of the curse of seven years' bad luck but the 'accident' was probably an unconscious reaction to what the mirror itself had brought into the room. It seemed as if something from outside had come into the room, a previously safe, protected space. As the mirror is such a diverse symbol, it was possible to understand this in several ways. One, that the mirror brought external reality into the room, in contrast to the acceptance and reflection that Ruth was receiving from the therapist's eyes; the mirror as a critical eye, of conscience, of society, disapproving of mess, make-up. Or, that the mirror showed an inward depth, the cracked self-image underlying the surface made-up image. If, as Freud suggests, the uncanny is really the secretly familiar, the repressed, then the feelings behind the breaking of the mirror must be contact with a 'broken' self-image which is familiar at an unconscious level (Freud 1919:219–52).

We have discussed earlier in the chapter the ideal mirroring that takes place between mother and child, the 'timeless' mirroring relationship with the mother' which Lacan (1977) describes. This also reflects the experience the therapist can give, of acceptance of the messy, unacceptable parts of the self, working to understand and integrate them. Before the entry of the mirror there had been a certain timelessness, and imaginary area in which play could take place, an unconscious working. The breaking of the mirror brought a harsh sense of the present time to the room, moving out of the imaginary into reality. A further facet may be that we had begun to weave a fragile sense of self which could be easily shattered.

The play with paint make-up has the innocence of children trying out their mothers' make-up, but is also a sign that girls will be women in the future where make-up has associations with sexuality and moral ambiguity. Make-up is almost a sign to the world that one is ready for flirtation. The painted image is perhaps the gap between what we would like to be and reality and also between our natural selves and what society demands of us. There is a suggestion that women need to be seen as the desirable object in male/female relationships. This is also what babies need to be seen as by their mothers. Feminist psychology suggests that because of problems of identification, women may never receive this from their mothers, whereas men may have experienced being the 'gleam in a mother's eye'. The mirror and make-up have powerful resonances of women's psychology and of fragility. There is a sense of the mirror being potentially more reliable than the eyes of another. It is written of Helena Rubinstein and Elizabeth Arden that:

> They created an image of beauty that was
> framed by the mirror instead of lit by the
> eyes of the beholder.
> (Quoted in Wilson 1985:110)

In her play with paint make-up Ruth may have experienced a premature 'adult' reflection, of a sophisticated self, a threshold she was not ready to cross. One could perceive her as asking to look into 'my mirror', that of the adult woman therapist, for which she is not yet ready. Looking into a mirror the observer perceives the image as if it were inside the mirror. 'The mirror as the moment when the reflected ego changes to social ego is a "structural crossroads" or, as we were saying before, a threshold phenomenon' (Eco 1984:203). One further thought will not exhaust the possible meanings in this 'accident'. The double image also represents Ruth, the looker and the mirror-image the internalized mother image:

> The experience is one in which the looker is also looked at. Yet, the looker experiences the image in the mirror as 'me' and yet 'not me'. It represents, I believe, a revival of experiences that the person must have had in the separation–individuation phase of development.
>
> (Fiegelson 1975:352)

Following the breaking of the mirror Ruth decided to have a bath early and to come back to my room, 'to sleep on my desk'. In the bath, all three girls lay flat together, pretending to be asleep. Ruth, when she got out, wanted to stay in a ball on the floor. Arriving back at the art therapy room, she made a bed from paper and old bits of material, settling under my desk. Then, she found she could not sleep, 'she had been so tired'. She ran up and down the room trying to get tired, feeling lost and uncontained. She came to sit by me, half-perched on my lap saying at first, 'She didn't like laps', then 'that's what mothers do isn't it?'. She got up and chalked on the board, lots of handprints, lots of crowns. She began to wonder where her mother might be, what she might be doing at home, her mother went to bed a lot, she might be there now. She made a new bed with lots of paper and spent the rest of the session curled up in the middle.

The bed-nest brought forcibly to mind the wandering lost part of her, like a tramp bedding down, but also the function of sleep in fairy tales. There the heroine often sleeps in a hollow tree or container, apart from the world. One is neither 'here' nor 'there' but set apart when entering a depression. The incident with the mirror had somehow shattered the omnipotent, contained world of play through the unconscious but may have brought to the fore a potentially growing side of experiencing depression. She was in contact with the lost part of herself and of her mother, but outside the world of action. It could be seen as regressing but with sleep also necessary for recovery and for renewed strength.

Bathing and beds

In the following 'clean' session Ruth made two black slimy paintings. She mixed very thick paint, making patterns in it with her fingers, adding coloured crepe paper. It was gradually mixed in with the black slime till it became a curved little foetus-shaped lump at the centre, an intense black on black. The second picture, ending as black slime, originally had colours beneath and was left with her initials clearly marked out on the surface. These felt very depressed pictures, like two most basic signs that would give her an identity from the blackness surrounding her.

Ruth appeared a few days later with Steven, a boy of 9, at the Centre, both asking if they could have a messy session together. After they had changed they started to paint make-up paint on themselves carefully. Ruth put on red paint 'lipstick' and then was very concerned to get it off. She separated black and white paint from the colours which she mixed together on the floor, placing a large bowl of water in the middle. She pretended to swim, lying across it, much splashing and laughter. At bathtime she washed in the hot water talking about her mother. 'I worry because I think she might be dead, I imagine it'. 'Because she might be lost, she might not find her way home'. She then went into a long description of the way from the Centre to her home. 'Did I think she had got home alright?' Both children came back to the art therapy room to continue working after their bath.

Ruth decided to paint a picture. She was very sad and depressed while she did it. It was of a house, sky and building lit up with flowing red paint, as if ablaze, in black crayon and red and white wash (*Plate 27*). There is a tree to one side which is almost washed out by the paint and a formless person on the left, featureless, head, hair and lines for a body which go straight to the bottom of the page. It feels both depressed and angry, on fire. From the elation of swimming before the bath, of pleasure in movement, there is a despondent reflection which she is unable to talk about. She then made a heart-shaped red felt pin-cushion and last, before the end of the session painted white a pebble which she had picked up from the grounds on the way back from the bath.

In the sessions a pattern has emerged, which alters and progresses. There is a contact with cold blackish slime and then a move to immersion in hot clean water. In the frame of the hot bath it feels as if the emotional content of the sessions can be verbalized, present worries, fears, and probably anger emerging at her sense of being lost and abandoned. Bathing is cleansing, releasing 'mother thoughts'. This last time she was able to give these thoughts about home and mother a concrete representation in the picture afterwards. The red heart is an ambivalent image, a heart for sticking pins in. The white pebble is like a talisman to hold on to.

Marie von Franz writes about bathing and cursing in *Redemption Motifs in Fairy Tales* (1980). In fairy tales, redemption refers specifically to a condition where someone has been bewitched or cursed and, through certain work in the story, is redeemed. Cursing is seen as a projection of a shadow part on to another person who takes it in, projective identification; it does not actually belong to the cursed person. Here, one might look upon the rejected child as cursed by parent(s), the recipient of projections of unacknowledged feelings in the family. In Ruth's case, this could be understood as the mother's own hurt, wounded child projected on to her.

A week or so later Ruth and Susie asked to have a messy session together. Both girls changed and then Susie took over the leadership for the first time. Water was poured on to the floor and Ruth was ordered to pour it into cardboard boxes. Both made paintings with powder-paint on top of sponges. There was rivalry as to whose paintings were best, both saying in sing-song voices, 'Nobody knows what I'm doing'. Ruth tried to use paper to make a picture while sitting in the minor flood, but this disintegrated. We found pieces of flat wood from the wood pile that would be more hardy. These were carefully chosen for each one and sprinkled on in place. A gentle shake dissolved them into the black background, starburst shapes. She was very anxious about each one, about being able to keep them, would they survive, could they come to the house with her? A lot of gentle singing, a lot of anxiety for her productions. There was a sense of pride in achievement and control of the media.

During bathtime, Ruth was asking me a lot of questions again, 'Will your mother hit you when you go home?', 'Does your mother do that?', 'Where do you live?', 'Do you live alone?'. In answering her questions this time, I acknowledged the strong underlying current of a fantasy of coming home with me, a very painful issue which arises particularly when working with children in care. For the therapist working with children of the same gender, empathy, identification, and counter-transference need to be carefully negotiated. All inform aspects of the work and can aid the drawing of necessary boundaries of role and function as well as blurring distinctions. After the bath, both girls decided to make beds in tea chests in the art therapy room. These were lined, like nests, with paper and material. Ruth continually hopped out to look at the pieces of sponge, wood, and card drying. All the rest of the day she came to the door or into the room, interrupting other sessions, to look at them, very anxious that they were there and surviving.

In the last two sessions the emphasis has moved away from 'being the slime' to being almost clean; swimming in the bowl, above the colours, making objects. This session, she might be seen to be a stage further in control of her creations. The slime, now clean, has separated into parts of black and all colours, crystallized into objects to keep from the session. The focus has shifted from her own person to the imbued objects. Now the time for slime has finished it can be seen to have been an ambiguous substance, representing an attempt to individualize out from the original substance. It has a consistency which could symbolize the psychic process of separation from mother.

Sartre, in his fascinating enquiry into the psychoanalysis of things, has a special discussion on slime. Slime is in the process of dissolving and in the process of solidification, this is its ambiguity and why it is disturbing. It might become a useful medium for exploring issues of separation because of its peculiar characteristics. 'Actually we have here the image of destruction-creation' (Sartre 1966:608). Slime and water played an important role for Ruth in aiding both non-verbal and verbal exploration of relationships and identity. Something of their relationship might be expressed in Sartre's work.

> Slime is the agony of water. It presents itself as a phenomenon in process of becoming; it does not have the permanence within change that water has but on the contrary represents an accomplished break in the change of state. . . . Nothing testifies more clearly to its ambiguous character as a 'structure in between two states' than the slowness with which slime melts into itself.
>
> (Sartre 1966:607)

Cyclops and swans

Sandplay became the main focus of two sessions with the theme of hiding small objects for each other to find. This hide-and-seek play variant, a play of trying to locate lost feeling has been discussed elsewhere (Case 1986). During this phase Ruth's interest in fairy tales had moved from Cinderella to three stories expressing aspects of the same motif, *The Six Swans*, *The Twelve Brothers*, and *The Seven Ravens*. In the stories a number of brothers are turned into swans or ravens and a single sister has to work to make reparation before they can be redeemed. Ruth spent one session making six swans out of plasticine with a lot of accompanying talk of how she missed her youngest brother of 4. She phoned him nearly every night. The swans were achieved with some difficulty, help was needed to form the bodies, all made of white, red, yellow, and blue colours.

The last messy session, the ninth, came out of a clean session with a group of girls, including Susie. One of the girls was telling and painting a story of a spaceman coming to earth. Ruth painted her family as spacemen; all are white in spacesuits except herself who is suitless in black. They meet a human and they all get killed. She painted them lying down dead. Then she said, 'They've just fainted. They walk home'. She next painted a large monster, hair all over his face, big teeth, and with three eyes, one in the middle of his forehead. Then she started talking. 'He is *so* angry, he puts paint all over him'. She does so.

Me: Why is he angry
Ruth: Someone has stolen his *sheep*. And he is *so angry*. [She adds colours whirls them all over the paper using both ends of the brush.] And then someone steals his *sheep*. [Lots of emphasis.] He is *black* with anger. He pours paint all over him.

The paper gradually rips and disintegrates.

She starts again, a new piece of paper. Wilder this time. Paint is going on the floor, all over the table, she is scratching at marks through the paint. A second, long, involved tale follows about the giant and his sheep. The giant eats humans trying to steal his sheep (this mainly follows the tale of Cyclops and Ulysses). In the story all the sheep are stolen except for his favourite sheep. His favourite sheep is a boy. Then the favourite is a caterpillar. Because he is the giant's favourite he only has one of his legs eaten. Then anxiously, 'caterpillars have lots of legs don't they', pause, 'five thousand'. The story ends with everyone getting thrown into a river. The river swirls around the table, she *is* the destructive river, off the table top and on to the floor. It is the end of the session.

In the Cyclops story anger at the separation from her family comes through strongly. She is able, through the giant's actions, to express anger and punishment for the loss, separation, and rejection. She punishes the family for leaving her, through the sheep that are punished for being stolen and the humans for stealing them. Her identification is with the uncontrolled destructive anger which destroys even the giant. The river washes all away. Only her younger brother about whom she had previously expressed concern, in the making of the six swans, is saved in the form of a caterpillar, just slightly damaged. Cyclops, born from Mother Earth and Father Heaven, does not have the usual significance of the third inner or spiritual eye but appears to symbolize the primary forces of nature (Cirlot 1962). There are no products at the end of this session. The final river of destruction completely disintegrated the paper but its flow has brought out ambivalent feelings about the family that were previously hidden in the sand tray and expressed in a more tender form through the making of the six gentle swans.

Three days later I was walking in the grounds at lunchtime and was joined by Ruth and Steven. Ruth decided to tell a fairy story about a Swan Princess. The story was a condensation of *The Twelve Brothers*, *The Seven Ravens* and *The Six Swans*, or which various versions were told. It expressed as a main image a beautiful velvet-clad princess with loving brothers around her, albeit in the form of swans, not humans, as if in this way love could be expressed by their mute presence. A wish to be important in the family and at its centre contrasted with reality. Contact with Ruth's family was becoming less frequent and it seemed less and less likely that a rejoining of her to the family group could take place, despite all the work in progress to achieve this end. It was now being suggested at assessment meetings that a placement in a small children's home for children lacking early mothering experience would be the most positive outcome. These future changes were being discussed with Ruth. Looking ahead, we had 5 weeks now until Christmas which would be a painful, difficult break and some uncertainty about when a place would be available at the children's home.

Queen of hearts

An extraordinary prolific session took place a week after the Cyclops story. Ruth began by painting a 'seasonal' picture of Father Christmas (*Plate 32*). He walks along laden down by sacks at the bottom of the brown paper. It is snowing heavily. The picture suggests the awful weight of depression that can be felt in institutions before these traditional family occasions. This was put on one side, and a second picture constructed, of a 'Dark lady from Egypt or India (*Plate 28*). Brown paper is again selected and raffia for her hair. She has three eyes, one in the middle of her forehead.

The next two pictures are both made by crayon and wash techniques. In the first, a vivid row of mountain peaks rises out of the sea, coloured brightly, with a powerful sun and moon (*Plate 29*). The second is of 'The Queen of Hearts' (*Plate 30*). She is in stark contrast to the 'Dark Lady', pale, almost pasty-faced, with blonde hair. Her crown does not have the base and form of the original blackboard queens, but a row of 'mountain peaks' across her head. There is a large orange sun and four tarts laid on a table. She looks sideways as if aware that they might be stolen. These pictures were all made with Ruth sitting beside me, with little comment, except for a title and a few words of explanation. We were nearly at the end of the session and I moved away to assist other children to look after their work. The fifth painting was on a small piece of white card, again in crayon and purple wash, of mountain peaks, a turbulent sea, and a sun. She was frantic not to have to go at the end of the session and began to attempt to lengthen it by pouring water over the card, over the desk, which descended to the floor as the river had done in the Cyclops session previously. She scratched angrily at the mountain peaks with the handle of the paintbrush, marking and mutilating them.

Several themes link across the last two sessions. The 'Father Christmas' painting felt like an initial attempt to 'fit in' to the beginning of a festive season, but the weight of the sacks showed the emotional load that the figure has to carry. The 'Dark Lady' symbolizes an ancient image of the cycle of creation–conservation–destruction, of Shiva. It is both a reference to, but a move forward from the Cyclops where the emphasis is on destruction, the end of a cycle, rather than a sense of renewal being possible. As a female image it feels more owned by Ruth.

The mountains, an extremely confident picture with a good technical use of the medium, is a powerful image. As a barrier they both give a sense of impossible heights to overcome, and have a loftiness of existence, above the ordinary world. There is a link between the purple wash over them and the purple sacks of Father Christmas. In the sequence of paintings they have a sense of being 'tips of the iceberg', standing out from the sea, because, in the next painting they have risen up on the Queen's head, or she has pushed them up from below as her crown. 'The Queen of Hearts' has a connection taking us back to the very first painting of the 'Pattern of the Heart' and the 'Heart Pin-Cushion'. She is also a feminine side of the Cyclops in that she too has her 'good objects', her tarts, stolen. The two images of 'Dark Lady' and pale 'Queen of Hearts' stand as archetypes of female experience, the ability to creatively make 'good objects', and the possibility of destruction and loss. 'The Queen of Hearts' feels conscious, wary of this world, and the 'Dark Lady' with her inner looking eye, otherworldly, both spiritual and unconscious. In the last mountain picture on the card there is anger and loss expressed to me at the end of the session, but it is also reminiscent of the scratching-out of the family and the destruction by flood of the previous session. This gives the peaks a further resonance of the resistant family who will not give to Ruth, give way, or allow her in.

From the beginning, with the first chalked queens and crowns, there has been a play between omnipotence and queens. There is a dual sense here of mothers being queens of hearts, experienced internally as all-giving or all-destructive and of Ruth's own sense of creativity and destruction. Omnipotence, the illusion of independence, is one defence against rejection. The five pictures stand as different parts of her and her experience during this period of transition; and also of our relationship as I am experienced as giving or withholding.

Ending

In this section, which marks the end of my work with Ruth and the end of the chapter, all the difficulties of finishing arise. How can one find a form for reflection within which both present loss and a future can be contemplated? The sessions were characterized by many different activities and attempts at making – some unfinished – and reflecting a range of emotions. Four themes have been selected which run through the last four weeks, until the Christmas break:

Sticking

The whole of this time was characterized by Ruth feeling stuck to me. She did not want the sessions to end, though this feeling was now no longer frantic but expressed in a depressed, sad way. She used an enormous amount of glue during these weeks. Pictures were attempted with ready-made sticky shapes, chaotically arranged on the paper, interspersed with flat, black paintings, completely featureless. There was a sense of formlessness, just sticking shapes anywhere, often accompanied by worries about and for her mother. 'She hasn't phoned', 'She might be dead'. A more manic form of these paintings was of black backgrounds mixed with an adhesive medium and colours sprayed or flicked on to them, also they were all mixed with glue, finally the whole surface was covered with layers of more transparent glue when it dried. The result was a shiny painting, unnaturally bright and fixed. Tearing, sticking, painting, and glueing also took place.

There was a saddening sense in these activities of sticking together, of being stuck in depression, and of putting a skin over fragmented pieces. A much earlier session, where torn fragments had been scattered round the room had had a partly joyful feel of a breaking down to make ready for a new formulation. Here, there was a powerful patching process going on. During this time of fragmentation and glueing, Ruth was often literally sticking to my side; feeling small, depressed, and lonely with the lack of support from her family. The term 'adhesive identification' has been developed by Esther Bick and described by Meltzer (1975) in relation to autistic children who tend to relate to the surface qualities of people, there is no sense of depth as the children have had no previous experience of containment or holding. Extreme anxiety also produces a desperate clinging to a surface, sometimes to the therapist, or the radiator, which is a basic need for warmth, giving the child security.

Merging

A second development was requests and then ordered commands for us to paint paintings together. There had been a previous phase of it being essential for me to have messy hands while in the messy sessions which had denied my separateness and boundaries, but this had been quite brief. Now, we had to paint exactly the same shapes on the picture surfaces, abstract shapes, usually rounded, and each had to be the same number and colour. Then a piece of tape was attached to the top and the bottom of the picture. At the top, 'By Ruth —', and at the bottom, 'By Caroline Case'. This merger on the picture was about a denial of our difference, a wish to return to a symbiotic relationship. These sessions were accompanied by pleasurable, even triumphant feelings, 'Nobody would know whose paintings they were!' Interestingly it was expressed in a symbolic way, not by regression to behaving like a younger child, but almost like an equal sharing, except that I was following orders.

Good and Bad

The Christmas season gave form to a different expression of parts of herself. Ruth began by showing me how they had made cards with angels on in the classroom and from this there developed several paintings of Yellow Angels and Red Devils. These too were interspersed with black, shapeless paintings and were sad, whiny, depressed sessions. The Yellow Angels and Red Devils seemed a more judgemental and punishing expression of 'goodness' and 'badness'. The more archaic images of Cyclops, the 'Dark Lady' and 'The Queen of Hearts', were able to tolerate creativity, rage, anger, and destruction. The Angels and Devils seemed a more dualistic representation, black or white, perfection or badness, with no room for acceptance of less desirable feelings within one.

Separation

In the last week of term Ruth again asked me to paint with her but this time to do separate paintings and she would choose the subjects. The subjects reflect and echo the conversation which concerned what we would be doing while we were apart.

(a) Our parents' house: Her parents' house has a protective rainbow above it, a sun, birds, and a tree with broken-off branches beside it.

(b) Our family members: The family scene is her step-father and brothers playing on one side of the picture. A large cooking stove divides her and her mother from them. Her mother is cooking. No one has facial features but she is able to draw each person roughly in paint.

(c) Ourselves: Her realistic self-image is extremely accurate, her own expression, thick hair, and freckles. She is painted all in shades of brown and auburn with orangey-red lips.

(d) Our own choice: Her choice is a pattern. A circle is divided by a cross, four black blobs at the centre, eight orangey-red ones round the circle. Waves and curves, at the edge, in browns and auburns reflect exactly the colours in the self-portrait. In the pictures we have before us there is a sense of separate identities, but shared experience, a statement of difference and the coming parting (*Plate 33*).

The last day of term, she ran into the room, grabbed some paper, which she painted, roughly, yellow. She scattered a handful of sand over it and placed a few animals in the desert. This was to remain intact until my return after the holiday; which it did, bridging and surviving the separation.

Last session

In January, the first session in the first week of term was to be our last session together at the Centre, a far from ideal arrangement, prompted by sudden changes at the Children's Home making a place available. Ruth came in and we talked about the new home which she had been visiting over the holiday. She checked to see if the animals were still on the yellow paper and then decided to paint. The picture had green grass, a yellow sun and roughly painted blue sky, like rain. It was left unfinished. Her thoughts turned to houses. The doll's house was explored and then she began to make a house from cardboard boxes to take away. All the structure was made and painted and it was ready for things to be added to the inside. Finally, she chalked a figure on the blackboard asking me to keep it there always. It was of a baby with ribs showing, a heart and a belly button. It had hooves for hands and feet. It was chalked in white but had eyes the same colour as hers.

The three elements in the last session suggest the position that had been reached. The unfinished painting reflected all the work that still needed to be done. The house returned in theme to the first sessions and the changes that she was again facing. Here, she took with her a structure that hopefully she could add to. The little chalked baby with hooves, heart, and belly button did represent that this 'bad' baby had had recognition and acceptance in art therapy. We had been able to explore the messy side, with the exposed vulnerable heart at the centre.

The need to continue art therapy with rejected children in care like Ruth and Susie was recognized within the Social Services Department and it became possible to establish part-time sessional work at their Children's Home. In this way some continuity was kept for them. This did prove to be a support for them especially over the transition period, while relationships were made with the therapeutic team of houseparents.

At the time of writing, many such posts have depended on good will established between particular members of staff who have recognized and seen the importance of supporting the work. Sadly, they often fail to be replaced as staff change and individuals leave. This will continue, unless it is possible to establish permanent posts for art therapists within the educational and social services.

Figure 8.1 Author's line drawing from blackboard

© 1990 Caroline Case

References

Axline, V. (1947) *Play Therapy*, New York: Ballantine Books.
Bick, E. (1968) 'The experience of the skin in early object relations', *International Journal of Psychoanalysis* 49, pts 2–3: 484–6.
Bion, W.R. (1959) 'Attacks on linking', *International Journal of Psychoanalysis* 40, pts 5–6: 90–1, 102–5.
Bion, W.R. (1962) *Learning from Experience*, London: Heinemann.
Boston, M., and Szur, R. (eds) (1983) *Psychotherapy with Severely Deprived Children*, London: Routledge & Kegan Paul.
Britton, R.S. (1978) 'The deprived child', *The Practitioner* 221, Sept.: 373–8.
Case, C. (1986) 'Hide and seek: a struggle for meaning', in 'Looking at Childhood', *Inscape*, Winter.
Case, C. (1987) 'Loss and transition in art therapy with children', in T. Dalley, C. Case, J. Schaverien, F. Weir, D. Halliday, P. Nowell Hall, and D. Waller, *Images of Art Therapy*, London: Tavistock.
Chodorow, N. (1978) *The Reproduction of Mothering*, Berkeley, Calif.: University of California Press.
Cirlot, J.E. (1962) *A Dictionary of Symbols*, London: Routledge & Kegan Paul.
Douglas, M. (1984) *Purity and Danger*, London: Art Paperbacks.
Eco, U. (1984) *Semiotics and the Philosophy of Language*, London: Macmillan.
Eichenbaum, L. and Orbach, S. (1982) *Outside In, Inside Out*, Harmondsworth: Penguin.
Eichenbaum, L. and Orbach, S. (1987) 'Separation and intimacy: crucial practice issues in working with women in therapy', in S. Ernst and M. Maguire (eds) *Living with the Sphinx*, London: The Women's Press.
Ernst, S. (1987) 'Can a daughter be a woman? Women's identity and psychological separation', in S. Ernst and M. Maguire (eds) *Living with the Sphinx*, London: The Women's Press.
Fiegelson, C. (1975) 'The Mirror Dream', *Psychoanalytical Study of the Child* 30: 341–55.
Franz, M. von (1980) *Redemption Motifs in Fairy Tales*, Toronto: Inner City Books.
Freud, S. (1919) *The Uncanny*, Standard Edition XVII, London: The Hogarth Press.
Grimm's Tales for Young and Old. The Complete Stories (1978) trans. Ralph Manheim, London: Victor Gollancz.
Henry, G. (1983) 'Difficulties about thinking and learning', in M. Boston and R. Szur (eds) *Psychotherapy with Severely Deprived Children*, London: Routledge & Kegan Paul.
Hillman, J. (1979) *The Dream and the Underworld*, New York: Harper & Row.
Holmes, E. (1977) 'The educational needs of children in care', *Concern* 26: 22–5.
Klein, M. (1940) 'Mourning and its relation to manic-depressive states', *Contributions to Psychoanalysis*, London: Hogarth Press.
Klein, M. (1957) *Envy and Gratitude*, London: Tavistock.
Klein, M. (1975) *Collected Works Vol. I: The Importance of Symbol Formation in the Developing Ego*, London: Hogarth Press.
Lacan, J. (1977) *The Four Fundamental Concepts of Psycho-analysis*, London: Hogarth Press.
Mahler, M. (1968) *On Human Symbiosis and the Vicissitudes of Individuation*, New York: International University Press.
Meltzer, D. (1975) 'Adhesive identification', *Contemporary Psychoanalysis* 11(3), 289–303.
Parkes, C. (1976) *Bereavement*, Harmondsworth: Penguin.

Pines, M. (1982) 'Reflections on mirroring', *Group Analysis* 15(2) (supplement): 1–26.

Rubin, J. (1978) *Child Art Therapy*, New York: Van Nostrand Reinhold.

Sartre, J.P. (1966) *Being and Nothingness*, trans. Hazel E. Barnes, London: Methuen.

Stott, J. and Males, B. (1984) 'Art therapy for people who are mentally handicapped', in T. Dalley (ed.) *Art as Therapy*, London: Tavistock.

Wilson, E. (1985) *Adorned in Dreams*, London: Virago (quotes A. Lewis and C. Wordsworth, Miss Elizabeth Arden, W.H. Allen, 1973).

Winnicott, D. (1965) *The Maturational Process and the Facilitating Environment*, London: Hogarth Press and the Institute of Psychoanalysis.

Winnicott, D. (1971) *Playing and Reality*, Harmondsworth: Penguin.

Wolkind, S.N. (1977) 'Women who have been in care: psychological and social status during pregnancy', *Journal of Child Psychology and Psychiatry* 18(2): 179–82.

Wolkind, S.N., Hall, F., and Pawlby, S. (1977) 'Individual differences in mothering behaviour: a combined epidemiological and observational approach', in P.J. Graham (ed.) *Epidemiological Approaches in Child Psychiatry*, London: Academic Press.

Wolkind, S.N. and Rutter, M. (1973) 'Children who have been in care', *Journal of Child Psychology and Psychiatry* 14(2): 97–105.

Acknowledgements

First, thanks to Iris O'Brien who helped to create a situation in which art therapy could be made available to children at the Assessment Centre. Second, thanks to Nick Cocks and David Punter who have helped to make possible my writing of the work described.

Chapter nine

Images and integration: art therapy in a multi-cultural school
Tessa Dalley

'Both therapists and teachers are ultimately ''enablers'' – they can do no more than harness a child's own capacity for discovery, mental growth and change. Psychodynamic theory has made an important contribution in affirming whether in healing or in education it is ultimately the agent, the child, who can bring about change for himself' (Reeves 1983:27).

Introduction

This paper is divided into two parts. First, it will examine how the practice of art therapy can offer a valuable resource in the special needs area of mainstream education. Where art therapy is established in schools, it can been seen to benefit those children who have particular emotional or behavioural difficulties and whose special needs cannot be met in the classroom. Various models of working with children in art therapy have been put forward in the relevant literature and in this book (Case 1987, Dalley 1987, Halliday 1987, Kramer 1979, Rubin 1978, and Wood 1984). The argument for using art therapy in schools will be based on my experience of working as an art therapist in an inner city primary school. By considering briefly the educational debate surrounding the idea of integration of children with special needs into mainstream education, the role of art therapy as a central means of working with the child's emotional needs to help the achievement of learning potential is stressed.

The second part will specifically consider the issues that arise when working in art therapy with children from different ethnic minorities, in particular children of Afro-Caribbean origin. The school in which I work has a high proportion of non-white children, the majority of whom are black, and some of them feel doubly isolated, lacking in self-esteem, and are 'underachieving' at school. Inter-cultural psychotherapy has recently been given more attention and the interest has important implications in terms of addressing racism, prejudice, and the experience of racial difference. This paper will attempt to examine the many complex issues that are encountered when working in art

161

therapy with these children and how images are used to communicate their experience.

Integration of children with special needs into mainstream education

In 1944, children were given the right to compulsory secondary education and eleven categories of special education were laid down. The 1981 Education Act followed the *Warnock Report's* recommendations to integrate children with special educational needs into mainstream schools. This follows from their view that

> the form of special educational provision that a child requires is not necessarily conditioned by his disability alone, but should reflect a full assessment of his individual needs . . .
>
> Special educational provision, in whatever shape, will only be effective if informed by an accurate assessment of all the factors – physical, mental and emotional – which condition a child's performance.
>
> (HMSO 1981:112)

These radical ideas have been slow in being implemented as responses from the local authorities have varied greatly. The onus, it seem, has fallen on the teachers to accept these changes but their job, as perceived by most parents and society as a whole, is to adhere to the curriculum and help children through the educational milestones of the examination system. This will be further exacerbated if the recent *Baker Recommendations*, which propose more frequent and rigorous examination procedures, reach the statute books. Their close daily contact with children means that teachers can readily identify individual needs and concerns of their pupils, and in many ways, when doing their job are forced into the role of friend, ally, mother, father, counsellor, and so on.

Without additional qualified staff it is difficult to see how the Warnock ideas can succeed. Her proposals necessitate some inclusion into the system of more specialist staff who can help those children in need of individual time, attention, help, and indeed therapy. This applies particularly to those children coming from special schools, and also helps to maintain those 'statemented' children in ordinary schools. There is increasing support for this argument as can be seen by recent literature which addresses many aspects of problems surrounding educational integration (Goacher *et al.* 1988 and Mittler 1988).

Recognizing these different factors, and working with the whole child alongside other children, regardless of ability, difficulty, or handicap, presents a radical concept and a daunting challenge for educators. Some of these changes in educational thinking were reflected in the 1960s with the publication of the *Plowden Report on Children in their Primary Schools* (1967:48). The basic philosophy was one of controlled progressivism and its most far reaching contribution was in connection with the relationship between the primary school and the home and the social background. It recalled that the *Crowther*, *Robbins* and other reports had 'produced evidence that shows how closely associated are social circumstances and academic achievement' and established Educational Priority Areas for which extra funds and resources were designated with the aim to develop ways of establishing closer links between home, school and community.

The many teachers who do so well in the face of adversity cannot manage without cost to themselves. They carry the burdens of parents, probation officers and welfare officers on top of their classroom duties. It is time the nation came to their aid. The principle, already accepted, that special needs calls for special help, should be given a new cutting edge. We ask for "positive discrimination" in favour of such schools and the children in them, going well beyond an attempt to equalize resources. Schools in deprived areas should be given priority in many respects. The first step must be to raise the schools with low standards to the national average; the second, quite deliberately to make them better. The justification is that the homes and neighbourhood from which many of their children come provide little support and stimulus for learning. The schools must supply a compensating environment. The attempts so far made within the educational system to do this have not been sufficiently generous or sustained, because the handicaps imposed by the environment have not been explicitly and sufficiently allowed for. They should be.

(*Plowden Report* 1967:para. 151)

Attempts were thus made to take into account the social environment of the child. Incorporated within this philosophy, the change in emphasis from 'being told' to 'finding out' was an important aspect as it gave emphasis to the less academic features of the junior school programme. These ideas encouraged further research where discrepancy remained between the child's performance and potential in schools. Attempts were made to analyse the complexity of the situation, and to address the problem of how best to educate those children with acute difficulties. Woolf (1969) suggests that behaviour disorders evoke negative responses which causes motivation to drop and success to become more remote. The frustration of educational failure leads to aggressive anti-social behaviour which leads to disapproval of teachers, and it is from this pool of socially and educationally limited and discouraged children that delinquent teenagers come. Woolf maintains that they cannot identify with the adult world from which they see themselves excluded, and so create their own adolescent world.

In this dilemma, we look perhaps over-optimistically, to our education system in the hope that changes in school organisation and teaching techniques can halt the process by which increasing numbers of our children are excluded from the mainstream of society.

(Woolf 1969:172)

Thus the problems of children with emotional difficulties have been in the minds of educationalists for many years. 'What troubles teachers is not so much the varying intellectual capacity of their children, as their varying emotional needs' (Winnicott 1964:206). As early as 1942, Herbert Read wrote, 'One of the most certain lessons of modern psychology and of recent historical experiences, is that education must be a process of individuation, but also of integration, which is the reconciliation of individual uniqueness with social unity' (1942:5).

Professionals working in special education have the greatest experience of teaching children whose emotional difficulties have prevented them from entering mainstream education. Their contribution to the debate regarding integration is invaluable, particularly in their understanding of the term 'maladjustment'. In her paper 'Special educational treatment', Patricia Howlin (1985) outlines the main arguments in favour of integration. First, it avoids the need to classify a child according to a single handicapping condition, thereby affecting teachers' expectancies of attainments and perceptions of individual needs. Second, by allowing the handicapped child to mix with non-handicapped peers, the child should learn appropriate social skills. Third, integration should avoid the stigma of labelling and result in better social adjustment and improved self-esteem. Finally and most important, since the majority of children will ultimately have to be integrated into society, it would seem essential to prepare them for this during their school time. (Howlin 1985:852)

Other writers concentrate on the difficulties and disadvantages of this process which stems from the special problems that these children have (Lubbe 1986, Reynolds 1984). The essence of their argument is that it is assumed that the school is not the causal factor, and the problems of delinquency, deviance, and maladjustment are caused by the pathology that is internal to the child, the family, the neighbourhood, the culture, and thus are individually not institutionally based. 'The aim is to fit the deviant who is malfunctioning into the school system that is assumed to be functioning properly' (Reynolds 1984:16).

David Hargreaves (1981) speaks of the 'cult of the individual' as the greatest obstacle to progress in meeting special educational needs in mainstream schools. He suggests that it is a false premise that professional efforts should be directed at helping the child adjust to the demands of the school. His contention is that the school environment is maladjusted to the needs of the child, and professional efforts should be directed primarily at helping teachers in mainstream schools adjust to the demands imposed by pupils with special needs. The crucial factor of pupil-satisfaction can be understood as one of self-esteem and the so-called disruptive behaviour seen as an attempt to gain some dignity by the development with peers of a 'counter-culture' to that of the school. 'Pupil dissatisfaction does not arise from some intrinsic defect' (Hargreaves 1981:188). He maintains that it develops over a period of time during which pupils are exposed to constant failure and feelings of inadequacy. Many of these children have emotional problems and difficulties at home, but the cause of the dissatisfaction is the combination of these problems and the deficiency of the school environment when it comes to accommodating pupils with special needs. Hargreaves points out that what the children need is the opportunity to express fears and frustrations and since they get little chance to do so, these emotions are expressed behaviourally, then interpreted as 'maladjusted'.

Those who fail in our society are lonely – only anger, frustration, suffering and withdrawal are available which leads to a 'failure identity'.

(Glasser 1969)

Therapy and education

Writing in his preface to Aichorn's *Wayward Youth*, Freud (1925) recalled that there are 'three impossible professions – educating, healing and governing'. In being a teacher and a psychoanalyst, Freud suggested his colleague had taken on two impossible professions. The nature of the relationship between child, school, and home, are central to the child's development, especially in the areas of learning and socialization. Both educator and therapist are aided in their handling of a child by the knowledge of normal developmental processes and stages. Where young children are suffering from delays or distortions in this developmental process, the distinction between therapy and education is to be found in the different ways of using this understanding. 'There is no border at all between education and therapy as far as the usefulness of psychoanalytic theory of childhood development is concerned' (Edgcumbe 1975:133). In her article, 'The border between education and therapy', Rose Edgcumbe distinguishes between the inward-looking process of therapy which may run counter to that of the outward-orientated process of education 'at any rate until therapy has enabled the child's ego to arrive at better adapted compromises between the demands of id, superego and external world, thus feeling the child's capacity to benefit from educational opportunities' (Edgcumbe 1975:134).

She describes how the teacher and therapist make different uses of the capacities of the child. The teacher offers herself as a model with which the child can identify and this positive relationship fosters reward and achievement as success becomes an internalized source of self-esteem and the child moves towards autonomy in areas of functioning. On the other hand, the therapist and child form a therapeutic alliance in which both can work with needs and conflicts, in spite of the temporary loss of self-esteem and increase in anxiety, guilt, shame this process may arouse in the child. One important part of the process is the transference on to the therapist of negative and positive aspects of relationships. Edgcumbe concludes that where a child's ability to profit from educational experience is being interfered with by internalized conflicts, or by distortions in ways of relating which prevent making a predominantly positive and trusting relationship with the teacher, then individual therapy is required. 'Such children require analytic explorations and interpretation of their internal world, in a one-to-one relationship, away from the distractions of the school group' (Edgcumbe 1975:146).

It is clear that problems of learning, behaviour, and emotional development are inter-related in many ways. Many children have missing areas of experience and there are established links between early deprivation and the child's ability to acquire and retain knowledge and particularly the capacity to think. As the school is part of the child's ordinary experience, important in healthy emotional development, there is a persuasive argument for the establishment of a therapy resource in the school environment, as opposed to the more rarified atmosphere of a clinic. But what is the case for school-based therapy?

One interesting study carried out by Kolvin et al. (1981), attempted to clarify some of these issues. The main object of the research was to find ways of developing mental health services in the community, particularly in ordinary schools, in an attempt to counteract the modern society's high incidence of psychological problems. 'Essentially we were concerned with finding ways of identifying maladjusted children in ordinary schools and, more important, evaluating the effectiveness of different types of treatment, administered within the school' (Kolvin et al. 1981:3). The study identifies the normal school as the frame of reference because the school is second only to the home in its potential for influencing child development. The study offered a variety of therapies to 7- and 11-year-old children who had been screened as being maladjusted or at risk from maladjustment: parent–teacher counselling, group therapy, behaviour modification, playgroups, and nurture work. These were compared with each other and with a control group, the subjects being randomly allocated to the different groups. There were a number of home and school-based outcome measures of change. Those interventions that focused skilled attention on the child directly, were found to be most successful and are clearly effective – that is to say behaviour modification, group therapy, and playgroups. One of the most important findings was that the effects of treatment seemed to increase with time, even though active therapy had finished. One explanation was that the immediate result of the therapy was to trigger a more constructive relationship between the child and the school.

These findings suggest that there are complex effects between school and therapist when therapy is conducted in a school setting, and are findings of utmost importance.

It merits urgent replication and further study, since it indicated an effect of conducting therapy in the school which could not possibly be reproduced in clinic based therapy. . . . They should be additionally attractive to health and education administration because of their short-term natures and relatively low costs.

(Nicol 1987:332)

There are several examples in the 1960s and 1970s where the idea of trained counsellors began to be accepted as a feature of school life (Hughes 1985) and the core of their training was based on the non-directive approach of Carl Rogers (1952). This therapy model has a particularly clear value system based on the idea of personal growth and self-realization. But this movement has, to some extent, been eclipsed and it seemed likely that some of these counsellors had succumbed to the many roles demanded by the school and that their 'therapist's' function had been submerged.

So, the idea of introducing a therapy resource in schools has been under discussion for several years. The pervasive social system of a school causes many pitfalls for therapeutic practice but, as Nicol (1987) points out, the system can provide the structure to more relevant and effective approaches to therapy. The key lies in a better understanding of the school as a social system and in finding ways to increase the diversity of focused activities that can take place within it.

We have seen that effective therapies, even for learning problems, can take place outside the school and it is no doubt easier to organise the complex assessment and the vigorous, focused therapeutic effort that seems to be one of the hallmarks of effectiveness in clinic settings. Therapy in the school takes place within a tight organised social system, with its own value system, which is primarily geared to a different end. This makes the mounting of effective therapy much more difficult.

(Nicol 1987:663)

He continues that the therapists may find their energies directed to different ends dictated by the social system of the school and will run into difficulties if the values implicit in their intervention do not coincide with that of the school at large. On the other hand, the right kind of school system does seem to be a powerful source for promoting adaptive development and the potential for school-based therapy that can capitalize on this phenomenon is great.

Art therapy in schools

The practice of art therapy within the school can run in conjunction with and indeed facilitate the educational process. The regularity and recognition of the smooth functioning of the school day is crucial, and the therapist works as a member of staff alongside the teachers, sharing the same overall objectives. Understanding is essential with mutual professional respect for each others' objectives.

In art therapy the art materials provide a tangible medium through which a child can express him or herself. As children often have difficulty in expressing their feelings verbally, the process of art provides the child with a less problematic, more spontaneous means of communication. This approach differs from art teaching in that the learning skills and the aesthetic quality of the image, are not the primary concern of the art therapist. Another difference from an art lesson is the importance of the boundaries of the session, for the safe containment of the child while in therapy. The time allocated to the child must be held without interruption. This prevents the intrusion of the 'school' for the duration of the session so that the child can concentrate on inner conflicts and personal exploration. It is often the case that it is the internal conflicts that interfere with the educational experience of these children. By working with these conflicts within the art therapy sessions, with both negative and positive transference, the child can then begin to establish some ability to work within the classroom to enable better relationships with teacher and peers.

I work with those children from each class who are seen to be having particular emotional difficulties. Behaviour problems are often means through which some children can communicate their distress or unhappiness. The children come to art therapy either individually or in small groups according to the needs of the particular child. My timetable is worked out in close liaison with the teachers and is constantly in review. Working within the constraints of a school system is possible if clear, therapeutic boundaries and goals are maintained. For instance, adherence to the timetable worked out with both children and staff – the children themselves remember from week to week, and seldom have to be reminded, or ask to come outside of their time or interfere with any other child's time. If possible the times that children come to art therapy are worked out so that the end of the sessions coincide with breaks or dinner times. This helps the re-integration into the classroom which might otherwise be problematic as the child needs to find his or her place again back with his peers. Fascination and envy as to what happens in the art therapy room is a constant factor, and might have the effect of the child being rejected when returning from a session. Likewise, feeling this projection, the child might do something 'naughty' to make his or her presence felt and help acceptance back into the room. Returning to the more neutral territory of the playground or dinner hall helps this integration process.

From the other perspective, I have noticed that my work with certain children and the removal from their normal class situation albeit for half-an-hour, helps to diffuse potentially difficult situations. This change can help the other children to get some space and possibly more attention from the teacher, with the removal of a demanding or attention-seeking, disruptive child. This can be supportive both to other children and staff members alike. There is an argument against withdrawing children from the classroom, but in most cases, the value of removing one child and working individually far outweighs continuing the experience of the competition and battlegrounds within the classroom. At the end of each term, or when asked for a specific occasion such as a case conference, I write about my work with each child. This, I have discovered, helps communication and outlines aims and objectives in therapy. This has helped considerably by informing the more sceptical members of staff and preventing the development of misunderstanding in what I am actually doing which at first glance, might seem very little to an already overworked and busy class teacher having the stressful task of containing twenty children.

The room in which I work is full of art materials, clay, sand, water, and junk – boxes, shells, stones, etc. The art therapy sessions are unstructured in the sense of being non-directive. The child is free to chose his or her own activity within the boundaries of the time available which is in sharp contrast to the more structured ethos of the lessons. The important feature is the therapeutic space in which the children can feel able to explore and work through some unresolved conflicts and difficult issues. Even though reasons for attendance are always explained to them, the children seem to have an intrinsic understanding about why they come to art therapy. Very few actually say 'Why do I come here?' and then they can usually answer the question in some way themselves. The question usually arises when the child is making some progress or is working through some particular issue that feels difficult and awkward.

Using the art materials, their feelings are expressed and contained in the session in a safe and non-threatening way – which for some of the more disturbed children provides an enormous relief. For some of them, the classroom situation sets up the worst areas of conflict and they end up behaving badly because of the attention that they crave and have to compete for. The knowledge that at some time in the week they will have an attentive adult to themselves, in itself gives a sense of security for that particular child as there is no competition for that time or space. This provides an environment in which the child can safely explore infantile aspects of the self in a contained setting. This is one main advantage of building, into the school day, a space in which children can creatively explore their imagination, fantasies and fears, and can be seen as part of their overall learning experience rather than being separate from it.

Why art therapy?

Thus, art therapy provides the child with a therapeutic space to choose a wide range of media to help express, often unconsciously, particular needs, concerns, phantasies, and wishes. This approach to art therapy has a psychoanalytic perspective based on the ideas of Melanie Klein and Donald Winnicott, and corresponds to a fundamental principle of psychoanalysis – free association and the exploration of the unconscious are the main tasks of the procedure using the analysis of the transference as the means of achieving this. Klein's work differed from Freud's in the development of her emphasis of working with anxiety. Her conviction was that it was the interpretation of the anxiety that made it greatly diminish. This she clearly describes with her first patient Fritz – a 5-year-old boy with whom she 'interpreted what I thought to be most urgent in the material the child presented to me and found my interest focusing on his anxieties and the defences against them' (Klein 1955:4). Her psychoanalytic play technique involved consistent interpretation of the anxiety and phantasies that the child expressed in play, with the result that additional material came up in the play.

> The case strengthened my growing conviction that a precondition for the psycho-analysis of a child is to understand and to interpret the phantasies, feelings, anxieties and experiences expressed by play or, if play activities are inhibited the causes of the inhibition.
>
> (Klein 1955:6)

This understanding of anxiety is of particular interest to us in terms of her work with children experiencing difficulties at school.

> It was always part of my technique not to use educative or moral influence, but to keep to the psycho-analytic procedure only, which to put it in a nutshell, consists in understanding the patient's mind and in conveying to him what goes on in it.
>
> (Klein 1955:10)

She cites the example of a 7-year-old girl in 1923, whose neurotic difficulties were apparently not serious, but her parents had for some time been concerned about her intellectual development. Although quite intelligent, she did not keep up with her age group, she disliked school, and sometimes played truant. Since starting school her affectionate and trusting relationship with her mother had changed. In the sessions she communicated through her play, with mounting anxiety, some difficulties with a boy at school, and when this was interpreted her anxiety and distrust first increased but soon gave way to obvious relief. The analysis progressed well and there were favourable changes in relation to her family, her dislike of school diminished, and she became more interested in her lessons. Her inhibition in learning, which was rooted in deep anxieties was gradually resolved in the course of the treatment (Klein 1923).

Art and play, like dreams, manifest expression with latent unconscious content. Klein paid attention to the ego's early mechanism of defence which can be seen in the relationship between therapist and child when communicating an experience that cannot be verbalized. When these are put into words, an interpretation can bring clarity and relief. This is particularly relevant when working with aggressive children and again her examples are most useful. Aggressiveness is expressed in many ways in the child's play or contact with the art media, either directly or indirectly. Breaking a piece that has been made, attacks with scissors on the table or with paper, water or paint that is splashed around. The room can become a battlefield.

> It is essential that the child can bring out his aggressiveness, but what counts most is to understand why at this particular moment in the transference situation destructive impulses come up and to observe their consequences in the child's mind.
>
> (Klein 1955:9)

The importance of this interpretation is in the control of this aggressiveness, and to prevent the therapist becoming the object of this aggression. 'The more I was able to interpret in time the motives of the child's aggressiveness the more the situation could be kept under control' (Klein 1955:9).

In art therapy, the focus of the session revolves around the making or not making of an art object, and it is here that the emphasis differs from Kleinian analysis. Art therapy is process not product orientated and there is greater emphasis on the process of making or creating rather than the verbal analysis of it. The process of making an image, for example, can act as a therapeutic agent for expression in itself. This tends to make the sessions less verbal, with less interpretation, as much of the work is done through the art process. The third object made within the therapy creates another dimension within the transference and counter-transference process and tends to hold the significance of what is being communicated by the child.

The art materials are used as a means of communication – in much the same way as Klein used her toys – but have an added importance in that the child can make, symbolize, or create images which are central to the communication of anxiety. These are usually solid, permanent, and can be secured in the safe-keeping of the therapy room. The folder for the work takes on a great significance in terms of the trust, communication, and safety that are established within the therapeutic alliance. Children regularly remember what they did the previous week and return to it immediately, as a way of maintaining the continuity of experience. The child feels shattered when some item might have broken or in some way deteriorated during the week, as this symbolizes the safe-holding by the art therapist. The child has the experience of either being kept in mind or of that link being broken.

One way that jealousy or envy of the other children is conveyed is the blaming of the other children for breaking or damaging the pieces. Curiosity about the other children and attempts to spoil are conveyed through the art work that is made, and stays within the therapy room.

Where all the art materials are available, the choice of activity is one of the most important means of communication for the child. For example, sometimes much of the activity is carried out in the basin with water and the child becomes totally absorbed in the water, mixing colours together, splashing, messing, smearing. He or she has some valuable space to safely experience some earlier stage of development, which can then be worked through. Mary, a 9-year-old girl spent most of her time initially in the sessions squeezing wet clay through her hands. She continued to do this until she felt able to move on to other more 'constructive' work and this coincided with an increased ability to maintain the boundaries of the session. At first, she would never come on time, and would seldom leave without a fuss. As the work progressed, she became more able to negotiate her own boundaries and work with some of her acute dependancy issues.

For young children, who seem neat, correct, and well-behaved but are underachieving in their school work, it takes some time for them to feel able to express their inner feelings. Hassan, a very quiet 5-year-old boy, recently arrived in this country, spent a lot of time stacking boxes, sorting out the crayons, ordering the paints as an attempt to control his underlying anxiety. Once this was made conscious he began to explore using the water, endlessly but excitedly pouring water from one container to the other. He moved on to mixing in the paint and using the colours, smearing and mixing in a regressive way. The process enabled him to express some very strong feelings through his activity in which he became completely engrossed.

Other children use picture-making more specifically, drawing pictures of their experiences, their feelings, or their fears and they can choose to talk about them if they wish. The art materials provide an important starting point for the child in their desire to communicate their experience. This may have many stages and the therapist must be aware of the whole process in order to understand the anxiety that is underlying it. An image, begun with skill and precision, can develop into a black monster, smeared with paint, which is then cut up, mashed up into pulp with water, sand, or other available materials, and possibly ultimately destroyed. The making of art objects can also take on more specific enactment where games are played, in which the child allots roles to each individual such as patient and doctor, playing shops, mother and child. A piece of paper is made into a map, a piece of clay into sausages and chips, a piece of wood, a lock, and so on and these are used in the games in which the child's phantasy, which is triggered in the process of making the object, is played out. In many of these games the child frequently takes the part of the adult, expressing the wish to reverse the roles, but also demonstrating how he feels that his parents or other people in authority behave towards him. Sometimes, there is aggressiveness and resentment, when in that role, the parent is sadistic towards the child. In the small groups, many of these games and pretend roles that are enacted offer important ways that the children can work out many of their relationship issues together. This frequently happens in both the groups and individual sessions and can give clear indications as to the child's inner experience of himself and others around him.

One example, of a 6-year-old boy, full of thoughts of destruction and violence, would come into the art room and begin to systematically destroy whatever he felt that I would most mind about. Interpretations as to why he might be doing this and the nature of its attack seemed to help him reflect on his actions and begin to understand them. Containment of his aggressiveness, which he was most frightened of, was something which was central to our work in the session. When he was overwhelmed by it, he would ask me to put him into a box and put the lid on – a kind of psychical as well as physical containment for his own protection. Sometimes, he would attempt a picture and then begin to destroy it, first by ripping, then spoiling and smearing in a most destructive way. It felt that it was also to deny me the pleasure of seeing him 'produce' something which was a strong dynamic played out from his classroom.

The variety of emotional situations which can be expressed through art and play is unlimited. Feelings of frustration and rejection, jealousy of father and mother or siblings and aggressiveness that accompany this, feelings of love and hate towards a new born baby as well as the ensuing anxiety, guilt, and urge to make reparation. The space of the session gives an opportunity for the child to renegotiate that essential space with mother. Linda, a withdrawn, rather sad 6-year-old girl, spent many sessions drawing her mother pushing the pram of the new baby, and she placed herself in different positions with her many siblings as a way of working out her ambivalent feelings about the new arrival. She would always say cheerfully that this was her new baby but soon the jealousy and the rage were apparent and important for her to express. She was continually preoccupied in her classroom about this, saying she wanted to go home as she was worried about the new baby.

The repetition of actual experiences and details of everyday life, often interwoven with phantasy, is very common and it is revealing that often very important events fail to enter into the images, play, or associations. The emphasis tends to lie in minor happenings, but these are most important because they have stirred up emotions and phantasies. Any activity, such as changes in posture or in facial expression, can give a clue to what is going on in the child's mind. The art therapist must therefore watch closely and be in touch with the child during the whole session and not feel because he or she is busily painting, that contact can be temporarily halted. It is this psychic holding during the activity of the session that creates the trust and develops the transference. It is as if the mother is ever-present for her infant. The child can thus be helped fundamentally by taking anxieties back to where they originated – namely in infancy and in relation to first objects. For by re-experiencing early emotions and understanding them in relation to primal objects, the child can, as it were, revise these relations at their root, and thus effectively diminish them.

Many children keep some small but precious store of symbols representing their earliest experiences, but often there has been nobody to whom they felt that they could communicate the meaning of these. Children working in art therapy are able to symbolize and communicate these experiences through their imagery and art work. It is important that these communications are received and responded to. Children who are able to communicate in this symbolic way will be able to convey their own inner worlds, which otherwise might not be reached. Charles was intelligent but exasperated the teachers with his indolence and lethargy in class. He was a large, overweight but emotionally immature 9-year-old and began his work in therapy with a minute model of an aeroplane. At first he worked so secretively with his back to me that he refused to let me see what he was doing for several weeks. Feelings about his intrusive, over-protective mother, competition from his older brothers, and his difficulties with his own self-esteem became apparent as the therapy proceeded. His confidence and ability to be open and spontaneous grew as his anxiety was addressed and he was able to express his internal chaos and mess, which on the surface were heavily controlled and repressed. His final image on leaving the sessions and the school, was a huge model aeroplane which filled the hall. His difficulties about control and personal expectations of failure had been worked with, and on leaving the school he seemed a more mature 11-year-old.

Jo was an insecure and anxious child who, at first, was so easily distracted that he would begin to draw and leave unfinished up to twenty drawings in one session. He tried cutting them up using scissors in an attempt to make his images solid and three-dimensional. His concentration was such, that he would literally leave the scissors in the paper as his anxiety stopped that process and caused him to jump to an alternative activity. Gradually he became more able to sit, concentrate, and feel sure enough in himself to pursue his images for himself, rather than worrying about other factors. He was becoming in touch with his inner world and as his anxiety was contained, he was able to work with some deeper aspects of his experience. Martin, a 7-year-old, made a box which he lavished with care and attention which symbolized for him the containment that he wanted but was unobtainable from a neglectful mother; Serena attempted to take control of her internal chaos, made efforts to keep the paint on the paper and create an image rather than resorting to mess and chaos.

Louise, a precocious and intelligent child, had by the age of 8 been to many different schools and lived in many places. Her instability and precarious homelife were reflected in the sessions as each week, she would come and do something completely different. The only consistency was her chaos, which mirrored her experience, and it was difficult to know what was phantasy and what was reality for this child. Most of her behavioural difficulties stemmed from acute sensitivity to rejection, which was an indication of her extremely poor self-image. In the classroom, she expressed this by being verbally abusive and physically violent with peers. As she was so large for her age, she would choose to pick fights with the older children, and she came to realize this was a dramatic way of drawing attention to herself, as her reputation went before her. She sought this attention but it had the effect of making other children and teachers extremely angry with her. She found it difficult to make friends or sustain lasting relationships as they seemed to end in a fight – for Louise, difficulties were about winning rather than resolution. She found it hard to take criticism from teachers about her school work and so would react by creating chaos and confusion around her.

After some weeks in art therapy, gradually some images appeared that began to repeat themselves as she became more settled, and she was beginning to feel safe enough and contained to be calm and create some solidity to her experience. For example, her love of animals and riding began to feature in pictures and she made several clay models of farm animals to which she became extremely attached. It emerged that these animals were connected to parts of her life that she could feel part of and attached to. The stories and phantasies which she associated with these animals helped her to verbalize much of her inner distress and uncontained disturbance which she experienced most of the time.

'Now what shall I do?' she thought out loud, looking around the room. 'I did a pig last week – perhaps I should do another animal – a farm animal.'

'Do you like farm animals?' I asked.

'Yes I used to live on a farm in Wales until I was 4 – then we moved to London. I don't remember it really except it was a white house.' She explained that she loved cows and used to milk them when she was 4. 'I don't think I could use the machines though.' She thought for a minute in silence and turning to me asked, 'What shall I do? Tell me what to do.' She picked up the clay, squeezed it in her hands and through her fingers. She was stroking the clay with her thumb, enjoying the sensation and the shapes it was making. 'I need some water – it's too dry,' and got up a brought a jar of water back to the table and sat down. She put her fingers into the water: 'Look they go all fat,' and then put a piece of clay into the water and putting it in, caused the water to overflow over the table. 'It doesn't matter if it spills and I make a mess does it?' I reassured her that it did not and then, pulling the clay out of the jar – water and clay oozing everywhere – she asked again what she might make. 'I could make a mouse – rats – rats that bite – and lots of pigs that bit on the farm. I can remember my dad being bitten by the pigs – I was afraid of them – he came out of the shed all covered in bites.'

I reflected that I did not know that pigs bit people – 'yes', was the reply, 'I know a lot about pigs – there was a programme about them on Channel 4 on Thursday at seven – did you see it – what channel do you watch on Thursday at seven?'

Later in the same session she continued to squeeze the clay through her fingers – the sausage shape remained. 'Look that's where Tracy bit me – can you see?' she asked, pushing her wrist towards me.

'Why was that?' I enquired.

'She just did – it really hurt –'

'You think she did it for no reason.'

'She did – and Mr J. saw and didn't say nothing.' She continued to make her clay object.

This session is one example of Louise trying to express her muddle and confusion of events that seem to 'happen' to her and others which she seemed unable to comprehend. At the same time she was beginning to express some underlying conflicts. In art therapy, the experience of finding a safe place in which she could express this disturbance and be understood became to be of value to her as she began to gain some sort of understanding of herself. She was enthusiastic and looked forward to coming to the sessions where progress was beginning before her mother removed her to yet another school.

The child versus society

Sceptical of the use of these ideas and pessimistic of any real hope of change are those that believe it is ultimately our society that militates against disadvantaged children. Feeling alienated from home, school, and other institutions, the child has little chance of making any real change. In his penetrating book, *The Politics of Psychoanalysis* (1987), Stephen Frosch addresses this complicated issue and begins with a common criticism that psychoanalysis is by nature a 'bourgeois discipline' (1987:10). But as his argument unfolds, he distinguishes the different analytic approaches which show varying degrees of awareness of the power relations present in therapy, and how these can and should be worked with. When these power relations are recognized and used to explore the internalized power structures that have been embedded in the client's personality, then, he argues, psychoanalysis begins to contribute to social change (Frosch 1987:210).

Frosch points out Freud's therapeutic pessimism in his interest in psychoanalysis as an instrument of knowledge rather than a therapeutic system. Freud's purpose was to understand, to develop a system of ideas that could make sense of people, of their individual psychology, and in the structures they create for themselves. Frosch argues that psychoanalytic psychotherapy is capable of offering insights and experiences which are congruent with, and can contribute to, progressive political changes. 'The crucial point is to maintain the distinction between modifying distress and creating real change' (Frosch 1987:213). He maintains that it is precisely because psychoanalytic theory so convincingly demonstrates that social forces are internalized by each individual and live on inside to form the basis of personality, that it is politically relevant to develop ways of acting directly on these internalized forces, as well as upon the external structures which give rise to them.

> This is not confusing therapy with politics, but it is rescuing therapy for a potential role in politics, based on the idea that individual change is not completely determined by social change, and requires methods tuned to the uncovering of unconscious structures.
>
> (Frosch 1987:215)

Klein remains close to Freudian ideas of what is possible, and she states that 'the ultimate aim of psychoanalysis is integration of the patients' personality (Klein 1957:231). Her notion of integration does not mean freedom from conflict, but rather in the Freudian style, it requires the ability to live in ambivalence, tolerant and aware of the conflicting forces that, under different circumstances might tear one apart. Klein stresses the aim of deepening the personality, with a particular emphasis on developing a rich phantasy life with a capacity to experience emotions.

> Analysis leads to a growth in integration which in turn leads to a strengthening of the ego so that it is able to recover good experiences and tolerate the recognition of the bad experiences of the past; hence also one source of the optimism that Kleinians have concerning the analysis of psychotics.
>
> (Frosch 1987:234)

These political implications are important to our work in art therapy with children. The question is that if one attempts to help the individual to change, is there any way that this can be given permanence with the constraints of the social and political situation in which the child finds itself? Certain things will never be changed – cultural traditions, religious views for example – are social phenomena which create division and maintain separateness. But the possibility that there is room for individual or internal change, however bleak, is the basis for work in art therapy. By helping children come to terms with many of their own conflicts, which are probably compounded by their social situation, then perhaps there is a way in which they can live more easily with this ambivalence and tension that Klein speaks about.

The black child's experience

All children experience chaos, joy, envy, misery and these are communicated through images in art therapy. In the previous section, the racial origin of the children has deliberately been omitted in order to describe clearly the process of art therapy when working with the inner world of the child, and how this is communicated through the images and within the therapeutic relationship. However difference of race and colour adds an important element in terms of the communication and understanding of the child in art therapy.

In the school, there is a high percentage of children from ethnic minorities, the great majority of which are of Afro-Caribbean origin. These children have particular difficulties in terms of their experience of being black in a fundamentally non-accepting society. The political and social implications of the black child's experience mirrors that of their parents in terms of racial alienation and discrimination. The complexity of working with children who might be disruptive and aggressive but who basically feel discriminated against in a 'white' culture must be addressed. It is for this reason that I want to explore issues of racism and other social pressures that surround and complicate the black child's experience, as they inevitably affect the work in any therapeutic relationship.

'It has been clear that in order for black children to realize their real potential they must be respected as equal participants capable of full educational attainment' (First Afro-Caribbean Educational Resource Project which began in 1976).

> The identity of a child or what it inherits is important to his or her self-esteem; to deny this is to deprive the individual of a basic human right. The school should become an enriched intercultural learning environment for the non-racist society that we all hope for.
>
> (Afro-Caribbean Educational Resource Project 1977:4)

It is not my intention to discuss and analyse the origins and complexities of racial tensions and prejudice currently existing in our multi-cultural society. The events of Brixton and Bristol, for example, are salutory reminders of the intensity of the feelings of the communities, particularly black, in their struggle against what they see as white oppression. Black people generally lose out in jobs, homes, and schools when there is competition from whites. It is not surprising that they then group together, as any minority group struggling for survival, identity, and self-esteem, but this happens in the urban overcrowding of the inner cities.

Anyone living in contemporary Britain must also be aware that the black–white difficulty is compounded by other rivalrous groups causing conflict and tensions between them based on difference of colour, religion, and class. It is unfortunate that, in Britain, it is a deeply suspicious, largely ignorant community that maintains prejudice and separateness that itself needs re-educating to gain some understanding of the problems encountered by people whom they see as different and also inferior. Racial prejudice is as deep as it is destructive. It is a particular type of attitude.

It concerns racial or ethnic groups and is based on faulty and inflexible generalisation. It may be felt or expressed. It may be directed towards a (racial or ethnic) group as a whole or toward an individual because he is a member of that group.

(Allport 1958:10)

Prejudice adds to these ethnic categorizations an additional component of rigidity and hostility.

A vast literature considers many aspects of the subject of race relations, particularly the issues surrounding education and social work. There are many explicit accounts of the experience of living in multi-cultural Britain. (Brah and Minhas 1985, Carling 1986). In his book, *Black Youth in Crisis* (1982), Cashmore points out the special experience of being black and how this structures the position of black youth. He maintains that youth has its own problems; being black its own problems; put them together and there is a whole set of problems which tends to dispel the optimism of those who believe that youthful exuberance will subside as maturity comes to the fore.

We have drawn on our own empirical work to suggest that, as young blacks become aware of their colour and realise that this can be depreciated and used as a basis for exclusion, they fuse this blackness with a new significance, incorporate it into their consciousness, organise their subjective biographies so as to include it, strike up allegiances and perceive adversaries on the understanding of it; in general position themselves in relation to that quality of blackness.

(Cashmore 1982:26).

He continues that social experience give support to their belief that blackness means being different, usually in an inferior way. This crucial realization of being different, being black causes the emergence of 'culture of disengagement' – the extreme example of which is the Rastafarian movement.

Cashmore describes how black people therefore adopt strategies for survival which possibly involve non-differentiation of white attitudes and degrees of prejudice. He cites Muhammad Ali who once gave his explanation for this kind of thinking suggesting that, a nest of vipers may only have one venomous snake, but who can ask a man to put his hand into the nest to differentiate. 'Put differently tell a black person that not every white man is bad, but do not expect him to be bothered to sort out the good from the not-so-good at his own expense' (Cashmore 1982:29). It seems that this is where the school experience can be crucial – the dissatisfaction with school broadens into a dissatisfaction with society generally which, in turn, translates into a desire to have nothing to do with it. Cashmore ends on a pessimistic note:

> The prospect is not pleasant, but it has to be faced; the situation is dire but it has to be reckoned with. Measures we have at our disposal are cosmetic; they mask the real discontent beneath the surface. Nothing short of a wholesale transformation of attitudes, orientations and postures towards young blacks and, crucially, on behalf of young blacks, will suffice in diffusing a potentially explosive situation. People expect things of black youths and the latter expect things of others; both sets of expectations are usually fulfilled. These expectations are therefore unlikely to be changed and, without such changes, there can only be a further slide into the kind of ugly crisis of violence that we both find abhorrent, yet have unwillingly to concede is a menacing probability.
>
> (Cashmore 1982:34)

Room for change

Working closely with young black children makes clear the conflicts experienced by these children who, having been born and brought up in this country are faced with the prospect of discrimination and non-acceptance based on the colour of their skin. The children do experience being different and have already adopted the strategies that Cashmore so clearly describes. Many of these children are referred to art therapy for unruly, sometimes aggressive anti-social behaviour which manifests itself in the classroom and playground. Their concentration is sometimes poor, and their attention lacking, but it seems that much of this is based on the idea of disengagement – there seems to be no meaning in the classroom. There is the feeling of alienation – a point supported by Malcolm Cross (1982) who uses the term 'marginality'. 'Change the child or change the curriculum', seems to be an ongoing educational debate. Most educators agree on the latter alternative and feel that they follow it. But, Torrance and White ask, is this the case in the education of black children? How can a curriculum be tailored to the needs of these children when the teachers and curriculum writers know little about or simply disdain black culture? 'Educators who view black culture as a sick white culture are hardly qualified to make useful curriculum changes' (Torrance and White 1975:252).

However, anti-racism in schools is an essential policy that most authorities and teachers have begun to work with, and the legal requirements of race relations and the establishment of the CRE have attempted to bring employers and other institutions into line with these rulings. The more recent initiatives of non-racist policy in schools is an indication that schools are trying to change and move towards integration and positive images for black pupils.

Black children, white children

To understand more clearly the issues involved when working with black children, I feel it is important to consider how racial attitudes are transmitted. The complexity of the subject thwarts any simple answer to the questions about the genesis of prevailing prejudice or existing attitudes around race. Indeed one of the stumbling blocks might be the resistance of many people to give serious consideration to this subject which has the potential of being sensitive and difficult.

One of the most interesting studies that looks into racial attitudes among sub-groups of children is *Black Child, White Child* by Judith Porter (1971). Even though this is an American-based study, much of it has relevance for our purposes. She observes the way the development of racial attitudes and preferences affect self-esteem and interaction patterns and she delineates the mechanisms by which these racial feelings are actually transmitted to the young child. Her suggestion is that this process of transmission involves significant people in the child's environment and his or her cognitive and emotional development. All children become aware at some point of the existence within the dominant cultural system of racial prejudice which is directed against either their own or other groups. However, the extent and intensity of the child's attitudes and the nature of the response varies. Inter-related causes of prejudice are fundamental in the development of children's racial attitudes, and Porter suggests that white children cannot help but be exposed to racial evaluations of black children which are unfavourable. The black child also recognizes these negative feelings about his colour, even if there is little contact with whites. The black child is exposed to anti-white feelings and/or pro-black feelings within the black community at the same time and so he may internalize conflicting sets of attitudes (Porter 1971).

There are various mechanisms by which these racial attitudes are conveyed from the cultural system to the child. A child becomes aware that racial differences exist – that is the child is learning both that different categories exist and that people are classified into these divisions on the basis of certain perceptual cues. The child learns of the existence of racial categories and at the same time becomes aware of the evaluations attached to them. The family is one of the most important agents of attitude transmission. The child may accept the parents' norms, values, and behaviour patterns as his own. These racial attitudes may be transmitted directly and explicitly by parents. But they can also be powerfully transmitted through overhead conversations or implied by subtle behavioural cues and it is probably in this fashion rather than by direct instruction that such attitudes are primarily learnt. 'Minute displays of emotion such as affection, pride, anger, guilt, anxiety . . . (rather than the words used, the meanings intended or the philosophy implied) transmit to the child the outlines of what really counts in the world' (Erikson 1964:30). So, by the time a white child is explicitly told for the first time that black people are inferior, he may already be convinced of the fact. For the black child, this sense of discrimination that their parents experience is transmitted and powerfully reinforced.

Children can acquire different attitudes to those of their parents which are transmitted from the peer group. The real implication of race is strikingly pointed out to many children when they first enter school. Members of his own or other racial groups may make positive or negative comments about the child's appearance or racial membership. Hence the atmosphere of the school in inter-racial understanding is crucial. Admiration of personal appearance whether by peers, play group, parents, or others is a highly important mechanism of transmission. The fair skinned blue-eyed blonde child is admired, and this may imply that other skin or hair colours are less acceptable. For white girls concerned with physical appearance, whiteness as an attribute of beauty assumes particular significance (Porter 1971:106). Particularly, for black children, admiration of personal appearance may be crucial in the image they have of their black peer group. In some situations, the more they approach white standards of attractiveness, the more they may be envied by children with darker skin. In some instances, one black child will point out to the other how important the shade of skin colour is. Where a negative affect becomes attached to the colour brown, the children can generalize this to their brown skin as well. 'This crayon is brown. I'll take pink because I like pink, it's a lighter colour, and it's better than all the rest. Myself's not pink' – a 5-year-old child.

Racial awareness

There is much evidence to suggest that the first five years of life are impor-tant for the development of racial attitudes (Porter 1971). One of the first empirical studies of nursery school children was done in the 1930s (Horowitz 1939). Clark and Clark (1939), using Horowitz's line drawings of children and their own doll-play techniques, demonstrated that for some black children basic knowledge of racial differences may begin even as early as age 3, developing from year to year until reaching a point of stability at around age 7.

It seems by the age of 5, children have clear knowledge of racial differences and their racial attitudes are already rather sophisticated. White children may realize that blatant and overt expressions of prejudice are somehow unacceptable, and the black child may be developing complex feel-ings toward both his own and the opposite race. But even at 4, children have internalized the affective connotations of colour and begin to generalize these meanings to people. Although the 3-year-old white child does not on the whole invest colour with social meaning, the black child of this age does perceive vaguely that colour differences are important and may be personally relevant. Therefore even pre-school children are not exempt from the prevalent racial attitudes characteristic of a large section of the adult society. James Baldwin says that even before the black child fully understands racial distinctions 'he has begun to react to them, he has begun to be controlled by them' (Baldwin 1962:65).

Other studies have shown the damaging effect of prejudice on the self-esteem of black children (Clark and Clark 1958). The black child is exposed to negative attitudes about his race and to factors like discrimination. Thus he or she must learn to adapt to pressures in some way. Racial evaluations affect black children more directly and personally than they do whites, who are forced to cope with the problem of being stigmatized because of skin colour. Devaluation of one's racial group can create not only a negative group identity but also feelings of inadequacy and insecurity on a deeper level as well for the individual child. In her study, Porter looks at this component of self-concept which she calls the 'personal identity' dimension. She uses a picture-drawing and story method which provides an operational definition of personal self-esteem and discovers that this varies by both race and class. Each child was asked to tell a story about the self-portrait and those pictures which indicated poor self-image tended to be accompanied by stories in which themes of fear and powerlessness were stressed.

Porter gives the following example of one white child who drew a large figure, centred in the middle of the page The body was outlined in yellow and pink, and the figure had not only eyes, nose, and smiling mouth in appropriate colours but also curly brown hair and a colourful blue and white dress. Arms, legs, hands, and feet were present. In sharp contrast, a black boy who drew himself as a small grey blob in the corner of the page, asking that it be labelled with his name, or a black girl who carefully drew a person and then picked up a blue crayon and obliterated the figure completely with systematic strokes. When asked what she had drawn, she said sadly that she had produced a picture of herself. She makes the point that the white child was middle class, and the two black children came from poorer, 'lower class' homes (Porter 1971).

Our experience of working in art therapy enables us to understand that it is not only differences in either racial or social terms that produce self-images of this nature. Poor self-esteem is a dominant feature of many children who are referred to art therapy. Kathy, for example, an intelligent, highly capable child suffered acute bouts of depression and withdrawn, uncooperative behaviour. Her main difficulties lay in her lack of confidence and inability to understand her own sense of worth which had never been emphasized at home. Her poor self-esteem was the biggest obstacle to achieving her real personal and educational potential. In spite of being well-liked in the school and having many friends, indeed many children relied upon her for support and stability, Kathy felt her situation was compounded by the fact she was black.

The general pattern of the findings from the Porter study suggest that black people, with a host of economic and familial problems have especially high rates of poor personal self-esteem, which is associated with racial self-rejection. It seems that these can also apply to the British experience. On the basis of her findings she recommends quality integration for schools which is not based on a *laissez-faire* policy. In order to counteract attitudes which are already in the process of development, pre-school programmes must stress inter-racial tolerance in both direct and subtle ways. In a quality inter-racial setting, white children have an opportunity to have their stereotypes corrected by actual association with black children and if the black child is accepted by whites in an atmosphere which stresses the importance of all races, he learns that others respect him.

Thus, continuing efforts must be made to confirm a strong sense of black identity but this should be in terms of equality and integration and distinguished from institutionalized separatism. Black Power movements have been most influential in the various political arenas and have raised racial consciousness. But laws regulating equal opportunity for employment, education, and housing must be enforced to enable our society to become fully responsive to the needs of black people. A black student says 'All white people are racist, you, not us are the problem'. Being part of the problem is hard for white 'liberals' to take on. Banton *et al.* (1985) points out in their work in anti-racist workshops that it is easier to see the cause of racism as a product of the socio-economic relations of capitalism, unemployment, or the cuts. They suggest it is easier to be in opposition, to identify with the oppressed as women, as gays, as the disabled, as the unemployed or to be against the bomb. 'To be part of the problem is much more difficult' (ibid.:119). They continue

> The education, culture, institutions and the consequent socialisation of white people are essentially racist. Resistance to change (to active adoption of an anti-racist policy) arises from the internalisation of privilege, which is not only material benefit, but is also concerned with power. Racism is part of ourselves as white people.
>
> (Ibid.)

This institutional factor of racism raises many implications for working with black children. Racism exists and escapes no one. 'It is part of us all and has deeply infiltrated the lives and psyches of both the oppressed and oppressors' (Katz 1978). Where the power base lies within an institution, racism occurs, but within this, unconscious racism can operate on a personal basis but may be rationalized in terms of institutional factors. In other words, the institution is blamed for the racism when this might being projected onto it by the unconscious processes of the individuals. I encounter aspects of unconscious racism in my work and must be aware when it is made conscious both within transference and counter-transference processes.

Instances happen in a flash and are often difficult to comprehend at the time. Examples such as suddenly becoming aware of colour difference during the session, when the work is centred on the communication of the child's inner world, it is important to analyse the process of the session to understand this. Once working with a group, I was suddenly struck half way into the session that there were four black children sitting with me – it was interesting to explore dynamically what was happening in the transference to make me react and consciously take note of difference at that time. In the counter-transference, the therapist may also move away from the inner world of the child in response to some unconscious process.

Other examples might occur such as toleration of aspects of the black child's experience, over-compensation for the child's situation where there might be resistance to exploring areas of real difficulty or where potential areas of non-acceptance happen in a momentary interaction. Equally from the child's point of view, she might resort to patois in a confused or difficult moment and the complaint, 'you don't understand', takes on another dimension for the black child. Attempts at understanding these transference and counter-transference responses can be difficult to acknowledge, but they must be explored by the white therapist.

Banton et al. (1985), describes this process of unconscious racism in the following way.

> Just as children must accept the often unpredictable arbitrary and brutal experience of school life as part of their maturation, so by implication must blacks rise above their experience irrespective of its nature. The unconscious racist association between blacks and other children is extremely powerful – 'It takes time for them to learn our culture and our ways' and has the effect of creating the conditions whereby the authenticity of black experience can be overlooked, which in turn avoids the necessity of criticising those forces that determine the experience. Just as children are seen as irrational, demanding and subversive, so blacks consistent with the historical view of them as sub-human (and certainly not adults) are required to learn from their oppression. Here the analogy breaks down, since for children the prize of learning is acceptance into the adult world; for blacks they must stay as children.
>
> (Ibid.:119)

In their forceful book *Sexism, Racism and Oppression*, Brittan and Maynard (1984) attack the school as being one of the main institutions for racism and sexism. 'It is not disadvantage that is at work in schools in these sorts of instances but prejudice and discrimination as well' (1984:154). They describe how this manifests itself:

West Indian children, for example, are more likely to be regarded and treated as if they always behave aggressively, unresponsively or in a restless fashion. Accordingly they tend to be seen as presenting special educational and disciplinary problems. . . . Black culture is viewed in a stereotyped way and cultural difference tends to be treated as a deficit, particularly in relation to educability. For many teachers, the black family is considered as unable to provide the conditions for, or as actually inhibiting, the successful educational progress of the West Indian child'.

(Brittan and Maynard 1984:166)

They raise another central point in that the literature within schools provides black children, and indeed all ethnic groups, with few significant role models and concerns itself with issues in which they are only marginally featured. Thus the curriculum can actively foster disenchantment with education. The teachers' negative expectations affects the child's school performance and the tendency to encourage involvement in school sports and music promotes school failure by channelling the black child away from the academic mainstream. Brittan and Maynard (1984) are again scathing as to the implications of this in terms of the black child's education.

Moreover, the 'sports and music' curriculum can be regarded as a form of social control aimed at 'cooling out' Blacks by using their anticipated interests to contain or neutralise disaffection caused by lack of educational success. Such a curriculum may also provide a justification for giving those pupils in these non-academic streams a 'watered down' form of schooling. It is for these kinds of reasons, that teachers' expectations are an important factor in the educational career of the black child. They help to create, however inadvertently, an environment in which Blacks are assumed not to have and treated as if they lack, the ability and potential to 'achieve' in the conventionally accepted sense.

(Ibid.:167)

However, it seems that this is where the value of certain curriculum activities might be made distinct from the personal needs of the children. In a wider social context, all children need role models or idols, yet the black child, living in the urban inner city, has difficulty in finding that identification. There are some black actors in central roles, although these characters are usually removed from the average black child's experience. Prominent musicians, singers, and poets have, over the years, been of great significance to their young audience. The biggest area of change seems to be in the area of competitive sport where outstanding achievements by black athletes can meet the admiration of the child and indeed evoke some degree of aspiration – crucial in the young child's ego development.

In my experience, when given the chance in the safety and space of an art therapy session, where judgement is suspended and there are no expectations of achievement, part of the process of self-exploration and self-discovery is the child's search for heroes and part of their experience of disillusionment seems to lie in the fact that this quest is seldom satisfied. The actor Eddie Murphy, featured strongly in several sessions with a 10-year-old boy. An idol who felt estranged and alienated himself. More mythical figures tend to take the place of real people. The 'successful' black people have by and large been accepted and integrated into the white world and media and this felt as though for this boy, they were in some way tainted or not pure enough for his own needs for identification and idolatory. When these children suffer the experience of a negative stereotype, who can they follow and model themselves upon in their approaching adolescence?

Working in art therapy

With these issues in mind, I want to examine the complex issues involved when white children and black children work together, sharing and exploring art materials. More specifically, does the black child have an added difficulty in communicating his or her experience when working with a white therapist?

In art therapy, acceptance of the experience of the child and the visual statements that derive from their values is fundamental. Art is used as the means of communication of this experience and central to this process is the expression of deep feelings, unconscious wishes, and phantasies. Does any cross-cultural difference or even surface difference of skin colour effect this process and set up conflicts for the child involved? In Philip Rack's book (1982), he points to the 'grotesquely unbalanced scene' in which the practitioner is depicted as an intelligent, skillful, wise, compassionate, high status member of the dominant culture (white). Rack speaks of the representative of the ethnic minority as cast in the supplicant role: it is his cultural peculiarities, his unfortunate experiences, his failures of adaptation that cause the problems.

This worrying attitude has caused me to reflect on the processes involved with those children who not only feel in personal difficulty and conflict but also are deprived and oppressed by their situation as well. As a white therapist I am implicated in some way in their situation and therefore have experienced some very complicated aspects within our relationship. This stems from the fact that issues around colour and race are evident and it is essential to acknowledge and work with them. The feelings of the child towards the therapist in the therapeutic situation are held to be of crucial importance. Becoming aware of these feelings, sometimes by monitoring one's own feelings to reflect back to the child and to gain an empathetic understanding of him or her is the fundamental task of both psychotherapy and art therapy.

Currently there is more attention being paid to issues around inter-cultural psychotherapy and the increase in available literature will help all professionals working with ethnic minority groups. Studies looking at general issues of inter-cultural psychotherapy (Atkinson 1985, Gilbert 1986, and Munoz

1986) are equally useful as those which consider the subject more centrally concerned with this paper – black and white therapists working with black and white patients (Griffith 1977, Jones and Gray 1985, Mouzon 1987).

In a recent article, Jung's ideas have come under close scrutiny and it is argued that his perception of black people is racist and that these same views permeate the entire fabric of Jung's psychological theory (Dalal 1988). Dalal argues that these views are woven into the theoretical foundations of two major Jungian concepts – the Collective Unconscious and Individuation and specifies Jung's racism in that he explicitly equates the modern black with the prehistoric human, the modern black conscious with the white unconscious and the modern black adult with the white child. 'It is this that constitutes the racist core of Jungian Psychology on which all else is based. The equations are where he begins; these are the idea and beliefs that he accepts without question.' (Dalal 1988:263.) Jung accepts stereotypes without question but as he does question any deviation from them, Dalal concludes that the consequences of his theories, if true, are serious for any practising psychotherapist because this would mean dealing differently with black and white clients in order to remain within a Jungian framework and be consistent with it.

Whatever one might think of these views, the ideas are certainly worth consideration if only to question the validity of some psychoanalytic theory and its application in our contemporary multi-cultural society. This certainly adds to the upsurge of interest in this field and no doubt will be commented upon in the forthcoming volume of the *Journal of Social Work Practice* (November 1988) which will be a special issue on inter-cultural psychotherapy and social work. It does seem surprising, however, that this area of work had been so badly documented and that, until recently, such scant attention had been paid in the literature to the effect of the therapist's visible racial characteristics on the psychotherapeutic relationship. This may be because of the sensitivity of the subject but also because of the wide influence of the 'transference' model which in its simplest form sees all the child's feelings toward the therapist as stemming from past relationships. Using a Kleinian model there is emphasis on the importance of the child's inner world which is free from external factors and influence.

Yet Freud was aware that the personal features of the therapist could significantly alter the content and expression of what he called transferences. In one of the earliest formulations on the concept (1925) he noted that some transferences are 'Ingeniously constructed; the content being subjected to a moderating influence . . . by cleverly taking advantage of some real peculiarity in the physician's person or circumstances and attaching themselves to that' (Sandler *et al.* 1973). Although Freud does not refer specifically to racial difference, the idea is still valid for this 'real peculiarity' or difference in racial origin surfaces regularly in my work. There is constant reference to cultural issues on a conscious level but the feelings that are expressed sometimes derive from unconscious processes. Phrases have ambiguous meanings, frequent references to classroom maps on the wall saying, 'That is where I come from', and the difficulty that is encountered when the island is so small that it does not feature on the map of the Caribbean; images of islands, palm trees, and attempts to draw or articulate visually some land or idea of origin; when asked to write the Caribbean into her sand picture, embarrassment on my part and frustration on the child's at my hesitation of the spelling.

More personal references are frequent. These may include self-confidence and pride in the communication of sense of difference, particularly where cultural traditions create a strong black identity. Others struggle with acknowledgement of conflict within their experience and lack of self-esteem abounding from that, 'Miss I have got the darkest skin in the school', 'I wish I didn't have black skin', 'She is everybody's friend – she is the only white girl'. Children seek acceptance and reassurance but also need time to establish enough trust within the relationship not only to speak about their experience but also to be able to look at the underlying, perhaps unconscious issues such as envy, jealousy, hate which are central to their concerns and are communicated in the transference. These difficulties can be expressed by reference to skin colour, but it is the underlying feelings central to the effects of racism that are important to explore and this is where the real area of sensitivity lies. Racially prejudiced people use reaction to skin colour as a way of preventing themselves exploring their real feelings about the situation and indeed it maintains the distance that prevents them from having to get close enough to do so.

Varghese (1983), himself of Indian origin working with white Australians, suggests that the race of the therapist can play a significant role in the manifestation of transference and counter-transference phenomena. References to the colour of the therapist may be the first sign of a developing transference relationship. He suggests that failure to appreciate the impact of racial differences can impede therapeutic progress while sensitive confrontation may be a valuable tool in the recognition and communication of emotionally charged feelings in therapy. He suggests that dream material is influenced by the race of the therapist who may be less easy to disguise in dreams, and the therapist may avoid certain dream interpretations because of unacknowledged discomfort about race. He cites one case where failure to confront the issue of race early in psychotherapy contributed to lack of progress, frustration with the procedure on the part of both patient and therapist, and ultimately to a negative reaction. The bringing into the open of unacknowledged feelings about race was a turning point in therapy and brought home to the therapist the powerful impact of racial difference on the patient's interaction and the importance of racially different identity in the therapeutic situation.

Problems around racial differences and skin colour are expressed in many ways during the process of making images in art therapy. One example that springs particularly to mind was when a 10-year-old boy I had worked with for about two years excitedly brought in a photo of himself taken at nursery school. In our relationship, he had a tendency to idealize in an attempt to work with the conflicts that he experienced concerning his mother. As he lacked a father he felt extremely loyal to and protective of her, and yet felt abandoned by her as a recent care order had been implemented temporarily removing him from the home and her care. Mother had accused the authorities of racial discrimination as the reason for the removal of her children and so as a white person, at some level I was responsible for this. He was presented with many conflicting and complex problems which he was attempting to sort out in the sessions.

I saw the nursery picture as some attempt to return to his pre-school years, where mother was the dominant carer and difficulties with racial issues were at a minimum. At a more personal level, I felt this was about establishing some identity for himself, independently from me and also to some extent from his mother. He demonstrated this, in his usual 'macho' fashion on the surface, but underneath he was displaying his real need for mother and a nurturing experience. In the execution of this painting he took great care to draw it as carefully as possible, and then the next week began to paint it. He painted the tee-shirt, then the arms, and the neck with great precision and enthusiasm until the end of the session. He left his painting carefully with the rest of his work in the folder with the intention of resuming it the following week. When he came the next week, he was rather subdued and rather reluctantly fetched the painting. As he was free to choose his own activity, there was no encouragement to finish pieces of work and indeed, continuity of work was only established after weeks of working with this boy. His initial confusion and distractedness at first made him forget what he had been doing in the same session, let alone from week to week.

After therapy had progressed and he was becoming able to make links and establish continuity and investment in the sessions and our relationship, I saw this reluctance as something significant. He sat for a long time with the picture in front of him, and made some excuse that he had forgotten the photo. He then said that his mother would not let him bring the photo in again to school and so he could not possibly carry on with it that day. As he had originally intended the picture to be for his mother, I suggested that this must be causing him some difficulty – not only that it was intended for his mother but also that he was finding it difficult to complete. It was the difficulties that he was encountering within the transference that were making him anxious.

He first asked me to fill in the face as he could not get the features right. When I reflected that I wondered what was his concern with the features and the face, he said he did not know what colour to paint it. 'You don't want to paint the face the same as the arms and neck?'

'No I can't', was the reply.

'Can you say why not?'

'Because I don't want to – and anyway I don't like the colour.' There followed a long discussion about this and he declared he wanted to paint the face white – he could not say why, said it had no connection to me, or that he himself wanted to have white skin. This was a tense and difficult session for him as it gave expression to his phantasies but also he had to look at aspects of himself, significantly using the face, as this is what people see. 'People won't like it – they won't think it is good', and as he spoke he was experimenting with different colours, several times changing the tone and the features.

The picture was 'completed' by him cutting out a white piece of paper and sticking it on top of the face, thereby leaving it blank and featureless. He seemed more resolved in himself about the issues that were raised by its execution and we experienced some real conflicts surrounding his feelings about his mother, her beliefs, his colour, and some issues that face him at school and outside. An interesting development from that session in that sense of differentiation had taken place in his ability to separate the stereotype 'white man' with long, straight hair, and white skin which he tended to ask me to draw or pick out of a magazine.

Difference of skin colour and racial origin may be the most distinct characteristic of an otherwise opaque and unknown therapist. Failure to note the child's attempt to come to grips with the difference and to allow the exploration of feelings, may impede therapy. It is important that every child has the opportunity and safety to express their feelings and phantasies. For white therapists working with black children, part of the task is to come to terms with and understand our own sensitivities, fears, and identities as different coloured people.

Colour is an area of difference within the therapeutic relationship that will be explored and it can be an important first stage to acknowledge this. Alternatively, it might emerge as a central issue to the child's experience much later as therapy progresses. For example, a 12-year-old boy, working with a white male art therapist, struggled with feelings about sexuality, anxiety, issues around his mother and absent father. He communicated this through many images of modes of transport – initially submarines, boats, cars, and finally aeroplanes. His communication could be understood in terms of emergence, becoming grounded, turning into defendedness and flight, as underlying this process was his search for self and concern about his identity which he was trying to consolidate.

During the last session, he began to draw a 'Ninja' which he made half black, half white. Unable to complete this, he painted an aeroplane, solid, brightly coloured in reds and greens and airworthy. Recognizing the flight from his problem, he returned to the completion of the 'Ninja', down to the detail of the spear which also remained half black and half white. It is interesting to think about the fact that the white parts were those he failed to colour in black – they were left blank, without colour. It seemed that this was an indication that he was able to express some inner conflict, but also come to some confirmation about his own identity as a black child. It seems that by internalizing some aspects of the white therapist, he had been sufficiently contained in the art therapy to allow the unconscious issues to surface, non-verbally, through the imagery, which enabled him to come to some more understanding about himself and verbalize that he wanted to be an Olympic runner.

The unwillingness to pick up references to oneself when the child is making thinly disguised allusions to his feelings towards the therapist and the coyness in dealing with these feelings when they are noted, particularly through the imagery, is certainly not restricted to inter-racial situations. 'Attuning oneself to the nuances of another's feeling while monitoring one's own, however uncomfortable they both might be, is a task that is clearly not restricted to inter-racial psychotherapy' (Varghese 1983:333). With this in mind, when working with a group of children, of different ethnic origin, eruptions of anger and competitiveness are sometimes expressed in racial terms. The effects of racism and the experience of being different become crystallized in antagonism with remarks that compare shades of skin colour to establish some pecking order, or to the extreme of offensive racist remarks made in retaliation or self-defence. Similar feelings of competitiveness or issues around self-esteem are expressed between white children, and even though they may be equally extreme, are couched in different terms. By my presence and colour, I become embroiled as the focus of complex transference processes. For the black children, these interactions seem to be internalized responses in terms of their own identity, and give some indication of the level of frustration that these children experience and also an expression of their hopelessness.

The intensity of these situations seems to elicit real racial feelings and attitudes. But it is important, in these small groups, to contain and work with these feelings, hopefully towards some tolerance and understanding. There are many examples of therapeutic intervention and containment which can begin to help children in understanding the intensity and nature of their interactions. Simply asking them to reflect on their actions helps this process. For example, children working together often take on roles which have personal implications in the choice of their games. They can attempt to work through some of the concerns that close relationships might bring. In a recent session with a group of four children, two boys wanted to play draughts – the black child adamantly wanted to be 'blacks', the white child agreed to be 'whites'. Frustrated by the rules of the game, they began to fight verbally. Later in the same session, they came together and chose to make a battleship, and with negotiation and some disagreement, constructed it, spontaneously painting it half white and half black. They then symbolically played out their racial battle, in their activity, at times with bitterness, but it reached a sense of resolution at its natural end.

In another group of four children, two black girls and one black 10-year-old boy and one white 8-year-old boy, the white child, tense, anxious, and vulnerable chose to work with the older boy. This child had a tendency to lose his temper at the slightest provocation, had a superficial arrogant air, and negotiated all his reactions to his peers through aggressiveness. Underneath he was a clumsy, uncoordinated, immature, young boy. These two came together, initially because of their mutual passion for football, but it soon became clear that each offered something to the other. They worked together for several weeks, drawing, painting, modelling, playing – establishing a relationship that involved negotiation and understanding. In their drawings, there was no evidence of different coloured people in the two teams that they each represented and drew together – the players were tackling hard and were highly competitive but not racially divided. This partnership was an important one for both of them and had some beneficial effects – the white child was able to be more assertive, his self-confidence grew when he realized he could achieve something with someone older who seemingly had the characteristics he lacked – and for the older boy, it helped him to see that it was possible to express vulnerability more openly.

To reflect for a moment on the differences in the children that I work with in terms of their sex, some extra difficulties have been expressed by black girls as they grow towards puberty. As was previously mentioned, issues surrounding idealization of whiteness and beauty can effect self-esteem. One 11-year-old girl, having reached puberty, seemed unable to find in herself the possibility of ever being attractive. Her self-image was poor, confidence low and waning, and her early physical development certainly compounded her difficulty of approaching adolescence. She spent many sessions using plasticine, making a world of 'aliens' as she called them. These creatures were a strange mixture of black figures, in many different postures, with white eyes and hair. It felt as though she was trying to come to terms with her changing body and what she might become. Physically embarrassed and emotionally fragile, with no stable mother figure at home to help her feelings of vulnerability, her body and outward skin colour were those aspects of herself that she could hate most. From this point she was able to move into painting and drawing and explore wider and deeper issues that she had felt previously unable to look at. Being shy and withdrawn, the lack of pressure to talk helped her face up to some of these difficulties as she began to emerge with a new self-confidence for her secondary transfer.

For boys, this process takes on a different dimension. Ambivalence about body image and sexuality seems to manifest itself in aggression and 'macho' type behaviour which seeks to threaten others who might come near. Underlying this is a deep need for love and acceptance which they are unable to communicate or admit to but which their behaviour actively sabotages. Disruptive and disturbed behaviour is one of the main reasons that children are referred to art therapy, and increasingly I have come to the understanding that this is an expression of need for attention and emotional acceptance which cannot be expressed in any other, more 'socially' accepted way.

> Children are expected to be tough and invulnerable to all emotional onslaughts. But they develop the wrong sort of toughness on the outside with no inner resources to face the sort of world that is thrown at them by their families, the media and increasingly, school.
>
> (Yule 1985:470)

This behaviour seems to be the way to be noticed – the point has already been made in terms of the difficulty that black youths have to feel accepted and integrated. Institutional racism is experienced from a very young age and can manifest the same type of behaviour in a 5-year-old.

One example of a black child with whom I have worked since he started school two years ago, gives a clear picture of the difficulties he faced with the school situation. Daniel is a lively, volatile child, with a small, compact, and agile body. He is very disruptive in class and finds it hard to sustain any degree of concentration or activity for very long. In assembly he is usually taken out for restlessness and unruliness. He is constantly moving around, fighting with his peers, and seems content only with the full attention of the teacher. He is left-handed rather unco-ordinated, and usually writes backwards and from left to right. His home situation lacks stability. His very young mother found him, as a baby, very unsettled and his distress was compounded by severe infantile eczema which still causes him extreme irritation and flakiness of the skin. His condition also causes him to have a constant runny nose which the other children always tease him about. Daniel was fostered at the age of 2, and attempts by the foster parents to adopt him were cut short when his natural father, who had had no contact since birth, appeared and wanted to adopt his son. So Daniel now lives with father, but his aggressive behaviour at school and general level of disturbance and confusion have caused serious questions to be asked about father's parenting.

I worked with him throughout this time of instability and uncertainty for one hour once a week. At first he came to the sessions with enthusiasm and motivation. He tried to draw and paint quite realistically, as though his work had some degree of structure, and even though he is quite uncoordinated he was not messy and even quite fastidious about clearing up the mess he made. However, the turbulence at home seemed to coincide with a notable change in the sessions as his work moved into chaos and mess. He just did not care. At times of acute distress he just lay around with his thumb in his mouth, apathetic and depressed.

He continues to come to the sessions regularly and always remembers to come at the appropriate time. As we have worked with his difficulties, he is able to feel, his distress can be contained. His sense of abandonment is acute and often uppermost in his mind. He occasionally comes with an idea – one week he wanted to draw a giant picture of a bogey man which had to have large green mucus coming from the nose and other orifices. This I felt was some real attempt to look at aspects of himself, his condition, and explore this with me. Much of the session remains non-verbal in that he finds it hard to speak about himself in any real way, but the extent that he can communicate his feelings and inner chaos through the media is most important. The unpredictability of his mood is reflected by his choice of media and he uses this to work through and express the turmoil that he continually experiences. This allows him to experience very early times through water, play, mess, sand, and can begin to form new patterns of relating with paint and crayons, progressing to models and containers which he has made with great pride.

Clay has provided an important medium for him as this can be messy, provide solid structures that he can paint, which he can also choose to destroy or in some way change. This enables him to discover that he has some control. On painful incident happened when, I fetched him from the classroom, disturbed and disruptive, kicking everything in sight, and when we got into the room he roamed around trying to find the clay piece he had made the week before. It was a cup and saucer and when he found it he said in exasperation, 'Oh no it's broken.' We looked at it together and the feeling was that his whole world, fragile as it was, had shattered yet again. I reassured him that it was not and that it seemed whole to me. He took them to the table, examined them carefully and noticed a tiny hole. He said, 'Oh I can mend it,' and charged off to find the glue, paint, and other materials to make it alright. That one moment was important for him – the devastation of the feared broken pieces seemed to be the expectation of his inner experience – constantly broken and shattered by events and relationships. In the session the anxiety about this was held, and enabled him to make the change and feel that he himself could make it whole again.

Without these kinds of intense experiences, Daniel's world will continue to be the victim of broken containment. If no one is capable of holding his emotional needs and anxieties, his capacity to take in, grasp, or hold on to thoughts, feelings, and experiences will remain impaired. His difficulties in the classroom can never be sorted out, given that it is the competition of his peers that set up the worst conflict that makes him suffer most. His early experience of exclusion seems to be repeating itself at school. 'Being' excluded was, and still is, his 'normal' experience and as he struggles to find another role or way to be, he forces people to exclude him. He is labelled 'the naughty boy' by his peers and one also wonders to what extent he is the victim of institutional racism which manifests itself in his chaotic behaviour. 'I'm bad, no good, can't think', sums up the deprivation cycle but one hopes that by working with him in art therapy in his school setting this will give him an opportunity to be understood and a chance to make relationships and for hope to appear.

Daniel is just one child who must be helped to come to terms with the acute difficulties that he experiences at school and at home. Working with him in the school, it is possible to enable that integration to take place without making him feel more stigmatized and discriminated against. Art therapy gives him a safe space to explore his thoughts and feelings and phantasies, feelings of abandonment by mother, and other important people in his life. A consistent and accepting approach to Daniel by myself and others concerned with his education and care will help him to come to terms with his own personal distress, but also with the hostility he will encounter in the attitudes towards race and black children that currently exist. This is the essence of real integration in schools – where the whole child can be helped to feel an integrated member of the society to which he rightfully belongs.

© 1990 Tessa Dalley

References

Afro-Caribbean Educational Resource Project, Full Report of (1977) *Words and Faces: a Resource for the Middle Years of Schooling*, London: Afro-Caribbean Educational Resource Project (ACER).

Aichorn, A. (1957) *Wayward Youth* (2nd edn), London: Hogarth Press.

Allport, G. (1958) *The Nature of Prejudice*, New York: Doubleday.

Atkinson, D.R. (1985) 'A meta-review of research on cross-culture counselling and psychotherapy', *Journal of Multiculture Counselling and Development* (Oct.) 13(4): 138–53.

Baldwin, J. (1962) 'Letter from a region in my mind', *New Yorker* (Nov.) 17.

Banton, R., Clifford, P., Frosch, S., Lousada, J., and Rosenthall, J. (1985) *The Politics of Mental Health*, London: Macmillan.

Brah, A. and Minhas, R. (1985) 'Structural racism or cultural difference: schooling for Asian girls', in G. Weiner (ed.) *Just a Bunch of Girls*, Milton Keynes: Open University Press.

Brittan, A. and Maynard, M. (1984) *Sexism, Racism and Oppression*, Oxford: Blackwell.

Carling, C. (1986) 'Kids Creole', *Guardian* (29 Oct.).

Case, C. (1987) 'A search for meaning: loss and transition in art therapy with children', in T. Dalley, C. Case, J. Schaverien, F. Weir, D. Halliday, P. Nowell Hall, and D. Waller *Images of Art Therapy*, London: Tavistock.

Cashmore, E. (1982) 'Black youth in crisis', in E. Cashmore and B. Troyna (eds) *Black Youth in Crisis*, London: Allen & Unwin.

Clark, K. and Clark, M. (1939) 'The development of consciousness of self and the emergence of racial identity in Negro pre-school children', *Journal of Social Psychology* 10: 591–9.

Clark, K. and Clark, M. (1958) 'Racial identification and preference in Negro children', in Maccoby, Newcomb and Hartley (eds) *Readings in Social Psychology*, New York: 602–11.

Cross, M. (1982) 'The manufacture of marginality', in E. Cashmore and B. Troyna (eds) *Black Youth in Crisis*, London: Allen & Unwin.

Dalal, F. (1988) 'Jung: a racist?', *British Journal of Psychotherapy* (Spring) 4(3).

Dalley, T. (1987) 'Art as therapy: some new perspectives', in T. Dalley, C. Case, J. Schaverien, F. Weir, D. Halliday, P. Nowell Hall, and D. Waller *Images of Art Therapy*, London: Tavistock.

Dunn, L.M. (1968) 'Special education for the mildly retarded: is much of it justified?', *Exceptional Children* 35: 5–22.

Edgcumbe, R. (1975) 'The border between education and therapy', in *Studies in Child Analysis*, Monogram Series.

Erikson, E. (1964) 'Memorandum on identity and negro youth', *Journal of Social Issues* (Oct.) 20: 30.

Freud, S. (1925) 'Preface to Aichorn's *Wayward Youth*', *Standard Edition*, 19, London: Hogarth Press, p. 273.

Frosch, S. (1987) *The Politics of Psychoanalysis*, London: Macmillan.

Gilbert, J.E. (1986) 'The association of a clinician's ethnic background and socio-economic status', *Dissertation Abstracts International* (Aug.) 47: 786.

Glasser, W. (1969) *Schools Without Failure*, London: Harper & Row.

Goacher, B., Evans, J., Welton, J., and Wedell, K. (1988) *Policy and Provision for Special Educational Needs: Implementing the 1981 Education Act*, London: Cassell.

Griffith, M. (1977) 'The influence of race on the psychotherapeutic relationship', *Psychiatry* 40: 27–40.

Halliday, D. (1987) 'Peak experiences: the individuation of children', in T. Dalley, C. Case, J. Schaverien, F. Weir, D. Halliday, P. Nowel Hall, and D. Waller *Images of Art Therapy*, London: Tavistock.

Hargreaves, D. (1981) *Challenge for the Comprehensive School*, London: Harper & Row.

Horowitz, R. (1939) 'Racial aspects of self-identification in nursery school age children', *Journal of Psychology* 7: 91–9.

Howlin, P. (1985) 'Special educational treatment', in M. Rutter (ed.) *Child and Adolescent Psychiatry: Modern Approaches*, Oxford: Blackwell.

Hughes, P. (1985) 'Guidance and counselling in schools', *British Journal of Guidance and Counselling* 13: 11–21.

Jones, B.E. and Gray, B.A. (1985) 'Black and white psychiatrists: therapy with Blacks', *Journal of the National Medical Association* (Jan.) 77 (1): 19–25.

Katz, J. (1978) *White Awareness*, Norman: University of Oklahoma Press.

Klein, M. (1923) *Writings of Melanie Klein*, London: Hogarth Press.

Klein, M. (1955) 'The psychoanalytic play technique. Its history and significance', in M. Klein, P. Heimann and R.E. Money-Kyrle (eds) *New Directions in Psychoanalysis*, London: Tavistock.

Klein, M. (1957) 'Envy and gratitude', *Envy and Gratitude and Other Works*, London: Hogarth Press.

Kolvin, I., Garside, R.F., Nicol, A.R., Macmillan, A., Wostenholme, E., and Leitch, I.M. (1981) *Help Starts Here. The Maladjusted Child in the Ordinary School*, London: Tavistock.

Kramer, E. (1979) *Children and Art Therapy*, New York: Schocken.

Lubbe, T. (1986) 'Some disturbed pupils' perceptions of their teachers – a psychotherapist's viewpoint', *Maladjustment and Therapeutic Education* (Spring) 4(1): 29–35.

Mittler, P. (1988) *Special Needs in Ordinary Schools*, London: Cassell.

Mouzon, R.R. (1987) 'Difference between the practices of black and white therapists with black patients', *Dissertation Abstracts International* (Nov.) 46: 1695.

Munoz, J.A. (1986) 'Countertransference and its implementation in the treatment of a Hispanic adolescent boy', *Psychiatry* (May) 49(2): 169–79.

Nicol, A.R. (1987) 'Psychotherapy and the school: an update', *Journal of Child Psychology and Psychiatry* 28(5): 657–65.

Plowden Report (1967) *Children in their Primary Schools: a Report of the Central Advisory Council for Education*, London: HMSO.

Porter, J. (1971) *Black Child, White Child: the Development of Racial Attitudes*, Cambridge, Mass.: Harvard University Press.

Rack P. (1982) *Race, Culture and Mental Disorder*, London: Tavistock.

Read, H. (1942) *Education through Art*, London: Faber & Faber.

Reeves, C. (1983) 'Maladjustment: psycho-dynamic theory and the role of therapeutic education in a residential setting', *Maladjustment and Therapeutic Education. Journal of the Association of Workers for Maladjusted Children* (Spring) 1: 25–31.

Reynolds, D. (1984) 'Creative conflict: the implications of recent educational research to those concerned with children', *Maladjusted and Therapeutic Education* (Spring) 1: 15–23.

Rogers, C. (1952) *Client Centred Therapy*, Boston: Houghton Mifflin.

Rubin, J. (1978) *Child Art Therapy*, New York: Van Nostrand Reinhold Co. Inc.

Sandler, J., Dare, C., and Holder, A. (1973) *The Patient and the Analyst*, London: Allen & Unwin.

Torrance, P. and White, W. (1975) *Issues and Advances in Educational Psychology* (2nd edn) Ill.: Peacock Publishers.

Varghese, F.T. (1983) 'The racially different psychiatrist: implications for psychotherapy', *Australian and New Zealand Journal of Psychiatry* (Dec.) 17(4): 329–33.

Warnock Report (1981) *Special Educational Needs. Report of the Committee of Enquiry into the Education of Handicapped People and Young Children*, London: HMSO, Cmnd 7212.

Winnicott, D.W. (1964) *The Child, the Family and the Outside World*, London: Penguin.

Wood, M. (1984) 'The child and art therapy: a psychodynamic viewpoint', in T. Dalley (ed.) *Art as Therapy*, London: Tavistock.

Woolf, S. (1969) *Children under Stress*, London: Penguin.

Yule, V. (1985) 'Violence and Imagination', *New Society*, 28 June.

Chapter ten

'I show you': children in art therapy
Roger Arguile

This chapter is based on my work at a school for children with special needs, and centres on Charles, a boy with a severe language disorder. It was, in part, the therapeutic work I did with Charles and his school friend Graham, that led me to be an art therapist.

Within the school, art therapy has evolved from a seed to a flourishing and expanding discipline. There is now a positive interest in art therapy from the teaching, care, and medical practices along with direct and frequent liaison with the school's visiting consultant psychiatrist through whom referrals are received either directly or indirectly. I am interested in role and performance in art and art therapy regarding both client and therapist. I see it as a medium of art rather like paint or pencil. It becomes part of an holistic experience in therapy that is essentially rooted in art in the historical, aesthetic, and primitive contexts.

My knowing Charles inspired me to create a series of drawn writings and photographic portraits based on word signing. In this chapter I will discuss and illustrate how art and art-making processes played an important and therapeutically beneficial role in the development of language and interaction between Charles, and myself. In conclusion I will look at similar qualities that materialize in a closed one-to-one art therapy setting, noting elements of performance and role that also operate.

Charles

Charles is a child with a severe language disorder. He has expressive and receptive aphasia in addition to severe speech dyspraxia. Aphasia is a language disorder due to damage in that part of the brain concerned with the cognition and production of speech. The two forms of aphasia are: (1) receptive aphasia, in which the child has great difficulty in learning to speak, and (2) expressive aphasia, in which the child readily learns to understand all or most of what is said to him but cannot learn to speak at the normal rate and in the usual manner. Often a child will have both aphasic conditions, as does

Figure 10.1 Charles standing

Charles. Dyspraxia is the inability to perform purposeful movements and is a neurological condition which again can occur alongside aphasia. Therefore, with speech dyspraxia, the child will need speech therapy in order to gain the ability to manipulate his mouth and tongue for correct speech.

Charles was born on 30 July 1973. For his first 18 months he underwent a perfectly normal development. During the next 12 months, although Charles was still trying to communicate normally, his vocabulary and clarity of speech were gradually lost. The cause of this problem has never been established as there were no obvious symptoms at the time. It was only in retrospect that a decline was traceable from the age of 18 months. By the time he was approximately 2½ years old, Charles realized for himself that he could no longer communicate, and he became very frustrated. Initially he was diagnosed as deaf and forced to wear an 'aid', which he could not tolerate. At this time he spent his mornings at a deaf unit attached to an infant school.

When Charles was approximately 3½ years of age he received a full assessment at Charing Cross Hospital. Aphasia was at last established as being the problem. It was the speech therapist at the Assessment Unit, Helen Haig, who introduced Charles to the Paget–Gorman Sign System which he responded to eagerly as a means of communication. Using Paget–Gorman as a signing system it is possible for a child to express conceptual ideas and subtle variations of grammar. Paget–Gorman is an aid for the acquisition of speech and language more than a complete language system in its own right as is the British Sign Language used more by the deaf. As a result of the assessment, Charles was referred to Mr Martin of the Nuffield Hearing and Speech Centre and accepted at a special nursery school for twelve children with speech disorders which Mr Martin ran at Ealing. It was at this time that the Nuffield Centre carried out an 'electrocochleagram' and proved that Charles had perfectly normal hearing. For 2 years from the age of 4 to 6, Charles attended Ealing as a weekly boarder and was given the grounding in Paget–Gorman.

At the age of 6 Charles had outgrown the nursery unit. As St Mary's School for Children with Special Needs had started to use Paget, and were suited to deal with Charles' then less disciplined behaviour, he was offered a place. He stayed there until he was nearly 10 during which time he received intensive speech therapy. Mrs D. Goodger, speech therapist at St Mary's comments on Charles's stay there:

Charles came to St Mary's School in 1979 when he was six years old. At this time his comprehension of speech was limited to a small number of single words and simple phrases which needed to be signed to him as well as spoken. He could express, through the Paget–Gorman System and gross gesture, up to three connected ideas only. His drawings were very imaginative and he often used pictures to express his ideas and experiences.

Figure 10.2 Charles with bells

He could articulate some isolated speech sounds but was unable to link vowels and consonants together to form words. Throughout his time at St Mary's he displayed extremely high motivation to communicate and progressed steadily in all areas of speech and language development, despite continuing severe problems in the auditory perception and reception of language, expressive language, and articulation, to the extent that he can now communicate intelligibly in simple sentences using an ever expanding vocabulary.

(Mrs D. Goodger 1983)

Charles moved to Moor House School for children with speech and language disorders, in September 1983 to continue his therapeutic language progress. I visited him there. He spoke with increasing fluency and a greater vocabulary, using better sentence structure, including correct use of more connecting words and parts of speech, with virtually no Paget. He was able to express himself more accurately and descriptively. His language expressed a larger percentage of his perception. It was just over 2 years, since he first struggled to utter my name, and Charles was confident in his ever-increasing new found speech.

Transition from Paget to speech

During his time at St Mary's School, Charles was popular with the staff and children, and formed a strong stable friendship with one of his peers in particular, called Graham, a very boisterous mischievous character of similar age to Charles. He was keen on football, and all the usual action adventure games that 9 to 10 year olds revel in. Charles was swept along by Graham's energy and vigour and thus the friendship grew. Charles, equal to Graham in terms of zest and enthusiasm, was at the time academically superior, but in speech, he was of course years behind. They grew to respect each other, and their play together led to an increasing desire for language interaction. Graham would shout out rules for a game but Charles would understand only in part. Charles would Paget to Graham, and slowly, backed up by Paget school lessons, Graham began to talk in signs, as well as speech, to Charles. This rapport strengthened and sometimes they would communicate messages across the busy school dining room or playground in Paget.

With speech therapy, Charles's language was becoming slowly more coherent and Graham was able to understand several of his spoken words. Charles found the ability to talk verbally in limited terms to Graham with the help of Paget. His desire to speak in words was being fuelled by this relationship. Graham was impatient and even aggressive if he did not get immediate response from his peers, but Charles was eager to remain friendly with him and because of this, there was an urgency for Charles in terms of language. It was vital to be one of the gang. Graham was always leader and Charles needed to be right near the top. He was compelled to communicate. Graham increased his use of Paget, and in a direct, almost charismatic way, dragged language out of Charles. Being of strong character, Charles could cope with this, and indeed revelled in this form of rather frantic learning.

As their communications improved, I remember often seeing Graham explaining to Charles in speech and signs, quite complex games, ideas and feelings. Charles would attempt to soak up all the words and then eagerly respond. I recall observing whole conversations, Graham speaking with some signing, and Charles, signing with some speech. The result was total language communication. At the age of 8, Charles was at last able to have simple but meaningful conversations with one of his friends as an equal. Because of this, and despite his handicap, Charles was secure within the hierarchy of his age group. Graham, Charles, and another boy were the terrible threesome! They were often in trouble, and always very boisterous and high spirited.

Charles's increasing spoken vocabulary meant that he was able to communicate with a greater number of children. He became more interested in football. His team-mates would shout for the ball and direct instructions during the game. Charles linked these words to the related movements and provided his own equally valid exclamations like, 'Gow!' (goal), 'Carr!' (come on). The link between those relationships and myself became more important. Charles wanted to talk to me about his attitude towards his peers and especially Graham. Sometimes he was able, in a few disjointed wrongly pronounced words, to express what he wished to say, without need of Paget. There grew within him a realization that there was greater possibility of expression in spoken language than in signing, thus his eagerness to extend and use his speech increased.

Throughout this period he was of course receiving regular speech therapy. In his art work with me, we had, with great determination, reached the stage where his pictures and models had become mediators through which increasing communication was made possible. It was at this time that I produced a series of photographs of Charles signing the letters of his name. He enjoyed this greatly and showed keen interest in the workings of the camera. In his own art he displayed great powers of observation for his age. Charles was now craving for language and knowledge.

Conversations

As Charles's ability to communicate with me developed, he became more confident in our friendship. The look in his eye was no longer one of frustration due to lack of language, but one of a self-assured individual communicating on equal terms. He knew he had a valid contribution to make in our conversations. The result was a fascinating mixture of maturity and naïveté – maturity in the desire to offer his ideas and concepts for discussion, and naïveté in his limited linguistic abilities. I became increasingly aware of the gap between Charles's understanding and his language. During the long period of Charles's language delay, his conceptual development had been progressing at a steady rate.

As his language increased, Charles became fascinated with various subjects. He showed particular interest in spiders, cartoon super heros such as Superman, maps, whales, and especially sharks. There was an increasing wonderment as he grappled with such topics as weight, distance, age, and families, plus the comprehension of life and death, all of which he introduced into conversations. I had long discussions with him dealing with such things as these. Many of his questions and comments were poignant in their depth. He demanded quite subtle yet lucid answers which I had to offer with a substantially reduced vocabulary. This put demands upon me that increased my own power of communication. Of course, I would introduce new words and explain them as we went along which in turn strengthened Charles's use of language. We sometimes became deeply involved as equals in our exploration of certain topics. Our conversations were a process of creative discovery where handicaps and distinctions were rendered void. There was a unity and power in our conversation in which language and the concept of language as art appeared to gell. I mention here a statement made by Matisse in an interview with Degand in 1945.

> Feeling is an enemy only when one doesn't know how to express it. And it is necessary to express it entirely. If you don't want to go to the limit, you only get approximations. An artist is an explorer. He should begin by seeking himself, seeing himself act; then, not restraining himself, and above all, not being easily satisfied.
>
> (Flam 1973:104)

Often Charles wanted to talk of his perceptions of life and death. One day he said 'What say you? I say, you don't know. You may die. No more life. You don't know. I don't know'. He spoke this slowly with single-minded resolution. By saying, 'you don't know', he wasn't being vague or negative about the mystery of death, rather the opposite. It was a statement of fact that he felt we ought to admit to, and in doing so, there lay perhaps a partial answer to the question of life and death. It reminds me of a verse in the New Testament: 'My knowledge now is partial. Then it will be whole, like God's knowledge of me'. I wanted to capture some of the potency of Charles's words in terms of my own work.

Language and art

I responded to Charles and his language problem from my standpoint as an artist. My concern was representing language in terms of visual art. My

Figure 10.3 One of Charles's school friends, drawn by Charles from life

subject for this was Charles and the verbal and non-verbal language he spoke was the raw material I used to create the final drawn writings and photographic pieces.

Let me expand on the drawings: 'Talking 12 May 1983', was produced following a conversation Charles and I had. Using only a little signing, Charles was talking verbally with great eagerness. He wanted to discuss the concept of life and age. Then he began to think of Father Christmas and had a clear idea of what he wanted to say. He looked at me with a powerful, almost primitive openness and tried to explain his thoughts. Although Father Christmas was a fully grown man, and despite his returning year upon year with wonderful gifts, he seemed somehow ageless. He was never too old to bring the presents. There was a poignant, silent pause, and then, as an explanation for all this Charles said of Father Christmas, 'He magic'. Then another thoughtful pause and he said again with wide eyes, 'He . . . magic . . . .' Silence.

These small childlike statements I later wrote down. Such language has a loaded simplicity. His perception was far more advanced than his spoken language. There was a void that Charles was battling to fill with language, to enable him to converse on equal footing with everyone around him. He was winning that battle despite great problems in his reception and expression of language. As an artist I find language of great import. By writing words we make speech visible, thus forming possible links between writing and visual art. Words then begin to work on two levels. They work in their own symbolized meaning, but also in their acquired visual context on a non-verbal level as part of the drawing process, and may function in their own right as images as, for example, the American painter Jasper Johns shows in some of his work. The space between Charles's speech and his fuller awareness can be visualized by making words become part of the drawn image, rather than just added on. This is what I began to explore.

I saw the problems Charles had and admired his progress, but found within his language development certain fundamental universal communicative qualities, which reveal to us the limitations of our greater word-based language. Charles, in a sense knew things at quite an advanced level before having to rely on symbolic language. Of course, it is good that he is now learning so much speech but I think we should learn his language too. With few words, Charles has said much.

When one draws something, one often draws more from word-based knowledge than from direct observation. When drawing a face one may form an eye, a nose relating observation to the familiar words 'eye' and 'nose'. To abandon 'eye' and 'nose' and to draw exactly what is seen will produce a more valid drawing. More knowledge may be gleaned in this way. This is what Charles had to do. He experienced the world intelligently without word props. Because of this he saw and knew things with a clarity that was exciting and refreshing. With great enthusiasm, he was finding the words to match his powerful language, and I was seeking to reveal an art language to match his words. A dual creative process.

I found interesting communication levels in Charles' spoken words, my drawn writings, and my performed spoken words. There are three different communication areas here. The first of these was Charles speaking. This was unselfconscious. It was the source material. It was his language, of his idea. By writing his statements I preserved them. Charles did not say them to be preserved. He spoke in passing like anyone else; but any passing remark if captured and preserved becomes special. It has a new context in which to exist. It is like a 'found object'. The Dada Art movement considered this. An object taken out of context and placed in an art context could become an art object. The viewer is forced to reassess the object or statement in this new environment without preconceived values and opinions being necessarily valid.

By taking Charles's words I had something rather rich as my 'found object'. Few people speak as normal chit-chat with the absolute vividness of Charles and so to collect these words and place them into the language of art, for me, was decidedly worthwhile. By writing them they become accessible to anyone. No longer was Charles speaking to me. He spoke through the written word to any reader. The words then became my work and Charles was untarnished by the exposure of his statements. By writing in crayon there was an association with drawing and by drawing over the words a crude and simple image of the subject matter (e.g. whale), they became part of the drawing, and no longer merely casual statements. They were integrated within a greater language, where words and image relate visually. Matisse again: 'In art what is most important is the relationship between things' (Flam 1973:60). When Charles spoke, the words emerged having come through his own non-verbal perception. When viewing the text drawings one may try to discern the statements by employing more vocabulary, but it is better to blot out other words in this case. The vague drawings should be sufficient as 'further explanation'. I wanted each piece to stand as an entity in itself rather than straightforward documentation of speech.

When performing the writings by reading to an audience we had a further communication development. The words returned to their original context as speech but no longer as naturally from Charles. I became the orator. Once again, the raw material was used to create a new experience, but with minimal change. An art of art is knowing how, and by what degree, to alter the raw material to establish clarity of an idea. With Charles's language there was need only for change of context rather than content.

Regarding Charles's speech, the psychologist will produce a statement, and the speech therapist or teacher will formulate their differing findings. I felt it necessary to portray an artist's statement. I did not carry out analytical speech tests on Charles. Rather, taking his language as it came I lifted qualities worth celebrating and began to work from there, dealing more with

Charles's language as portrait rather than Charles himself. My writings from his sayings do not require translations. That would only serve to make them clearly understandable which would lessen the struggle. For there ought to be a struggle to read and sense these writings just as there was a linguistic struggle for Charles in the speaking of the words.

The photographic sequences again use documentation but try to extend beyond that. I was concerned with the time-based quality of photographs in revealing language through Paget–Gorman signing, for example. One of the pieces is called 'photograph'. It is a mirror image of Charles signing the word photograph to himself, a girl and myself at the camera recording the event through the camera/film process. In this way Charles is also signing 'Photograph' to the viewer. Word as image. When I take a portrait photograph, I seek to capture a moment in a life, making it a preserved memory. It is still, silent, frozen for as long as the photograph exists. Looking at a photograph is like looking back in time. The image may be a recording of only 125th of a second but we are carried through time and memories to that moment. I like the image to contain the spontaneity of a snap but an awareness for the viewer that what is seen is more than just a snap. I like there to be a strong sense of time within the image and there to be a simplicity that can be felt at an almost primitive level transcending words. We can take time to read a portrait photograph. We oversee the image. We should view with respect. We need to remember that the photograph reveals an image of a life's moment.

A photograph is a recording of the real, whereas a painting or drawing in representing the real becomes its own reality. The created reality of painting or drawing and the time-fixed recorded evidence of a reality made visible in a photograph, are my dual concerns. The viewer responds to a photograph in a narrative-based, reflective way. We look back in time. However, when looking at, for example, oil paint on canvas, the senses are assaulted by the physicality of its live presence before us. It is a battleground of paint having been ordered into a visual language by the artist. In his interview with David Sylvester, Francis Bacon talks about the artist's desire for order:

> I think that great art is deeply ordered. Even if within the order there may be enormously instinctive and accidental things, nevertheless I think they come out of a desire for ordering and for returning fact on to the nervous system in a more violent way.
>
> (Sylvester 1975:59)

The aphasic child is involved in an inspiring battle to order his reality into verbal language, composing 'paintings' out of words. By responding in art to Charles's language, I found moments of unity between language, art, order, and disorder.

I could only have produced the work at that time, because Charles was

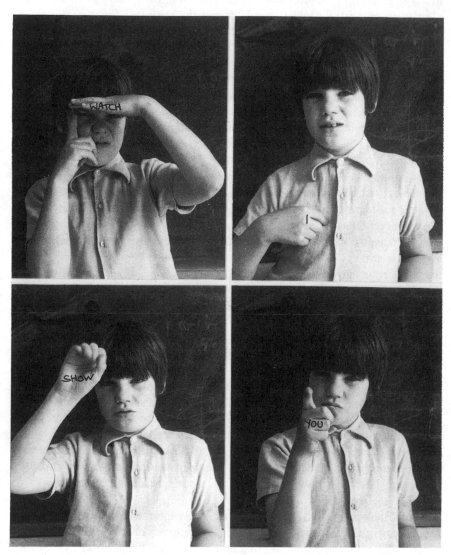

Figure 10.4 'Watch, I show you'

growing up and learning speech so quickly that those qualities in his language are now history. The spoken pieces that I remembered and worked from are as follows:

'Whale'
Bay be one huntred feet
Bay be one huntred tons
Whale – he big.
He no bite you
Shark. He bitey you
Naughty Shark
Whale Friend.

'Dog Fish'
Baby Shark. He swim
Sea water – swimmy
Sea water. Water go
No swimmy. He can't
He die
Baby Shark, he die
He didn't know
Its dangus – no water
Mummy daddy shark
Long way, sca
They didn't see
Baby shark
No swimmy
Ah, poor baby shark
No more life . . .

'Crab'
Water
Quicky
Takey home, crab
Tap water no good
Sea water good
It need sea water
Look, watch
I show you
Crab swimmy sea.

'Car'
Car
Quicky
Crash
Lots cuts
Breaky bones
No more life

'Aggerdabber'
I know
Give me cards, right
I know magic
Worn, two, tree
Look
Watch
I show you magic . . .

'Drakya'
I say Suman stwonges'
Suman first
Spiderman seyon
Womonwondon third
Huwk four
Drakya fife
Womonwondon bay be four?
Drakya ha ee big teeth
Look, see
He not life Englant
He from diffunt Cantree
He joke. He not here
He no heart – go AARRH!
He dead now. Not real
He joke – Drakya
Jays Bont clefer
Jays Bont
Jays Bont Street!
That funny!
I jokey!

'Talking 12 May 1983'
Kquisnus Father
Kquisnus Father not old
He man, but not old
He come evy 'ear
Lots of presee
Kquisnus Father not old
He magic . . .
He . . . magic . . .

'Life'
Life
Life
It good for you
What say you?
Say, what say you?
I say
I say you don't know
You may die No more life . . .
I say you don't know
I dunno

'I Catchy you'
Count one two
Count one two I catchy you
Me no silly
You silly
I know
I show you
Ar, pretty birds
They friends now
Quickly
Count one two
I catchy you

The creative process in the here and now

I am interested in role and performance in art therapy regarding both client
and therapist. My work with Charles was not experienced in a formal art
therapy setting. However, the relationship was therapeutic and to an extent
art-based. The transactions were on an equal level and were non-judgemental.
It is within this form of communication that qualities of performance can
enter the fine art process in art therapy.

The Olde Time music hall comedian, Max Wall, performs a one-man
show. He ponders, day-dreams, and leers at his audience. The audience is
a unit and though there are many people, it is essentially a one-to-one
communication. He picks up the 'feel' from the audience as he performs, and
carries it through different emotional responses by non-verbal gestures of
humorous subtlety. Like the artist at work, he knows intuitively when his
performance works and he knows how to monitor and maintain the performance. He knows his work so well, so can operate with total awareness to
the 'here and now' as he performs. The therapist functions with an accurate
empathy within the full experiential dynamics of the 'here and now' and as
such is also involved in role and performance. Moments of intervention are
the key to facilitating the therapeutic flow. Suggestions for acting or role play

Figure 10.5 'Dog Fish'

could easily divert the true flow into an artificial area of acting. The intervention must be absolute and unavoidable. D.W. Winnicott states:

> One can often rob an individual of a terribly important moment when the feeling is: 'I have an impulse to do such and such, but I also . . . .' and they come to some sort of personal developmental phase, which would have been completely broken across if somebody had said, 'You're not to do that, its wrong.' Then they would either comply, in which case they have given up, or else they would defy, in which case nobody has gained anything and there is no growth.
>
> (1986:149)

Figure 10.6 'Life'

The therapist clears the path for the child to achieve growth. The therapist clears the 'here and now' moment between past and future. Thus far and no farther. The child creates the prints that establish that path and can then achieve growth.

The conversations I had with Charles seemed complete. All energy was exhausted in the creative process of language interaction. Such a creative process is outlined by the painter Jasper Johns in an interview with David Sylvester about his work:

I think one has to work with everything and accept the kind of statement which results as unavoidable, or a helpless situation. I think that most art that begins to make a statement fails to make a statement because the methods used are too schematic or too artificial. I think that one wants from a painting a sense of life. The final suggestion, the final statement has to be not a deliberate statement but a helpless statement. It has to be what you can't avoid saying, not what you set out to say. I think one ought to use everything one can use, all of the energy should be wasted in painting it, so that one hasn't the reserve of energy which is able to use this thing. One should not really know what to do with it, because it should match what one is already; it should not be just something one likes.

(Sylvester 1974:14)

Charles's aim and objective was to speak. To say what he felt using ordinary words. The huge struggle was eventually successful. I engaged in the struggle. I picked up the poetic quality of his speech. Conversations were sustained by a non-verbal understanding that has an equivalent in two people playing improvised jazz together. The therapeutic benefit was experienced as much by me as artist as it was by Charles. After a conversation there was often silence or a change of venue. It was as if Charles was content with the outcome. Nothing else was necessary. I accepted this. To have pushed for more speech would have broken the final statement, the art performance.

Within the 'here and now', an art therapist can adopt a sense of free-floating attention with a client. By relaxing the conscious interpretive way of assessing events allowing the unconscious vision to scan the whole life experience, a deeper perception and awareness of the art-making process may be understood and experienced. Of course I have in mind here Ehrenzweig's term, 'unconscious scanning' (Ehrenzweig 1967). The therapist operates with automatic empathy. Intervention and pace occur intuitively in the therapeutic flow. A profound simplicity is happening. The painter, Francis Bacon, waits for an image to surface from his unconscious vision and he seizes it. He receives images with perfect timing. The art therapist's moment of intervention is a parallel equivalent of that. The therapist receives the client's images. The art-making process and image within the psychotherapeutic relationship forms the basis of art therapy. The powerful art and language dynamic that formed the core of my communications with Charles have been invaluable in my work as both artist and art therapist. It was largely due to speech therapy that Charles learnt how to speak, but it was through the language of art that he discovered much of what he wanted to say.

Conclusion

I must state the transitory nature of the period of Charles's development in which I found him. The fact that I discovered, for myself, qualities of enormous import at that stage of his development (and that I captured and recorded them in the way I did) does not mean I would have Charles remain at that point. Charles has progressed enormously since the days when his friend Graham used to will him to speak. They have maintained contact over the last 6 years. It is ironic that in 1987 Graham was referred to me for art therapy. Indeed the positive changes he has made for himself through therapy would form another chapter. This chapter closes, however, in the knowledge that Charles is now able to help his own toddler brother learn the art of language.

References

Ehrenzweig, A. (1967) *The Hidden Order of Art*, London: Paladin.
Flam, J.D. (1973) *Matisse on Art*, Oxford: Phaidon.
Sylvester, D. (1974) *Jasper Johns' Drawings*, London: Arts Council of Great Britain.
Sylvester, D. (1975) *Interviews with Francis Bacon*, Oxford: Alden.
Winnicott, D.W. (1986) *Home Is Where We Start From*, Harmondsworth: W.W. Norton & Co. and Pelican Books.

Acknowledgements

My thanks to Charles and his parents for their co-operation and support. Thanks also to Graham and his mother; St Mary's School for Children with Special Needs, Bexhill, East Sussex, England and Moor House School, Oxted, Surrey, England.

Name index

Subject index

abstraction: in autistic children 48; expressing feelings 9

accommodation syndrome in sexual abuse 99, 105

addictive patterns of sexual abuse 95–7

Afro-Caribbean children *see* black children

aggressiveness in children 171

anal stage (Freud's) 74–5, 79

anomalous draughtsman *see* unusual drawing development

anorexia 73, 76

anti-racism 180

aphasia 199, 201, 209

art: as alternative to language 10, 18–19; and communications 172; as component in education 39; development of and self 43; and language 205–9; and severe learning difficulties 25

art materials *see* materials

art therapy: and black children 187–96; and client-centred activities 119–20; and control 31, 85; daily impact 36; and Down's Syndrome 36–7; at Greyhound Centre 120–1, 128–9; in hospital setting 80; justification of 54; and language disorder 205–7; and mental handicap 23–4; and 'mess' 142–9, 152; perceived as abuse 78; potential to stimulate 87; and racial differences 189–90; and racial origin 178; role and performance of 212; in schools *see* art therapy and special needs; and sexual abuse 92, 100–1; and systems theory of human behaviour 118–19

art therapy in an assessment centre 131–60; and bathing 149–50; breaking taboos 142–4; function 131–2; 'heart' motif 141, 154–5; and rejected children 131, 133, 135–7; and sandplay 152; and slime 145–7, 150–2

art therapy and special needs 167–77; case for 169–77; focus of 171; materials 168, 169, 171; role of 167–9; *see also* case studies

'as if' concept 23, 24

Assessment Centre 131–60

assessment period in family centre 122–3

autism/autistic 51; and art media 34–5, 37; intervention with 25; lack of abstraction 48; and object-centred description 50; unusual drawing development 44–5, 48, 49

awareness in black children 182–3

babies: ego development in 133–4; merging with mother 133–4, 137–8; perception 41

Baker Recommendations 162

bathing 143, 149–50

bee circus 58–9

binding activities, and control 81–2

black children 177–98; acceptance into society 178; and art therapy 187–96; attitudes 181–2; awareness 182–3; and curriculum 180, 186; and prejudice 179–80; puberty 193; self-esteem 183–4, 189; and sex differences 193; and transference 189

Black Power 184

boundaries: body, loss of 80; in children 135; in families 117, 119; generational